Lincoln's Gift
from Homer, New York

Lincoln's Gift from Homer, New York

A Painter, an Editor and a Detective

MARTIN A. SWEENEY

McFarland & Company, Inc., Publishers
Jefferson, North Carolina, and London

LIBRARY OF CONGRESS CATALOGUING-IN-PUBLICATION DATA

Sweeney, Martin A., 1946–
  Lincoln's gift from Homer, New York : a painter, an editor and a detective / Martin A. Sweeney.
    p.   cm.
  Includes bibliographical references and index.

  ISBN 978-0-7864-6369-5
  softcover : 50# alkaline paper ∞

  1. Lincoln, Abraham, 1809–1865 — Friends and associates.
  2. Carpenter, F.B. (Francis Bicknell), 1830–1900.   3. Stoddard, William Osborn, 1835–1925.   4. DeVoe, Eli, 1809–1874.
  5. Homer (N.Y.) — Biography.   I. Title.
  E457.2.S93   2011
  973.7092'2 — dc23   2011026229

BRITISH LIBRARY CATALOGUING DATA ARE AVAILABLE

© 2011 Martin A. Sweeney. All rights reserved

No part of this book may be reproduced or transmitted in any form or by any means, electronic or mechanical, including photocopying or recording, or by any information storage and retrieval system, without permission in writing from the publisher.

Front cover: *The First Reading of the Emancipation Proclamation before the Cabinet*, painted by Francis Bicknell Carpenter, 1864 (Library of Congress); hand gestures © 2011 clipart.com

Manufactured in the United States of America

McFarland & Company, Inc., Publishers
  Box 611, Jefferson, North Carolina 28640
  www.mcfarlandpub.com

To the late and much beloved Professor Ralph Adams Brown of the State University College at Cortland, New York, who in the early 1970s urged me, a graduate student, to write biographical history, and to my wife, Carla, who was correct, as usual, when she advised me to write historical fact and not historical fiction.

Contents

Acknowledgments — ix
Preface — 1
Prologue — 3

1. Homer: The Place of the Silversmith — 7
2. "Proximus Ascendi" — 11
3. A Clever Drawing on the Schoolhouse Door — 22
4. Having Interests and Aspirations Different from Others — 26
5. "That Grim Object Lesson" — 31
6. Honing His Craft — 39
7. The Lemon Tree Comes into Bloom — 45
8. An Ambition Rising Fast — 55
9. "Something in This Man's Face and Manner" — 59
10. A Request "Bold, Even to Presumption" — 63
11. Foiling the Plot to Kill "Nuts" — 67
12. On Loan to the White House — 73
13. A Desk Near the President's Chamber — 79
14. The Sound of Breaking and Falling Chains — 87
15. "Do You Think You Can Make a Handsome Picture of *Me*?" — 92
16. "Turned in Loose" for Six Months at the White House — 97
17. "It Is as Good as It Can Be Made" — 102
18. Last Days in the Service of Lincoln — 108
19. Assassination and the Iconic Image of Lincoln — 116

20. Lobbying for Carpenter and the Painting	121
21. A Dream Fulfilled and Dark Days	125
22. Carpenter's Last Three Decades	129
23. "To Portray *the Man* as He Was Revealed to Me"	136
24. "I Have Certainly Not Stolen a March on Anybody"	144
25. Homer and the Lincoln Legacy	150
Epilogue	154
Appendix A: Central Illinois Gazette *Story (May 4, 1859)*	157
Appendix B: Central Illinois Gazette *Editorial (December 7, 1859)*	158
Appendix C: Gideon Welles's Version of the September 22, 1863, Cabinet Meeting	161
Appendix D: The Preliminary Emancipation Proclamation (September 22, 1862)	163
Appendix E: The Final Emancipation Proclamation (January 1, 1863)	166
Appendix F: Carpenter and Stoddard Describe Lincoln's Sleepless Nights	169
Appendix G: Remarks of William O. Stoddard of New York	172
Chapter Notes	177
Sources	193
Index	199

Acknowledgments

Undertaking this biographical study of the men from a Lincoln mecca in Central New York State would not have been possible without the inspiration and assistance provided by several individuals. Any errors or discrepancies in the content of the book are my responsibility alone and not theirs.

First, I am grateful to Francis Carpenter and William Stoddard. Without their memoirs and reminiscences, detailed and colorful stories and connections to Lincoln, would, as in the case of DeVoe, remain unchronicled. Without the efforts of William O. Stoddard, Jr., the 1955 novelized version of his father's memoirs would not have sparked a budding historian's interest in the intersection of local and national Civil War era history. The critical edition of the memoirs prepared by historian Michael Burlingame (2000) was examined carefully by me, but the greatest reliance was placed upon the annotated edition researched so well by my friend, the Lincoln scholar Harold Holzer. This book, published in such a timely fashion in 2007, and others by Holzer were invaluable for my research.

The impetus for this book is attributable to another friend, David Quinlan of Homer. Artist, art educator, fellow member of the Homer Central School's Board of Education, and avid scholar of Carpenter and his paintings, Quinlan was the one who conceived of honoring Homer's connections to Lincoln during the national bicentennial observance of Lincoln's birth. Out of that vision grew "Homer's Celebration of Lincoln in Paint & Print." This was a five-day series of events in mid–May 2009, with two of the days devoted to lectures in Homer by Harold Holzer, one of the co-commissioners of the national Abraham Lincoln Bicentennial Commission appointed by President William Jefferson Clinton. In preparation for this community-wide celebration and to inform the residents of the local area, I, as co-chair with Quinlan of the Planning Committee, penned a series of well-received articles for the

Cortland Standard newspaper on Homer's connection to Lincoln through Carpenter, Stoddard, and DeVoe. Out of these installments sprang this book. I am indebted to Mr. Quinlan for his encouragement, for bringing to my attention valuable primary and secondary source materials, for working on the graphics of this book, and for offering explanations that only an astute lover of art could provide.

Thanks, too, must go to Patricia Meola of the Summit Historical Society of Summit, New Jersey, for assistance in research on the detective born in Homer, Eli DeVoe. What people in mid-nineteenth century Homer thought and felt could not have been captured on paper without the late Herbert Barber Howe's well researched biographies of Jedediah and Paris Barber. These two men from Homer encouraged the portrait painter within a young Frank Carpenter to emerge.

Much gratitude must be extended to one of Howe's relatives, the late Mary Bartlett Cowdrey (1910–1974). An art historian, archivist, and curator, Cowdrey did extensive research on Carpenter and his paintings with hopes of publishing a catalogue of his body of work. The project never reached fruition, but fortunately her notes, letters, and manuscripts were donated as a collection to the Cortland County Historical Society in 1953. I am profoundly indebted to this woman for her extraordinary efforts. In some small way, I hope this biographical chronicle proves her labors were not in vain. I am equally indebted to the late grandson of Carpenter, Emerson Ives, for transcribing Carpenter's diary and letters of Daniel Webster Carpenter and William Wallace Carpenter. A copy of the transcriptions is also part of the society's archives. Mindy Leisenring and Anita Wright of the historical society showed an exuberant willingness to assist me in accessing the valuable Cowdrey notes and Ives transcriptions, and I thank them most sincerely.

Extensive assistance was provided by Laine Dunham and Gary Sloan. They provided copies of an incredible cache of letters to Carpenter that are archived at Hildene, the Lincoln Family Home, in The Shires of Vermont. The letters were gifted to Hildene by A. George and Carlin Scherer. George is a descendant of Francis Carpenter. Other letters to and from Carpenter, as transcribed by Pam Lange, were provided by the Lovejoy Homestead, Bureau County Historical Society, Princeton, Illinois.

On the Stoddard side, Margaret Tessler of Albuquerque, New Mexico, graciously provided a bound, transcribed, unpublished copy of her great-grandmother's journal. Titled "Recollections of Kate Stoddard Gibson," the journal offers Kate's perspective on Lincoln and on the life and times of her brother, William Stoddard. It proved to be a superb resource.

The book manuscript was initially submitted for editing to Stoddard's granddaughter, Eleanor Stoddard, of Chevy Chase, Maryland. With her experience as a former *Time* researcher, her eye for accuracy, and her generous gift of time, Eleanor offered suggestions that greatly improved the book and surely would be welcomed by her grandfather the journalist.

Several individuals of Cortland and Tompkins County also deserve recognition for the support they provided. They include Stephanie Urso Spina for her insightful and painstaking revisions, followed by the officials of the Town and Village of Homer, the Homer Central Schools, Matt Neuman and the Homer Education Foundation, the Homer Center for the Arts, the Phillips Free Library, the Town of Preble's Historian Anne Henderson , and various friends who contributed information and artifacts. In nearby Tompkins County, Cornell University, with its own connections to Lincoln, Stoddard, and Carpenter, allowed me ample time to carefully examine the copy of the Emancipation Proclamation archived in the rare books collection of Olin Library. In Trumansburg, Jill Swenson, Ph.D., served as my advocate, coaching me through revisions that her professional writer's eye correctly deemed to be imperative and suggesting the publisher.

Perhaps most importantly it is the bulk of the 4000 or so Homer Junior High students I taught over the past four decades that have convinced me that local history, especially where it intersects national history, can have value to the next generation of citizens, though it is not tested on New York State exams. I thank them for what they taught me.

Last, but not least, I am grateful for the support and encouragement of my loving wife, Carla, and of our two grown children, Charlotte ("Lottie") and Martin, Jr. They each share my value of education and made sacrifices through the years, especially with the family computer, while I immersed myself in the teaching, reading, and writing of American history and then in the telling of the story of small town kids who made it big and made their birthplace a Lincoln mecca.

Martin A. Sweeney • Homer • New York

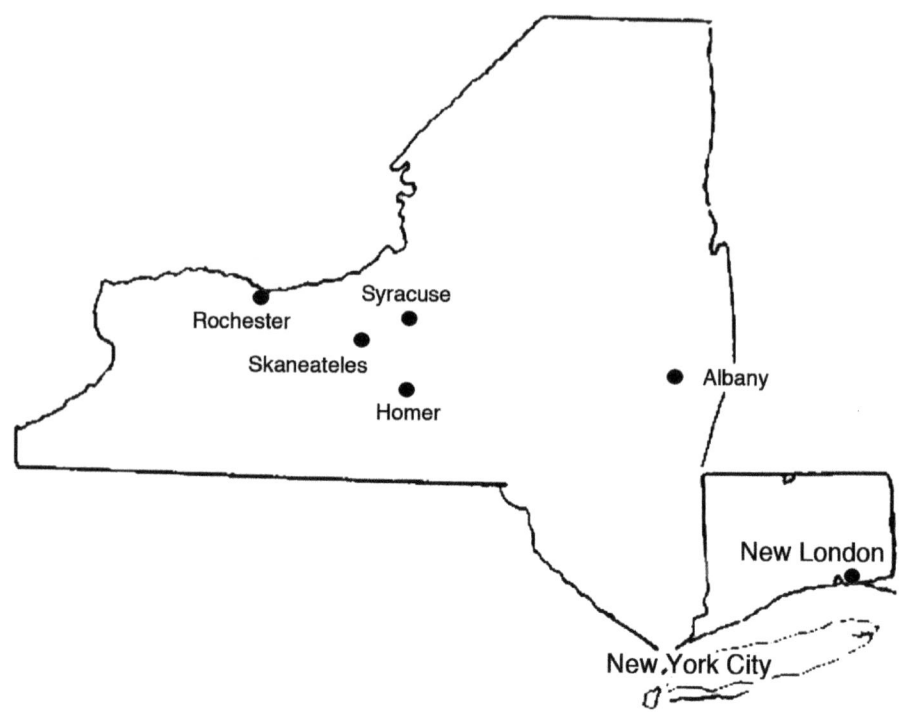

New York State (designed by David Quinlan).

Preface

Illinois indisputably deserves the title "Land of Lincoln," but New York State is home to the men who inscribed Abe's place in the nation's iconic imagery. Homer, NY, boasts of being the birthplace of three gentlemen — a detective, a portrait painter, and a journalist — who served the sixteenth president of the United States. Their lives are chronicled in this book.

The detective, Eli DeVoe, did his work so well that not much of a paper trail was left for historians. Yet, DeVoe was instrumental in foiling a plot to assassinate Abraham Lincoln before his first inauguration. Had DeVoe not done this, there would have been no President Lincoln and no remarkable story to tell of the lives of the other two men from Homer — Francis B. Carpenter and William O. Stoddard. These two men took separate career paths but their lives converged at the Lincoln White House where they shared a friendship based on more than common geographical origins. They forged a bond that resulted in Carpenter's most significant piece of artwork being accepted as a gift by the United States government in the Reconstruction era. This painting of *The First Reading of the Emancipation Proclamation before the Cabinet* has proven to be an integral part of the Lincoln legacy.

Not until this book has there been an effort at presenting the intertwined biographies of these three national figures under the same book cover. The story is a tribute to the town that produced the three men and to the village of the same name that boasts of 220 structures listed on the National Register of Historic Places. The place is justifiably named as "a new Lincoln Mecca" in *The Lincoln Forum Bulletin* of fall 2009, and its Green, according to internationally known Lincoln sculptor John McClarey, is "sacred geography." The institutions around this Green, both religious and secular, unconsciously played a role in "presidential image-making" in paint and print. What we know of significance about Lincoln today was provided through the efforts of Carpenter and Stoddard—men who traversed this Green.

Research for this study led to over fifty-five primary sources and forty-five secondary sources. Much material was collected over a lifetime by this native son of Homer who became increasingly intrigued over the years by his community's connection to the president he most admired. Access to additional valuable information was provided by those individuals and institutions gratefully listed in the Acknowledgements.

On Francis Bicknell Carpenter

"It has been my happiness to contribute *something* to the knowledge of, and love for the man who is certain to be regarded as the central man of the century."
— Francis B. Carpenter to Mrs. Lincoln in a letter dated January 5, 1867

"The most enduring accomplishments of that career were the creation of iconic portraits of Lincoln as an emancipator and father, as well as authorship of one of the most influential reminiscences [of Lincoln] ever published."
— Harold Holzer, in Introduction to the 2008 White House Historical Association edition of Carpenter's *Six Months at the White House with Abraham Lincoln: The Story of a Picture*, 1.

On William Osborn Stoddard

"Mr. Lincoln was the central figure of our age, and on him were concentrated the love, the faith, the reverence, the hate, the fear, and the calumny, of half the civilized world. The 'plain people' understood him better than did the politicians; and he in turn had a wonderful perception of the real condition of the popular heart and will."
— William O. Stoddard in *New York Citizen*, August 25, 1866, 1, col. 1.

"The presidential secretary who helped preserve Abraham Lincoln's memory in picture as well as word."
— Harold Holzer, in Afterword to his 2007 edited version of Stoddard's memoirs, *Lincoln's White House Secretary: The Adventurous Life of William O. Stoddard*, 348.

On Eli DeVoe

"Without DeVoe there would be no President Lincoln and no celebration of Homer's connection to the Great Emancipator in paint and print."
— Martin A. Sweeney, Homer Town Historian, opening of "Homer's Celebration of Lincoln in Paint and Print," May 13, 2009.

Prologue

Rights and freedom are significant concepts that predominate all through the history of the United States. After fighting unsuccessfully for one year for the rights of Englishmen, the delegates to the Second Continental Congress in colonial Philadelphia determined that the cause worth dying for was freedom from England. Thomas Paine made that point abundantly clear in his pamphlet *Common Sense*. In the summer of 1776, a Declaration of Independence was made public. Besides announcing the separation of the thirteen colonies from England and the creation of the United States of America, the document declared that "all men are created equal." It was understood that men referred to white males. Men was not a gender or race inclusive noun. Women were considered inferior to men and blacks inferior to whites. Black slaves were not men; they were property and could be bought and sold like cattle, horses, or swine. They had no rights. Thus, the seven year struggle for the United States' freedom from England did not encompass freedom for slaves. Neither did the Constitution ratified in 1787 nor the Bill of Rights added in 1791. The concept of freedom had its limits, but those limits would be addressed over time.

As payment for their fighting for freedom, soldiers in the Continental Army were to be paid in land. The State of New York set aside 1.75 million acres of land in the center of the state for that purpose. Known as the Military Tract, this area includes the present New York counties of Onondaga, Cortland, Cayuga, and Seneca as well as portions of Oswego, Schuyler, Tompkins, Yates and Wayne. The tract was surveyed and divided into twenty-eight townships (not to be confused with current towns) of 100 lots. Because a clerk named Robert Harpur in the office of the State Surveyor General was enamored of the Greek and Roman names he came across in his classical education, the tract townships were assigned these names: Aurelius, Brutus, Camillus,

Cato, Cicero, Cincinnatus, Dryden, Fabius, Galen, Hannibal, Hector, Homer, Junius, Locke, Lysander, Manlius, Marcellus, Milton, Ovid, Pompey, Romulus, Scipio, Sempronius, Solon, Sterling, Tully, Ulysses, and Virgil. A few names from British literature were slipped in as well.

Not until the middle of 1790 were the names of the eligible soldiers (or their heirs and assignees) placed in one barrel and matched with township lots from a list of numbers placed in the Township Box. After 94 lots in each township were balloted off, the remaining 6 lots were reserved for the development of places of worship and schools. Thus, in the case of the Town of Homer, in the center of the state, Lot 42 was settled by Amos Todd and Joseph and Rhoda Beebe in 1792. These first pioneers most likely purchased the lot from a Revolutionary soldier who preferred cash to a pig in a poke.

When Henry Godwin of Dutchess County drew Lot 11 in the Town of Homer as payment for his services as a captain in the Fifth Regiment of New York State, he felt he was too old to make the arduous trip to claim it. Instead, he sold the lot to his son-in-law, John DeVoe, a Revolutionary soldier of Hackensack, New Jersey. In 1808, John and Helena DeVoe took possession of their lot in the wilderness. There they raised a family of fifteen children and told them stories of the personal price paid for American freedom — of how their grandfather had been held captive for three years on the British prison ship, *Jersey*, and of how his home was plundered of all its goods before the very eyes of his wife and daughters.

Similar tales of hardship and deprivation were carried into the Town of Homer by those migrating from New England. The bulk of those early settlers traveled west from Connecticut and Massachusetts. The Noah Carpenters journeyed from Connecticut with stories of the exploits of a relative named Ethan Allen. The John Osborns moved to Connecticut from Massachusetts before crossing into New York. John's wife, Amelia Cotton, was a direct descendant of the Reverend John Cotton. When a Stoddard married into the family, that introduced a descendant of William Brewster, who arrived in Massachusetts in 1620 on the *Mayflower*.

When one knows the origins of Homer, New York, it comes as no surprise to find a picturesque piece of New England nestled there today in the form of the Homer Green. Lot No. 45 was set aside by the early settlers for worship and education. Since 1799, churches and a school have continued to be part of the landscape known as the Green. In that year, an organization was created that has endured and still maintains ownership of the Green. The organization is The First Religious Society of the town of Homer, and is still connected to the Congregational Church, which was established on October 12, 1801. Through the efforts of other denominations — Baptists, Methodists, and Episcopalians — a row of churches formed along the west side of the Green, with sheds out back for the horses and wagons of the devout who came down from the hills. Behind the sheds was the cemetery where frequently worshippers would tarry awhile among the tombstones, reading the inscriptions, visiting among the dead, and discussing the message of the day's sermon before departing for their homes.

Organized religion was and is frequently associated with efforts to mobilize public opinion to attain human rights, and with the migration from New England into Central New York in the early 1800s came Protestant clergy with notions of social reform. One such reformer was John Keep, the third settled pastor of the Congregational Church on the Green in Homer. Born and raised in Massachusetts and educated at Yale in Connecticut, the Reverend Keep received two calls in 1821, one from Brunswick, Maine, and one from Homer, New York. If he accepted the former, he would be the preacher to Bowdoin College and an instructor in moral philosophy. If he accepted the latter, he would be the pastor for four hundred Congregationalists in the wilderness of Central New York. After visiting both places, he chose Homer.

At first the community of Homer accepted Keep's call from the pulpit for temperance and for schooling for the girls, but the preacher as reformer ran into trouble when he joined the abolition movement and called for the emancipation of slaves in the southern states. The farmers and merchants of the town of Homer did not value the rights of black slaves as much as their own right to maintain a lucrative trade relationship with people in the slave state of Maryland. Advocating freedom for the slaves, as Keep wanted them to do, might threaten their economic livelihood. Folks in Baltimore might refuse to buy the pork and butter sent to them by river flatboats. With their consciences being uncomfortably pricked, the vocal elements of Homer deemed a change in pastors to be appropriate, and Keep agreed. He moved to Ohio in 1833. Joining other abolitionists, he helped to found Oberlin College, the first college to enroll females and blacks. In so doing, rights were extended at the grassroots level.

It seemed unlikely in 1833 that conservative Homer would ever contribute in any meaningful way at the grassroots level to the cause of emancipation, but Keep had planted seeds. The DeVoes and the Carpenters were Congregationalists. John and Helena DeVoe's third child, Eli, was twelve years old when Keep arrived in Homer. Eli was old enough to reason that if freedom was a right his grandparents thought Britain should not have denied the colonies, then freedom was a right that should not be denied the slaves. Noah Carpenter's grandson, Francis B. Carpenter, born three years after Keep left Homer, was impressed with the story of how close the Revolutionary struggle for freedom came to being betrayed by Benedict Arnold and he was told by his parents of the moral position espoused by Father Keep toward the black man's struggle for freedom. Freedom was connected to moral philosophy.

William Osborn Stoddard was born five years after Francis Carpenter into a Baptist family. He knew of a Revolutionary Stoddard's exploits in the Battle of White Plains and was brought up in an evangelical tradition that expressed concern for the rights of marginalized Americans, such as the Native Americans. William Stoddard discovered, at age ten, that his grandfather, John Osborn, was an abolitionist involved with transporting slaves to freedom in Canada. Later, in his teens, William Stoddard participated in the famous Jerry Rescue of 1851 in Syracuse, New York. The public demonstration of defiance against the Fugitive Slave Law of 1850 by abolitionists was "a grim object lesson" for Stoddard.

All three families—the DeVoes, the Carpenters, and the Stoddards—raised their children to appreciate their descendancy from Revolutionary patriots and imbued them with religiously based values of altruism. One son from each family would grow up and move away from Homer, taking the instilled values with them. They would enter upon distinctly different career paths. Eli DeVoe became a detective. Francis Carpenter became an artist. William Stoddard became a journalist. Yet, amazingly, each son of Homer became connected to President Abraham Lincoln. Through protection, paint, and print, each contributed to the story of The Great Emancipator, who pushed the nation through the earlier limitations to American rights.

To paraphrase Carpenter, if the Declaration of Independence was the assertion in 1776 that "all men are created equal," Lincoln's Emancipation Proclamation of 1863 was the consummation of this assertion. While Lincoln is technically not one of the Founding Fathers, he became one "four score and seven years" later by ultimately reconciling the Constitution with the Declaration of Independence. The Civil War and the Emancipation Proclamation were the origins of a "new birth of freedom" that would initiate an additional one hundred years of struggle in America for civil rights.

Within that age-old story of the American quest for the "inalienable rights" of "Life, Liberty, and the Pursuit of Happiness," three men arose from Homer and played their parts in shaping Lincoln's iconic presidential image. This is their remarkable story.

1

Homer: The Place of the Silversmith

It was late September 1866, and the word was out: "The painting has arrived!" The town of Homer's native son, the portrait painter Francis Bicknell Carpenter, had brought a canvas back by train from his studio in New York City. Folks from far and near arrived in buggies, surreys, Democrat wagons, and even lumber wagons. Horses from all over Cortland County waited patiently at the curb, swishing at flies with their tails, while their owners filed up the long flight of stairs in Barber's Hall on Homer's Main Street.[1] The curious pilgrims trod up to the third floor of what would be known a decade later as the Keator Opera House[2] to stand and gaze in amazement at the image of the assassinated president captured for all time in oil on canvas.

Carpenter's framed, unsigned painting on public display was nine feet high by fifteen feet wide, and its title was about as long as the canvas: *The First Reading of the Emancipation Proclamation before the Cabinet*. Depicted in oil was the likeness of Abraham Lincoln with members of his cabinet gathered at a table to hear the president present the document that initiated the process of freeing the slaves. For six months in 1864, Carpenter worked at the Executive Mansion in Washington, D.C., to prepare the painting while the War Between the States was being waged.[3]

Lincoln had recently and successfully steered the ship of state through four stormy years of civil strife. The Union was preserved, and the Thirteenth Amendment, at last, abolished slavery forever in the United States. Tragically, the president paid for it all with his life. On Good Friday, April 14, 1865, at Ford's Theater, a one ounce ball of lead fired from a derringer held by the disgruntled, pro–Confederate actor John Wilkes Booth altered the course of history. For those coming to see this painting, it was like coming to pay their

Carpenter's painting exhibited in Homer in 1866 (photography by Nelson Bakerman).

respects to their fallen leader. Seeing the portrait was the next best thing to seeing the real man. Shaking Frank Carpenter's hand at a tea party, hosted in his honor by Mrs. Jonah Stone of Homer,[4] meant shaking the hand that not only painted Lincoln's face but the hand that clasped Lincoln's hand in friendship — the same hand that penned the document that called for the liberation of slaves in the rebel states.

Unfortunately, the hand of the painter kept returning to the painting. Carpenter felt compelled to keep working on the painting. In his mind, the painting on exhibit in Homer was still a work in progress. Paint was still being applied here and there to the canvas — particularly to the images of Chase, Stanton, and Blair.[5]

Another of Homer's native sons, William Osborn Stoddard, was greatly troubled by his friend's compulsion. Stoddard once complained that Carpenter went about his craft like a farmer who could not stop building a fence; he simply had to keep adding one more rail across the top, just one more.[6] Carpenter listened to Stoddard's advice but, except for the visage of Lincoln, he was reluctant to heed it. Although Carpenter continued to apply paint, the two men continued to be friends.

Carpenter was born first, on August 6, 1830. Frank was one of eight children, the first son and second child of Asaph H. and Almira Clark Carpenter, who were members of the Congregational faith community in Homer.[7] Noah Carpenter, Frank's grandfather, migrated from Pomfret, Connecticut, in 1800 and settled in an area that eight years later became Cortland County. Noah's mother was Charity Allen Carpenter, a sister of the great Ethan Allen of Revolutionary War fame.[8] The Carpenters came from hardy New England stock, as did many who settled in Homer, and brought with them stirring accounts of fighting for freedom in an earlier time.

Another young man, William O. Stoddard, whose grandfather also migrated to Homer, similarly knew and depicted Lincoln, not in paint but in words. Stoddard, too, worked at the Executive Mansion. He occupied an office on the second floor directly across the hall from the president's office. From 1861 to 1864, he served as an assistant personal secretary to Mr. and Mrs. Lincoln. He, too, touched the hand that penned the Emancipation Proclamation. He held the original document and made handwritten copies for the president as the day of jubilee was fast approaching for those in chains.

Stoddard, whom Midwesterners like to claim as their own after his brief residence there, was born five years after Carpenter, on September 24, 1835, at his maternal grandfather's house on Albany Post Road in the freshly incorporated village of Homer.[9]

John and Amelia Osborn were Baptists who came to Homer from Albany, New York, in 1808, the same year the state legislature separated Cortland County from Onondaga County. In the wilderness of Central New York, the Osborns built a residence and John set up a silversmith shop nearby. To the Native Americans of the region, Homer was known as "the place of the silversmith."[10] The couple prospered and began adding onto their residence, building toward the road. It was the first brick house in the region, not palatial but with large, pleasant rooms. The brick was painted yellow, as was the custom in that day.[11] Amelia was known as "a handsome woman with beautiful black hair that curled in soft silky curls."[12] Squire Osborn became a respected justice of the peace for Homer and went on to represent Cortland County in the state legislature.[13] In 1819, he was one of the co-founders of the prestigious academy in Homer, which the state chartered that year.[14]

Stoddard's mother was Sara Ann Osborn, one of three daughters born to John and Amelia. Sara was sent to Rochester, New York, to attend Phipps Union Seminary. It was there that she met Samuel Prentice Stoddard, the deputy postmaster of Rochester, and fell in love. The young couple came to Homer to be married by the Baptist minister, the Reverend Alfred Bennett, another co-founder of the academy. The young couple took up residence in Richmond, a village south of Rochester, and Samuel became the operator of Henry Stanwood & Co., the first bookstore in the city. A daughter, Julia, was born three years before William, and other children — Kate, Henry, Charles, and John — followed to complete the family circle.[15]

While the Stoddards were visiting Sara's parents in Homer in 1835,

William was born in the upstairs back bedroom, the same room in which Sara had been born. He was named William John Stoddard after his grandfather. At age sixteen, with his father's permission, he replaced John with Osborn.[16]

In 1842, when Stoddard was seven years old, the bookstore in Rochester was sold, a victim of the depression that followed the Panic of 1837. The family relocated to Homer by a canal packet boat to Syracuse and then by stage.[17] Besides the house occupied by an extended Osborn family and the silversmith shop just around the corner on Main Street, the young boy had his grandfather's twenty-acre farm on East Hill to explore, as well as land the squire owned between Homer and Cortland village.[18]

Twelve-year-old Carpenter and seven-year-old Stoddard were not close childhood friends, but young Will had one close friend nearer to his own age. Across the road, at the intersection of Albany and Main, was a two story brick house in which Andrew Dickson White was born in 1833. Together, the two lads explored the wildflower-covered banks of the nearby Tioughnioga (pronounced *tie-off-ni-o-ga*) River and swam in the millponds at opposite ends of the village. They and other children loved to climb trees along the river, walk out on the limbs, and swing from one to the other while squirrels sat on mossy logs cracking nuts and chattering away at the intruders.[19] The two explorers remained life-long friends, even after they assumed different careers. White went on to become the first president of Cornell University in nearby Ithaca, New York, and later served as U.S. ambassador to Germany.[20]

Settled by religionists, Homer developed an early reputation for being a place conducive for raising a family within strict religious principles. Homer gave Carpenter and Stoddard their roots. Here they received their early schooling, and here they interacted with people whose values they absorbed. In Homer they learned that education, ambition, and adventure were worthwhile pursuits blessed by God. Ideas of unfettered possibilities were encouraged. They set upon career paths that converged in their adult lives during tumultuous years of human bondage and civil war. Together they were responsible for the only nineteenth-century history painting of Abraham Lincoln to hang in the U.S. Capitol Building. This and their written reminiscences about their time with Lincoln helped shape the sixteenth president into an American icon for generations to come. In accounts of the abolition movement, their names link the Great Emancipator to Homer forevermore.

2

"Proximus Ascendi"

The Tioughnioga River, the artery that brought the first pioneers and commerce into Homer after the Revolutionary War, flows effortlessly southward only yards from the farmhouse of John Osborn. Here, as a child, Stoddard used the garret on the second floor of his grandfather's house as a play room. He had heard stories of past events, but, here in this garret, history became very real. He had been told stories of the Revolutionary War and was proud to learn that his great-grandfather had been one of Israel Putnam's men and had sustained a wound at the battle of White Plains.[1]

The young, impressionable boy discovered a cavalry saber in the garret which particularly captured his imagination. In his mind, as he swung the saber through the air, it was gloriously associated with the fighting at White Plains. Perhaps it had been used to deprive General "Gentleman Johnny" Burgoyne of the precious fieldpiece, Old Brimfield, that was housed on the Green and patriotically fired every Fourth of July. No doubt, the notches along the saber's edge had come there through violent combat with saber-wielding British Redcoats. The several dark stains upon the relic were surely not rust but "the stains of the blood which had poured in battle from the many victims who had been mowed down by that tremendously curved scythe of war."[2] This and other items of military weaponry found in the garret contributed to the boy's appreciation of historical events and helped to instill in him a belief in service to one's country and to a cause worth fighting for—freedom.

Another garret over the red-painted granary on the same property in Homer was "swarming with ancient machinery and the wrecks of all manner of domestic and mechanical undertakings." Later, Stoddard reminisced that "these two garrets had much to do with some parts of my education." He explained that "I had more play room than any other boy in the village but I was not allowed to bring the other boys into my places of wonders."³ Alone in the garrets, the boy entered into the adventurous world of his imagination, which contributed later to his flair for writing adventure stories for young boys.

Once, he and another young friend, Hank Babcock, decided to go on an adventure upon the Tioughnioga River. A small, flat-bottomed sailboat carried them on a voyage of discovery upstream until stopped by the dam at the upper mill pond. In traversing the barrier twice, they managed to take a ducking twice. For his day's adventure, a drenched Hank Babcock received a strapping and a stern warning at home about "letting Willie Stoddard get him into any more wild escapades."⁴

From time to time, Stoddard could not resist the temptation to tease his younger siblings. Once, he took his sister Kate's doll, Anna, and hung her from the apple tree near the gate to the barnyard. Kate was much disturbed, convinced that Anna "was surely dead and suffering." On yet another occasion, Kate was shocked to find her brother had dissected her doll Flora. She was angry that he "let all her sawdust run out so that her legs were never right afterwards."⁵

West of the Osborn residence was Wisdom's Gate, a fairly large tavern, fronting Main Street, with a dining room to accommodate the many travelers brought by stagecoach. Here, since its opening in 1839, horse and traveler refreshed themselves while traversing the Albany Post Road, but alcoholic libations were not served. Hence, the establishment was also known as Temperance Tavern. An empty decanter, without a cork, was suspended from the ceiling in the barroom to signify to all the character of the premises. A sign out front read:

> Come, traveler, slack thy parching thirst
> And drive away dull care
> Thou needest not broach thy little purse
> For I am free as air.

The tee-totaling Quaker proprietor was George Washington Samson, a very fat and jolly man with a pet rooster trained to crow upon command.⁶ This man of principle made an impression upon young Stoddard, and the lad's association with the many interesting travelers passing through Wisdom's Gate introduced him to people and accounts of events outside of Homer.

Across Main Street from the tavern were the stately residences of the wealthy Schermerhorn and Williams families. Their children were Stoddard's playmates. Jacob Maus Schermerhorn of Rochester had married Louisa Anna Barber, the oldest of the five children of Jedediah and Matilda Barber of Homer in 1831. The Reverend John Keep officiated. In 1841, the couple purchased the

Birthplaces of Francis Carpenter (top) and William Stoddard (courtesy David Quinlan).

residence at what is now No. 90 South Main Street, Homer, and developed it into a lavish estate. With a beautiful formal garden, The Hedges was worthy of a man who was successful at banking, building, and farming. Later, profitable ventures in railroading and other growing corporations in the Northeast made Schermerhorn a prominent name in not just the community of Homer but in the national affairs of the Republican Party. By 1865 he had an income in excess of $43,000, the largest income in Cortland County, according to the *Cortland County Republican*.[7]

North of The Hedges was the Williams family. Stoddard's political education began with Mr. Williams, the owner of a woolen factory in the upper part of the village. Mr. Williams purchased wool from the sheep farmers of the area and manufactured good woolen cloth. Northern members of the Whig Party wanted a tariff passed to generate revenue for the federal government and to protect Northern factories from cheap foreign imports. Southern Democrats insisted upon a free-market approach that would increase the demand for their cotton crop. In this sectional tussle the latter won out. Stoddard's father and grandfather, who were both Whigs, explained to him the political causes of the decision by Cortland County farmers to cease raising sheep. This, in turn, caused the Williams woolen mill to shut down, the Williams family to move away, and Will Stoddard to lose little Eb Williams as a playmate.[8]

The Osborns may not have owned a fancy carriage like the Schermerhorns, but for young William Stoddard, there was one piece of furniture at his grandfather's house which was the object of a manner of respect bordering upon awe. This was a large mahogany secretary with a writing table covered in green cloth that could be drawn out for use. It had many drawers, but one was of special interest. This was the drawer containing two rifled derringer pistols that had been made for the boy and which he would, upon attaining the age of eight, be allowed to take out and frequently practice with — on the condition that he mold his own bullets. He became quite proficient with the derringer, knocking off the head of a daisy at ten paces with either hand. He also became quite aware of the costliness of powder and shot, since the purchase of these items required him to save up any money he might beg or earn.[9]

Respect for firearms, including knowing their proper maintenance and use, was typically part of any early nineteenth century male's education in Central New York State. Upon attaining the requisite age, Stoddard was taught how to use his grandfather's flintlock that hung near the staircase. He was expected to know how to disassemble it, clean it, and reassemble it. He was permitted to take it with him on forays into the deep woods, as long as he went alone and took no other boys with him. On long, solitary wanderings, the boy built up his physical endurance and developed a confidence at hunting and navigating his way through the dense wilderness. He said, "Not once did I get lost or feel any doubt as to the right way home from wherever I might be."[10]

Stoddard developed a great respect for nature, too. In his memoir, he attributes his botanical knowledge to his Grandmother Osborn. At an early age, Stoddard was instructed by her in "the names and qualities of every tree, flower, grass, root, and plant." Armed with that knowledge, he was sent forth by his grandmother to collect wild herbs. He returned with checkerberry, sarsaparilla, and other ingredients needed to make a tasty root beer. He would journey to the woods above the old stone quarry,[11] which was the best place to find sassafras, sarsaparilla, and an abundance of juicy, wild red and black raspberries.[12] For currants, which Grandmother Osborn made into jelly and wine, there was no need to travel far. The dark, glossy berries grew in abundance on luxuriant bushes lining the Osborn garden.[13] The boy was quite at home at the Osborn farm and in the natural environment of the Homer area, where he came by much of his informal education.

Here, too, at the school on the Common, young Stoddard received a portion of his formal education. The academy originated from a common school. The Green, or Common, was at the heart of the village, which consisted of only a few wooden-framed homes and businesses. Livestock were permitted to graze here, and the early settlers had decreed that the periphery should be dedicated to worship and education, as is still the norm. Thus, at the north end of the Green, a twenty-two by forty-four foot two-story structure was built by Nathan B. Darrow, the first pastor of the Congregational Church. It served a dual function: schoolhouse and house of worship. From 1805 to 1822, Major Adin Webb, a patriot transplanted from Connecticut, instructed the local youth in this building.[14]

In 1817, a group of twenty-one Homer men, anxious to promote literature in the new and growing county of Cortland, took it upon themselves to purchase a piece of land on the Common. Their plan was to erect a two-story structure, at the cost of $2,000, and to petition the Board of Regents at Albany to incorporate the school under the name of Homer Academy. The petition, dated March 1, 1817, nominated eighteen men to serve as trustees: Joshua Ballard, Hezekiah Roberts, Enos Stimson, George Rice, Dr. Lewis S. Owen, Andrew Dickson, Martin Keep, Matthias Cook, John Bement, Jesse Searl, William Lucas, the Rev. Elnathan Walker, Rufus Beach, Levi Bowen, Townsend Ross, David Coye, John Miller, and John Osborn, Will's grandfather.[15]

The requested charter of incorporation, bearing the signature of Chancellor John Tayler, was granted on February 2, 1819, by the Regents of the State of New York. The state required the name be changed to Cortland Academy, and the academy became one of the first twenty incorporated academies in the state. This was just eleven years after Cortland County was created.[16]

The trustees of the Cortland Academy went to work. It was their mission to educate the young people of Homer and its environs by hiring the best instructors. Teachers came from Amherst, Dartmouth, Hamilton, and Williams. Capable principals were hired to provide educational leadership and to supervise the elementary and upper level curricula. Three programs of study were available: classical, scientific, and teacher training. A vital part of the local economy was based on the boarding of students in the homes of Homer villagers. Student enrollment increased rapidly. In 1829, 197 students registered. The number was up to 575 by 1851. Eight years later it leveled off to 452, with some students coming from as far away as Iowa, Michigan, and Ohio.[17]

Much of this growth was credited to the progressive efforts of a Hamilton College graduate, Samuel Buell Woolworth. Samuel arrived in Homer in 1830. He served as the academy's principal for the next twenty-one years and as president of the New York State Teachers' Association from 1848 to 1849.[18] During his tenure in Homer, many students were fortunate to have him as their academic mentor, and that included William Stoddard and Francis Carpenter.

The twenty-one-year-old principal was a firm believer in the value of coeducation. He was most supportive of the Ladies' Department that had been established at the academy in 1821.[19] This was quite a progressive undertaking, but Woolworth's philosophy and efforts meshed well with those of John Keep, the Congregationalist pastor and social reformer who arrived in Homer in 1821 and successfully pushed for coeducation. Woolworth was not one of those who winced when, from the pulpit, Keep expressed his opposition to the consumption of alcohol and to the practice of slavery. Among some citizens Keep garnered a reputation as a liberal, if not radical, thinker.[20] Among the majority, his paternal regard for his flock earned him the affectionate title of Father Keep. He became a trustee of the academy, and, as such, he and Principal Woolworth were strong advocates for the advantages of education. The two worked tirelessly to serve as articulate role models for males coming of age in nineteenth century Central New York. While Keep left Homer before Carpenter and Stoddard enrolled, it was not unusual in their days at the academy to find Principal Woolworth on the Common with a group of students and a telescope making astronomical calculations.[21] Even Woolworth's home provided affordable room and board for out-of-state students; in 1848, the rate charged was two dollars per week.[22]

It was Samuel Woolworth who instituted Exhibition Day. This was a day-long event at the end of the academic year in which students publicly displayed their academic accomplishments. Exhibition Day commenced with a procession from the academy to the Congregational Church next door, the only edifice in town that could seat over nine hundred people — an edifice that the academy's young scholars somewhat irreverently nicknamed "God's Old Barn." Led by a band, the trustees, followed by the learned faculty and then the student body, marched forth from the academy and proceeded north past the white Episcopal Church and east along the north end of the Common. Upon reaching Main Street, the colorful pageant continued south until it came to the main walkway that crossed the Common. Boys in their Sunday go-to-meeting clothes and girls in white gowns with pink or blue sashes followed their mentors across the Common and up the front steps of the church past a good-sized assemblage of proud parents, supportive friends, and interested citizens.[23] No doubt, it was a sight to behold.

Once all had taken their places within the sanctuary, with the trustees and six faculty members seated facing the audience, the dignified Principal Woolworth arose and with the words "Proximus ascendi" introduced the young scholars whose names appeared on the program. One by one, students came to the stage. Some offered memorized recitations in Latin or Greek. Others delivered from memory essays they had crafted in the best style of the day. For their efforts, presenters received colorful and fragrant bouquets of flowers prepared by Robert Howard, the gardener employed by the wealthiest man in the village, Jedediah Barber. It was obvious to developing scholars like Stoddard and Carpenter that in this place on the Common learning and the learner were highly prized.[24]

Stoddard clearly knew that his grandfather also valued education. Not only was John Osborn one of the founders of the academy on the Common, but during the winter months, sons of old acquaintances boarded at the house on Albany Post Road while attending the academy. A number of them were allowed to board for free. The squire was considered to be truly a Christian pure of heart and was only too happy to help out those who could not afford to pay. He was quite proud to have given assistance to those young men who subsequently went on to successful careers.[25] And in the twenty-one years that Woolworth served as its principal, the academy churned out the likes of the Reverend Theodore T. Munger, a well-known anti-slavery preacher and theologian; Dr. Stephen Smith, who helped found the New York Health Department; and Almon Bacon, who added an "e" to his name and founded Bacone University in Oklahoma, a college for Native Americans. Then, too, there was Amelia Stone Quinton, co-founder of the Women's National Indian Association, and Dr. James Salisbury, originator of the germ theory in work antedating that of Pasteur, Huxley, and Tyndall.[26] For its day, it was a most impressive roster.

Now, appreciative of instruction as he was, young Stoddard was not above some classroom mischief. On one occasion, which he confessed to only some thirty years after the fact, he deftly managed to capture an assortment of stinging insects—wasps, hornets, and bees—and to place them in a lidded pasteboard box. He carried the box into the academy one morning and, during recitation, carefully placed it under an unoccupied desk near his own. With a stick he knocked off the lid, and, in his words, "the new candidates for admission to the academy were free to present their credentials." As the angrily humming throng of bugs arose in the classroom, Stoddard, as planned, scrambled out the window near his desk. Hanging onto a lightning rod, the little imp managed to observe the "scene of heterogeneous and exclamatory confusion" he had caused with this Pandora's Box. During the days that followed, he derived satisfaction from the efforts of the perplexed learned men of Homer in trying to determine "how so many different kinds of stinging insects could have broken out of the same nest and how and why they had made their nest in the schoolroom."[27]

Then, too, could it have been Stoddard who climbed to the school belfry one winter and packed the bell with so much snow that it was unable to ring in the morning? Could he have participated in the prank that resulted in Judge Keep's red cow making its way up the stairs of the school? Its bellowing horned head could be seen protruding out of an upper window. Stoddard took delight in telling of these schoolboy antics years later in his memoir.[28]

Another student's mischief once got Stoddard into trouble, and from this experience he learned early on of the concept of injustice. Squire Osborn decided to enroll his young grandson in the district school at the south end of Main Street instead of at the academy on the Common. The schoolteacher, Miss Hathaway, believed that if you spared the rod, you spoiled the child. Stoddard, years later, recalled, "One morning I was bending over my book at my desk when down over my shoulders came several sharp cuts of a heavy switch." The blows were delivered without explanation. Afterwards, Stoddard found that the teacher thought he was the boy who had been lobbing "paperballs" in class. Stoddard concluded: "That is the idea which lies at the bottom of most of the national declarations of war and the people who suffer are rarely the ones who were to blame." After this incident, John Osborn returned his grandson to his desk at the academy.[29]

Stoddard wrote of deriving enjoyment from working with his grandfather at his silversmith shop, assisting him in the stamping out of small articles. He was particularly fascinated by the process of melting down Mexican dollars and making silver ornaments for the Native Americans. Equally fascinating to him were the warriors and their squaws who visited the shop. It was obvious that they held the squire in high regard, for he was not only their silversmith but also a respected counselor in their affairs. This had been earned from his many years of legislative experience at the state capital where he had shown wisdom in dealing with the rights of a people assigned to a reservation existence. As the grandson of the silversmith esteemed by the Onondagas, young Stoddard was presented with a fine bow made for him by one of their warriors.[30] He learned that the Haudenosaunee, or "People of the Longhouse," were not the fearful, inebriated savages he might have expected from the story told of the damages they had done in 1800 to Major Enos Stimson's tavern when he refused to serve them any more whiskey.[31] On the contrary, these people of a different culture received increased admiration once he learned that, according to family lore, he had a paternal ancestor who had married the daughter of a Pequot or Narragansett chieftain. In his estimation, there was nothing quite like being a descendant "from the oldest families in the country."[32]

John Osborn, much respected deacon of the Baptist church where his brother-in-law, Edward Bright was the pastor, was a model of virtue for his grandchildren. They would remember the family patriarch fondly years later as "a lovely man; good to everyone ... and full of good works." They would recall, in particular, a holiday dinner in Homer for which their mother prepared a succulent roast pig with its tail tied with a festive blue ribbon and a savory potato stuck in its mouth. When their mother went to lift the large platter, their grandfather quickly stepped forward, saying, "Sara, do not lift that, tis too heavy for you." What remained in their memories was the tone of his voice—"so tender and kind"—and, of course, the toys he fashioned for them out of wood.[33]

Many events and individuals were influential in Stoddard's early development, but none made an impact upon him like the life-altering experience he had as a ten-year-old and described in his memoir with vivid detail. It was during a visit at his Grandfather Osborn's farmhouse in Homer that he thought he heard a strange noise, a singing sound, coming up through the broad wooden planks in the kitchen floor. Being a curious lad by nature, Stoddard went outside to the entrance to the cellar and threw back the doors. Stepping quietly down the cold stone steps, he entered the dank and musty cellar and squinted into the half-lit area from which the mysterious sounds were emanating. Soon, his eyes beheld a black man seated upon an upturned bushel basket. With his eyes closed, the man was rhythmically swaying back and forth and singing:

> I got a wife, an' she got a baby,
> 'Way up north in old Canaydy.
> Won't they shout when they see Old Shady
> Comin,' comin'?—Hail, mighty day!

Unnoticed by the man, the boy turned away and slowly walked back up the cellar stairs, much perplexed by what he had seen. Lost in thought, he came upon his grandfather at the top of the stairs. He was startled to find the tall, gaunt man did not have a happy visage. Quite the contrary, "there was the glitter of ice in eyes that had always been benevolent." With a voice of unusually stern admonishment, his grandfather simply said, "William, you have heard *nothing*, and you have seen *nothing*. Remember." The boy haltingly responded, "Yes, Grandfather," and the old man turned and left without uttering another word. What had young Stoddard heard and seen that he was not supposed to have heard and seen? This caused him much consternation.[34]

Why was there a black man in the corner of his grandfather's cellar? The man's skin color was not unusual to him; Stoddard had seen black people. A few, only a few, resided in the village of Homer. The wealthy Barber family had a black domestic, a fine cook named Hannah, and there was a mulatto barber in town known for his "vast personal dignity." Then, too, there was Don Brown from the north end of the village. Brown was a sawyer and delivered wood to the district schools. He walked with a noticeable up and down movement because one leg was shorter than the other. He was "very popular among the residents of Homer" because of his generosity and flair for amusing antics. In another fifteen years Don Brown would be known as "The Popcorn Man," earning four or five dollars a day (approximately $100 to $125 in today's

A SCENE IN DR. G. A. TOMPKINS' PASTORAL DRAMA, "THE VILLAGE GREEN."

From a daguerreotype by Professor Beck, handbill for play produced by Hose Co. 1 of Homer, New York, Keator Opera House, Barber Block, October 17, 1906 (author's collection).

money) as a purveyor of peanuts, candy, and popcorn balls the size of grapefruits.[35] So, where did this black person in the cellar come from — young Stoddard's over-active imagination?

The next morning, to convince himself that it had not been merely a dream, the boy carefully and noiselessly crept down the cellar steps again. Peering into the dark, he heard no singing; he saw no black man. But, there was the upturned bushel basket! No, the event, as he noted years later, had not been a dream.

Stoddard came to discover, in whispered conversations, that his grandfather, John Osborn, pillar of the community of Homer, was involved in something called the Underground Railroad. This was a secret organization determined to transport black people like Old Shady out of bondage in the South and into freedom in Canada across the New York State border. This was William Stoddard's introduction to the sinful practice of slavery and part of his education in abolitionism. He learned that his grandfather was an abolitionist, or one opposed to the practice of slavery in the United States of America. He was active as a conductor on the Underground Railroad.[36] The first brick house in Homer, the home of the silversmith, was a station where runaway slaves could find food and lodging. Then, at night, under the cover of darkness, the squire, it can be surmised, secretly transported them by his horse-pulled farm wagon up Cayuga Street and northward on the narrow West Road to the intersection of Cold Brook Road. There, at the farm of Oren Cravath, a respected deacon of the Congregational Church, refuge could be found at another station.[37] And so it went, from station to station, ever northward, the movement of human property through Cortland County, a region where not everyone was yet opposed to slavery and not everyone, like Cravath, was a member of the county's anti-slavery society.[38] Thus, William Osborn Stoddard, named after his grandfather, first approached the concept of human bondage in his grandfather's cellar and climbed up those cellar steps to share his grandfather's abolitionist values—"Proximus ascendi."

3

A Clever Drawing on the Schoolhouse Door

Meanwhile, Frank Carpenter's childhood in the town of Homer had its own singular life-shaping experiences. While Stoddard spent most of his childhood within the mercantile lifestyle of a village bookseller, Carpenter spent his within the frugal agrarian pursuits so typical of Central New York State in the early 1800s. As was the tradition of that pioneer era, farmers expected their sons to grow up to be like them — God-fearing, self-reliant farmers earning a decent living in a self-sufficient economy. Hard-working Asaph Carpenter was no exception. He expected as much of his son Frank. Deep was his disappointment. As soon as he was old enough to express any preferences, the boy wrinkled his brow and showed a stubborn disdain for the agrarian lifestyle.

Like other boys and girls in the area, Carpenter was sent to a nearby one-room district school for three years. He found himself in a gathering of stellar young classmates. The roster included names that would be of note in future years: Calvin Woolworth, Theodore Munger, Martius Lynde, and David Hannum.[1] Woolworth, the son of the academy's principal, became a successful patent attorney in Brooklyn; Munger flowered into a Yale theologian of renown; Lynde entered law and became a life member of the Brooklyn Art Association; and Hannum became the basis for the witty, horse-trading protagonist in Edward Noyes Westcott's best-selling novel of 1889, *David Harum: A Story of American Life*, later adapted to the screen in 1934 as a movie with the same title starring Will Rogers. The first three classmates remained close to Carpenter and followed his future career with interest.

While attending this one-room school, Carpenter, at the age of eight, first showed an interest in artistic endeavors. One day, during recess, a classmate named Fessenden Nott Otis did a clever drawing in pencil upon a panel of the wooden schoolhouse door — something that would, no doubt, be deemed in later years an act of graffiti or vandalism. Carpenter admired this handiwork by a lad who was destined to become a preeminent urologist and an author and illustrator of books on art and travel. From Otis' modeling, Carpenter resolved that he should like to become an artist. The seed had been planted.[2] It needed cultivation to bloom and to eventually bear fruit, but the day would come, in just a short thirteen years, when Carpenter paid a surprise visit to Fessenden N. Otis and thanked him for "the result of his school-day sketching."[3]

For the next five or six years, without the benefit of instruction, young Carpenter produced drawings of all sorts of things whenever time permitted and even when time did not permit. Often he would travel three miles down the road to the village to invest what limited funds he had in a sheet of unruled paper and a pencil. When paper of any kind ran out, the aspiring artist turned to whatever was immediately available: flat fieldstones, discarded wooden boards, and blank interior and exterior walls around the farm. At one point, much to his father's dismay, Carpenter chalked a scene depicting the famous capture of Major Andre with the British plans for capturing the fort at West Point. Another scene showed William Tell of Switzerland, a champion of freedom, shooting the apple placed upon his son's head.[4]

This penchant for artistic rendering of historic events was met with rebuke from his father. How mortified Asaph was to hear a respected church deacon speak scornfully of Frank: "Humph! You can't turn over a chip on his father's farm without findin' a pictur' of a chicken or sumthin' on t'other side on't!"[5] In spite of snubs and sneers from others and his father's admonitions to get this "nonsense" out of his head, young Carpenter persisted.

When Carpenter attained the age of thirteen years, his much exasperated father sent him to a grocer in Ithaca, New York. If the boy was determined to not follow in his father's footsteps, he might, instead, take to earning his living in this world as a merchant. Again, Asaph's efforts were met with disappointment. The grocer tried for six months to make a merchant of the boy. Finally, in despair, the grocer sent a letter to Asaph indicating that his son "showed nothing of the intelligence necessary for mercantile business," and that "drawing molasses was not the kind of drawing which the young gentleman preferred." The grocer sent the boy back to Homer with the advice that his father keep him on the farm.[6]

Still, the boy persisted. He was obsessed, and upon learning that George L. Clough, a painter from Auburn, New York, was coming to Homer to paint some portraits, Carpenter was determined to see the young artist at work. With permission reluctantly granted, the aspiring artist watched how paint was applied to canvas for the first time in his life. Inspired, he hurried home to try out his newly acquired ideas of color. But how was that possible? He had no paints or pencils. A neighbor suggested that house paint would do as well, and so the boy set about to improvise as best he could. A pound of white lead paint he got in the village. He scrounged up some lampblack, which was used for marking sheep. A reddish-brown pigment he concocted by pulverizing some lumps of iron oxide he found in the barn. Carriage-painters' pencils became his means of sketching. A piece of shingle became his pallet, and a portion of coat lining became his canvas. Now, all he lacked was a live model, but whom could he get?[7]

After much coaxing, the lad convinced his mother, Almira, to sit for him. However, because Asaph had become really angry in his opposition to his son's desires, both mother and son agreed that the portrait-making should be done in secret. Near its completion, the clandestine project was discovered. Looking for his "lazy boy" one day to assist with farm work, Asaph went straight to Frank's room. Coming into the room, Asaph found his son at work on the 30 in. by 25 in. portrait. Anger changed to awe as Asaph looked at the painting and came to terms with the fact that the boy had, indeed, captured a more than fair likeness of Almira. Perhaps it was true that this boy who had no mind for groceries actually had a mind for making likenesses. Perhaps this boy whose hands seemed unfit for farming actually had hands fit for painting something more than just the sides of a barn. "It is your mother, I suppose," he admitted somewhat gruffly. He then turned and left the room in haste, apparently forgetting the reason he had come there in the first place.[8]

Portrait in oil of Jedediah Barber by Carpenter (courtesy Phillips Free Library, Homer, New York; photograph by David Quinlan).

This event, documented by a Carpenter biographer, was a pivotal moment in young Carpenter's formative years. His father's manner toward him changed noticeably. He even agreed to sit for the boy to make his likeness, too—but only on rainy days, of course, when it was not fit for farm chores. At one sitting, Asaph, exhausted from his labors, fell asleep within ten minutes after being seated, making him an ideal model. The finished product met with approval. Even the neighbors attested that Frank's handiwork was better than the work of itinerant painters who had passed through the region. It was a small compliment but enough for the aspiring portraitist to feel encouraged to continue asking to receive professional instruction.[9]

At about this same time, another pivotal moment in Carpenter's life occurred. He met the Barbers, the wealthiest family in Homer. An acquaintance with the head of the Barber family, fifty-seven-year-old Jedediah, and more especially with Jedediah's third-born child, Paris, developed into a lifelong friendship that had a significant impact on Frank Carpenter's career.

4

Having Interests and Aspirations Different from Others

Jedediah Barber was the affable owner of the Great Western Store, a three-storied mercantile establishment on the east side of Main Street, in the village of Homer. The store employed about eight to ten clerks, including the fathers of William Stoddard and Andrew White. Samuel Stoddard and Horace White saw this as temporary work to tide them over until the depressed economy abated and better employment opportunities returned. Uncle Jed, as Barber was known, was said to offer "everything a farmer could raise or a skilled worker could make." He shipped firkins of white butter and barrels of succulent pork by flatboats down the Tioughnioga River that flowed behind the store. These waters moved goods southward, and ultimately the goods were purchased by folks in Baltimore, Maryland. People within a ten mile radius of Barber's store came to buy tobacco, maple syrup, tumblers, tea, sugar, wallpaper, nails, and, rum — all manner of goods that he brought to Homer from the Erie Canal that passed through Syracuse, some thirty miles to the north.[1]

Indeed, the folks of Homer boasted that "no one could ask for an article which the Great Western Store could not produce." A story once did the rounds that a stranger put the boast to the test by asking to purchase, of all things, a live toad. Uncle Jed directed the skeptic to go down in the cellar to the southwest corner and to lift up a four foot-long board. The fellow did so and discovered a live toad — and this was in the midst of winter! Through hard work, Jedediah Barber managed to establish a financial reputation rivaled only by the Honorable Henry S. Randall, a respected agriculturalist and politician of nearby Cortland. Symbolic of Barber's good fortune was his fine brick residence on North Main Street, constructed in the Neo-Greek style with columns along the south side.[2]

Around 1844, Jedediah traveled to New York City. He returned with a large sign for his store. It was the envy of all the other merchants on Main Street. They, too, wished they could have this new form of advertising, but the expense of bringing a sign all the way from the big city was cost-prohibitive. Nevertheless, new storefront signs began to appear along Main Street. Asaph Carpenter came into the village one day, making his way to the Albany Post Road, past the residence of Squire Osborn, and right to the blacksmith's shop near the bridge spanning the river. The smithy, named Mr. Tower,[3] called Asaph's attention to his sign — a new wooden sign bearing the image of a horse and the tools of the smithy's trade: horseshoe, hammer, and anvil. The name "Tower's" appeared, too, in neatly done lettering. Then, in a lower corner, Asaph spotted additional lettering: F.B. Carpenter, painter. Upon his arrival home, Asaph confronted his fourteen-year-old son, and Frank admitted that the reason he had been neglecting his chores was to make the new signs for Mr. Tower and the other businesses of Homer. In his defense, the boy quickly added that he got paid money to help the storeowners follow in the fashion established by Uncle Jed.[4]

Perhaps the boy had a head for business after all, but it was not signs he wanted to paint. Unfortunately, providing him schooling in portraiture would be costly. For some time, talk around the wood-burning stove at the back of the Great Western included stories of the contention that existed between poor Asaph Carpenter and his misguided son, Frank. Some voiced concern that the boy lacked good sense. Doesn't he understand that there's a good living to be made from the soil? One who overheard the conversation had an opinion at variance with the others, and that was Paris Barber, who had his own reputation in the village for being a rebellious sort.[5]

Paris, born in Homer on October 7, 1814, and named after the hero of Homer's *Illiad* who ran off with the beautiful Helen of Troy, was different ... and not just in name. What a shame, townsfolk thought, that Paris never showed any interest in joining his father, Jedediah, and his two brothers, George and Watts, in their successful work at the Great Western. Instead, Paris spent his time designing attractive gardens of shrubs and flowers and cultivating various species of daffodils, tulips, hyacinths, peonies, hollyhocks, and mignonette. His roses were the talk of the town. Beautiful cut flowers, artistically arranged by Paris, frequently were displayed before the pulpit of the Congregational Church. They were colorful and aromatic witnesses to this Barber's affinity for horticulture and not for merchandizing.[6]

Besides a merchant of renown, Jedediah was a prosperous farmer, owning many acres of land behind his house — essentially the land between present day Main Street and Route 281. Upon his graduation from the local academy, Paris went to work on his father's estate, earning a salary of fifty dollars a year and a home with his parents.[7] Father Keep felt compelled to intervene, in a paternal way, of course. He went to Jedediah and implored him to send Paris to Yale where his God-given interests in nature and aesthetics might be properly developed, where Paris might become a botanist or a landscapist, and where he might be trained to use his gifts to contribute to a wider world than just Homer. In the end, the minister's well-intended suggestion was vetoed by Paris's mother. Matilda convinced Jedediah that Paris's place was in Homer, on the farm "where he can raise all the things he wants to."[8] However, instead of raising a cash crop, Paris spent his time creating a garden to the south of the Barber mansion, filled with boxwood imported from Tarrytown, wild flowers he personally transplanted from the countryside, and flowers he had nurtured in a glass house. This landscaped area became the talk of the county and rivaled the gorgeous gardens of the Randalls of Cortland.[9]

Ever hopeful of turning his son into a farmer, Jedediah purchased one hundred acres of choice land located west of the village at the foot of West Hill and along Cayuga Street. This he gave to Paris who did manage to produce a bountiful yield of hay along with corn that was said to be the best in town. After three years, though, his interests gravitated back to flowers and horticulture.[10]

By 1844, the thirty-year-old Paris Barber had attained a greater degree of respectability in the community than he had enjoyed in his youth. After all, he was the one who had introduced "love apples," or tomatoes, to the town, along with articles in the paper on how to raise them. He had found an improved grade of oats and showed the other farmers how to get a greater yield. He had found a breed of shorthorn cattle for his father's farm that proved to have excellent results in the county. And what about that lemon tree he had growing in that innovative glass house of his? Now there was quite the conversation piece. Then, too, there was the Cortland County Agricultural Society and its annual fair. That was Paris's idea. Even Jedediah was forced to concede that Paris was "doing all right even if he ain't in the store."[11]

The Barber gardens and their architect, a veritable well-spring of horticultural information, was the source of much community pride in 1844. In addition to the community's respect, Paris was the recipient of the community's sympathy. His marriage to Mary Elizabeth McClellan of Nassau, New York, in April of 1840, ended abruptly in October 1843. Tragically, twenty-five-year-old Mary died three days after giving birth to their second child. Fortunately, the Barber mansion could accommodate multiple generations, and the extended Barber family helped to raise Paris' two little children, a girl and a boy.[12]

4. Having Interests and Aspirations Different from Others

One day, as the widower took in the conversation of the social club that frequented the back of his father's store, denigrating words spoken of young Frank Carpenter did not sit well with him.[13] Paris identified with this young man. Like Frank, in his own youth he had been called "lazy," "lackadaisical," and "a loony." And why? For having interests and aspirations different from others?[14] At least, he had Father Keep to come forth and champion his cause. Perhaps that was what Paris remembered. Maybe young Frank needed an advocate, too. Paris determined the only way to find out was to go out to the Carpenter farm and see for himself.

Paris Barber (courtesy Phillips Free Library, Homer, New York).

This Paris did, as described by his biographer. He was told he could find the fourteen-year-old out in the barn, up in the hayloft. Paris climbed the ladder to the loft. He was greeted with the sweet odor of clover and timothy and the sight of the farm boy working on some sketches of sheep. Scattered around were other examples of art work, which Paris examined and found to be quite appealing. He praised the boy's efforts and got him to open up to conversation. Paris learned that the boy was full of artistic ambition but had been sensitive to the derision it had caused. He wanted to produce more than store signs for the local merchants. His father, Asaph, had finally permitted him the use of this part of the loft as a studio. Best of all, through the intercession of a neighbor, Sylvester Nash, his father had, at last, agreed to find a way to send him to Syracuse for schooling in art. To this last piece of information, Paris responded with hearty approval.[15]

Out of that conversation in the hayloft developed a lasting friendship. In spite of a sixteen year difference in age, the merchant's son and the farmer's son found they had much in common. They were kindred spirits. Perhaps Paris felt that Frank was like the lemon tree in his glass house[16]; he was a natural-born artist who, with the proper cultivation and nurturing, was going to thrive and bear great fruit in the art world some day. This conviction he enthusiastically shared with the rest of the Barber family. And, thus, for the proper cultivation Frank Carpenter went off to Syracuse.[17] Down through the years, the question has lingered: Who financed Carpenter's schooling in Syracuse — his father, Paris Barber, or both? As Father Keep would surely explain, "God works in mysterious ways." At any rate, the means was found, and the aspiring artist headed off to follow his destiny with the full blessing of his future benefactor.

5

"That Grim Object Lesson"

In the autumn of the same year, 1844, Samuel and Sara Stoddard decided to commence preparations for removing themselves and their children from the Osborn house in Homer. Like Frank, the nine-year-old William Stoddard found himself on a stagecoach headed for Syracuse in the mid–1840s. Syracuse was, at the time, a mere village of some five thousand people,[1] but its location in the center of the state and on the Erie Canal would assure its future as an expanding urban hub of commerce. Next to William Winton's Hotel on Salina Street, a thoroughfare that crossed over the canal, the bookstore and publishing firm of Stoddard and Babcock opened for business. Here, Samuel made another attempt at selling books. He had come to Syracuse earlier to set up the shop and temporarily boarded at Robinson's Onondaga Temperance House at the corner of Church and Salina streets, while his family remained in good hands in Homer. Once he had made appropriate arrangements, his family joined him and took up residence in a two-story house of red brick on East Fayette Street.[2]

In Syracuse, young Stoddard manifested an instinct for entrepreneurial pursuits himself. With five dollars in seed money from his father, he purchased chickens and turkeys from farmers in the outlying rural areas and turned around and sold them for a higher price to the hoteliers and grocers of Syracuse. With the profits he constructed coops in the back yard and became a purveyor of eggs and fowl. A neighbor obtained a larger, harder-to-come-by species of chickens from China which commanded high prices. As a budding capitalist, Stoddard paid him two dollars for a dozen of the eggs instead of ten dollars for a pair of the birds and then sold off some of the chickens for five dollars per pair. One rooster he kept whose crow he maintained "would have put to shame a trombone in the middle of the German band." He also purchased a pair of Maryland game fowls known for their rarity of fight and beauty. From them he raised roosters for cock fights. He earned the nickname "Game Stoddard," and years later he was astonished to learn that a sporting event between Onondaga and Cortland counties had been won by "the Stoddard gamefowls."[3]

Here, in the community near Onondaga Lake, where salt was produced, young Stoddard had no shortage of friends and adventures. One of these adventures almost cost him his life. He and another boy decided at the end of March to go fishing out on the lake in a sailboat. The day was sunny but the lake water was icy cold. Half a mile from the eastern shore, the inexperienced sailors capsized the boat. The sail came down, forcing them to plunge below the surface to avoid being struck. Tugging the craft along, they managed to swim to shore, where a party of hunters pulled their chilled, nearly insensible forms out of the brine. They were revived and taken home. Stoddard later recalled, "We went to my house first, and found and drank all there was left in my father's bottle of old Madeira wine."[4]

The boy who delighted in hiking confidently through the hills of Homer made excursions into the region surrounding Syracuse. He formed a group of friends into the Rambler's Club and led them on hunting and small fishing expeditions along with the Stoddard family's dog, Dash. Sometimes they covered fifteen to twenty miles in a day. A favorite hike was to nearby Fayetteville, only eight miles away. The village would be the inspiration, in his later life, for writing *Crowded Out o' Crofield; or, The Boy Who Made His Way* (1890).[5]

Much to Stoddard's delight, another friend, one from Homer, was in Syracuse, too—Andrew Dickson White. Andrew's father, Horace, had also given up clerking at the Great Western and moved his family to Syracuse, where he was the cashier at the Onondaga County Bank. Purchasing houses on Fayette Street, the Stoddards and Whites were again close neighbors. Even after the Stoddards moved into a larger house on Onondaga Street, between Salina and Warren streets, the two boys remained close. Andrew went so far, one day, as to present William with a beautiful rifle with telescopic sights, which had been a gift from a friend of his father. He told his trusted friend, "I haven't any use for a rifle. You take it and use it as long as you want to, just as if it were your own. Take it home with you, flask, pouch, and all." Stoddard eagerly did so. He kept it through several years and named the future president of Cornell University as the one deserving credit for his future reputation at shooting a rifle.[6]

Both boys, later in life, sang the praises of Mr. James W. Hoyt, "a tall, handsome, pleasant-mannered young man," who served as their teacher in a private boys school they attended in the basement of the Congregational Church, opposite the park, in Syracuse. Hoyt made it his mission to make his twenty students into "young gentlemen" and without application of the rod. A Christian gentleman was defined as one who fundamentally practiced the Golden Rule and the Ten Commandments, and Mr. Hoyt modeled this well for his charges.[7]

Part of the curriculum involved writing compositions and preparing and editing weekly journals to be read aloud at monthly Saturday "elocutionary exercises" attended by the mothers of the students. Young Stoddard showed great interest and ability in writing. As the foreshadowing of a future career, for school he printed a little weekly he called *The Frolic Manual*. In this periodical he placed his own original poems. The verses were described by his sister Kate as "some very pretty ideas prettily expressed" and the source of pride for the author's mother.[8] At home, Stoddard built himself a little printing press, using a rolling pin for a roller and some second-hand type he obtained. The typesetting took a long time but ultimately he was able to laboriously print out several copies of the first and only issue of *The Gem*. The little press remained idle after that, but the experience was imprinted on his brain.[9]

In 1853, his first serious venture into journalism involved a trip taken to New York City to see the first World's Fair in America. With the use of a guide book, he spent days at the grand Crystal Palace documenting in writing the more striking sights. The long account was sent to the *Syracuse Chronicle*, where he found "my story was a good one and it was printed in full." This increased his standing among his classmates at school.[10]

Stoddard claimed that his teacher at school, Mr. Hoyt, "possessed a rare talent for getting young brains at work to the best advantage. He did his whole duty by us and made his mark upon every one of us."[11] White concurred with his classmate: "We doubtless agree in thinking that the lack of grammatical drill [in studying Virgil, Horace, and Xenophon] was more than made up by the love of manliness, and the dislike of meanness, which was in those days our very atmosphere."[12] With this educational underpinning, Andrew White left for Geneva College. There he prepared to attend Yale, where he was a classmate with Theodore Munger, another childhood friend from Homer. White's departure motivated Stoddard to seek higher education some day. As William put it, had he not, in a year and a half under Mr. Hoyt, "already mastered all the Latin and mathematics usually required in a freshman class at college?"[13]

Mr. Hoyt did his job well in character development. He instilled in his students the value of standing up for principles, something Stoddard had the opportunity to act upon under Hoyt's successor, the vile Mr. Caruth. Mr. Caruth believed in the all-too-liberal application of corporal punishment. One day Stoddard observed Joe May, son of the famous abolitionist preacher, the Rev. Dr. Samuel J. May, "one of the very best behaved and studious boys in the school," severely punished unjustly with a ruler. This was followed by a lashing of a three-foot length of cowhide upon another lad, a newcomer. The next day, it was Matthew Myers, another clergyman's son, who suddenly was the recipient of a similar fierce lashing. William heard poor Matthew cry out "O! Moses!" as the blows continued to rain down. Some of them drew blood. With this, Stoddard stood up and confronted Mr. Caruth. Screaming at the top of his lungs, he got the teacher to stop, and he forbade him "to strike another blow at any boy in that school." Mutiny ensued. The classroom was in an uproar. Was this flogging not similar to that experienced by some slaves and caused in them a desire for rebellion? Stoddard fed the ruler and the cowhide to the classroom stove, where "they burned well." After an investigation by the trustees, including an examination of the red marks upon Matthew Myers' neck, the school was shut down, never to open again.[14]

It was determined that William should next go to work at the bookstore, serving there as messenger, salesman, general clerk, and, of course, reader of all the books for sale. This last task he approached with great enthusiasm, thereby making himself quite well acquainted with the literature of the day. He devoured the writing of Washington Irving, James Fenimore Cooper, and Oliver Wendell Holmes. He delighted in the books of fiction by two Frenchmen named Alexandre Dumas and Victor Hugo, and he already knew of Sir Walter Scott.

Yet, the novel that made the most impression was the store's best-seller. They simply could not keep enough copies on hand of Harriet Beecher Stowe's *Uncle Tom's Cabin, or, Life Among the Lowly*. In 1852, in its first eight weeks, fifty thousand copies were sold across the land. This was an anti-slavery novel. It depicted a pious slave, Uncle Tom, being murdered by a cruel overseer named Simon Legree. It was quite incendiary reading for young William Stoddard, who just one year earlier, had been an eye-witness at both a memorable speech and at the famous Jerry Rescue.[15]

The speech was given in May 1851. The speaker was the fabled orator and senator from Massachusetts, Daniel Webster. From either a platform placed in front of Syracuse's City Hall or from a hotel balcony, the "Great Expounder," as Stoddard called him, spoke in "his deep, mellow, sonorous voice" on the moral issue of the day, slavery. Webster had supported the Compromise of 1850. This included the federal law passed in September of 1850 making it a crime punishable by fine or jailing if one did not help return runaway slaves to their owners. Standing in the forefront of the crowd gathered before this "very impersonation of political dignity, if not of national authority," Stoddard heard the stirring and challenging message delivered: "Fellow Citizens, the Fugitive Slave Law will be enforced! It will be enforced every-

5. "That Grim Object Lesson"

where and at all hazards. It will be enforced even in Syracuse and even if the Abolitionist Convention shall be here in session at the time."[16]

How prophetic were his words! Five months later, on the first of October 1851, William "Jerry" Henry, an escaped mulatto slave and cooper residing in Syracuse, was arrested ostensibly for theft. After he had been placed in manacles, it was announced that he was being arrested by federal marshals under the terms of the Fugitive Slave Law passed in September of 1850. An abolition convention was meeting in Syracuse, and a first attempt to free him occurred in the office of U.S. commissioner Joseph Sabine. With the help of abolitionists, Jerry was able to escape from the building, but he was recaptured at one of the bridges spanning the Erie Canal and taken to the Police Justice offices near Clinton Square.[17]

Jerry's rescue occurred that evening. People poured into Syracuse from outlying communities. Amid the tolling of church bells, a crowd of approximately three thousand people surrounded and stormed the building holding Jerry.[18] Stoddard was part of that mob. He described the scene: "As we surged onward, I saw several hack carriages, standing just beyond the Clinton Street crossing, at the curbstone, and among them was Charley Wheaton's team of fast trotters, and a top buggy.... Then followed a few minutes of the most utter confusion you ever saw or heard of. I was lost in the rush but was close enough to see the axes and crowbars go up and down upon those wooden window bars. In poured the mob."[19]

Pistol shots were fired, but the force of the mob was enough to carry Jerry out of federal hands. "The next thing," observed Stoddard, "I saw the several hacks set out in different directions, but I saw no more of Charley Wheaton's sorrel team." Jerry was successfully hidden in the city, then driven to Oswego, and later transported to freedom in Kingston, Ontario.[20] Across the country, the Jerry Rescue was celebrated with jubilation — as a great triumph of the antislavery movement. And young William Stoddard, proud of the bruises he had sustained in violating the Fugitive Slave Law, said "the whole devilishness of human slavery went through my mind like a red hot flash and I had been taught all I needed to know of it by that grim object lesson."[21]

During the presidential election of 1852, Stoddard began to take a more studied interest in politics. When the Whig candidate, General Winfield Scott, known as "Old Fuss and Feathers," made a whistle-stop speech in Syracuse from the back of a railway car, the curious young Stoddard came out to see and hear him. Hero of the recent war with Mexico, Scott was able to defeat New York's own Millard Fillmore, the incumbent president, for the party's nomination, but he was unable to get Stoddard to relinquish his admiration for Fillmore. The general tended to waffle, too, on the issue of slavery. In the

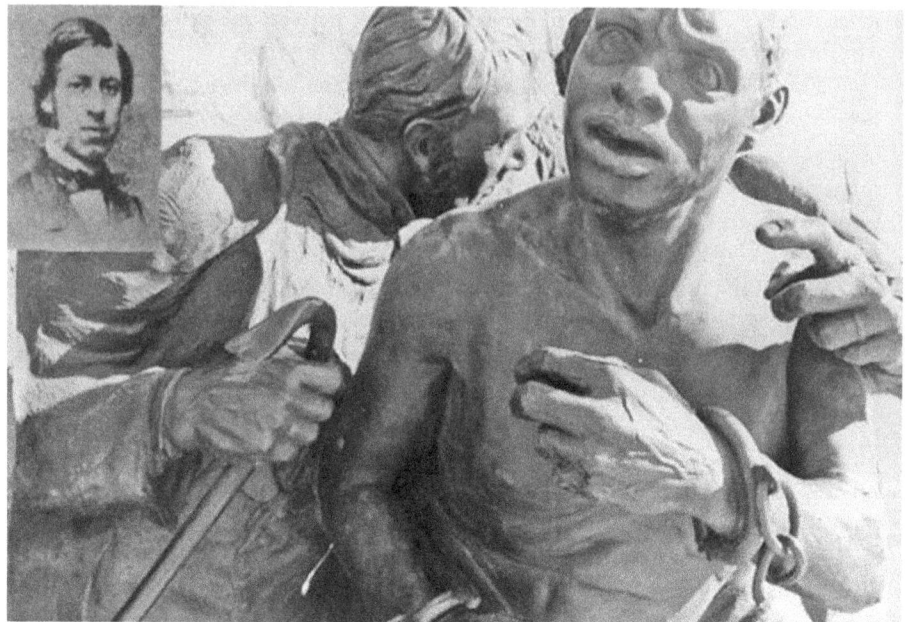

The Jerry Rescue Monument, Syracuse, New York. Inset: Young William Stoddard (courtesy Cortland County Historical Society, Cortland, New York).

election, Scott garnered the electoral votes of only four states, and the Democratic candidate, another veteran of the Mexican War, Franklin Pierce, carried the day. The election results served only to increase what Stoddard called "a rumbling and grumbling" among the anti-slavery elements.[22]

The next traumatic event Stoddard experienced was the death of his mother from consumption (tuberculosis) in 1853. She was the much loved link that held the family together. With that link gone, the family was never the same. Stoddard found he could not shed a tear at the deathbed. At the funeral, pent-up grief found release in a different form. He said, "Right there, however, relief came, for a torrent of blood burst out at my nose and mouth.... A blood vessel had broken under the pressure ... and this was the escape from the awful weight I was enduring. This was my first great sorrow."[23]

John Osborn took the loss of "his favorite daughter" as a severe blow and began to decline in health. The house on Albany Street in Homer was rented, and the squire and his wife went to board at Mr. Ford's, at the nearby intersection of Albany and River streets. After sustaining a fall there, John Osborn died, just two months to the day after his daughter died. William was unable to attend the funeral but was told that "such another had never been seen in Cortland County." His grandmother then came to live with the

Stoddards in Syracuse, "but she did not long survive her husband" and was taken back to Homer for burial.[24]

Before his passing, Squire Osborn, filled with premonition, shared his prophetic thoughts with his granddaughter Kate:

> I wish, child, that I could stand in your shoes from 1859–60 and on past 1870 years. You will see wonderful changes! During the years from 1860 to 1869 you will see and know a great civil war. This whole country will change with inventions that will turn all things over. You, child, will have a wonderful opportunity. I hope you will have knowledge given you to use and that you will live right and be a Christian woman in trying times.[25]

Samuel Stoddard remarried in 1856, but William never developed a close relationship with his step-mother, a Connecticut widow named Frances M. Bolles. Escape from an uncomfortable situation came upon his leaving for college. He had been accepted at the new university at nearby Rochester, New York. There, he excelled in his studies, kept up a high class ranking, and began "to enter into all social affairs with a great deal of zest." This included the practice the young male students dutifully took up of attending church services regularly since the female students in their fetching bonnets "needed company to and from the meetinghouses—at least, all the way home."[26]

In Rochester, Stoddard's abolitionist leanings were reinforced. As a student, one of the places where he boarded was Halsted Hall. This was a huge house, a former water-cure sanitarium, at the far west end of the city. The house was owned by three intelligent and well cultivated unmarried sisters, the Misses Porter, who also ran Halsted Hall as a station on the Underground Railroad. While there, William saw "more than one dark face come flitting by."[27]

Tragedy struck again when Stoddard, in his junior year of college, went home to Syracuse for the winter holidays. His sister Julia, who had just recovered from a severe bout with typhoid fever, was dealing with bronchial consumption. He returned home in February to be with her in her last days. In the end, she succumbed in his arms.[28] Life seemed to have no shortage of grim object lessons to impart to him.

He returned to his studies, broken-hearted, but managed to keep his class standing and his good reputation as a scholar with the faculty. However, by the end of his junior year, Stoddard amassed significant debts. His stepmother loaned him money, which he paid off with interest eventually. Although his father's business was flourishing, as managing deacon of the First Baptist Church, he had excessively committed personal funds to keeping the church financially afloat. His father sold the bookstore to Babcock and tried his hand at selling fire, life, and marine insurance. He even offered something called health insurance, but it did not pan out. According to Stoddard, "as soon as any man became insured he 'took sick' and became a pensioner, while the other subscribers were slow in making payments."[29]

William painfully concluded he must abandon his plans of finishing college and of continuing to seek a career in the law. His father urged him to stay at home, liquidate his debts, and then return to college. Instead, not without sadness, Stoddard elected to leave Syracuse and head out West. If he was determined to do this, his father cautioned him to do this on his own responsibility, meaning not to be writing soon for help. As Stoddard somewhat defiantly put it, "He did not know that I would have digged [sic] cellars first." So, with twelve dollars borrowed from his brother, Henry, who was called Harry, William Stoddard, vested with an adventurous spirit, headed out West at the age of twenty-two.[30]

6

Honing His Craft

While Stoddard spent close to eleven years in Syracuse (1846 to 1857), Carpenter spent approximately six months there. From the end of 1844 to early 1845, the fifteen-year-old art student studied under Sanford Thayer, a twenty-four-year-old artist who had gained renown for his portraits and Adirondack scenes.

Thayer, at age 14, was "thrown on his own resources," and somewhere around age 17 found employment at a wagon shop in Skaneateles, New York, at the northern tip of Skaneateles Lake. At the shop, he and another aspiring artist, Charles Loring Elliot, painted designs on the backs of sleighs. Elliot did a portrait of Sanford Thayer which was shown internationally and advanced Elliot's reputation as an artist.[1] Under Elliot's tutelage, Thayer and young George Clough of Auburn, whom Carpenter first met in Homer, gained their own reputations as artists in Central New York.[2] As luck would have it, when young Carpenter was receiving instruction in Syracuse, the eminent portraitist Elliot visited and painted several portraits in Thayer's studio. From the instructive comments of both Thayer and Elliot, Frank Carpenter learned the techniques that would serve him well in his career.[3]

From then on there would be no more improvising of paints and brushes. Tubes of oil paint were readily available in Syracuse or ordered from New York City. There were shops that filled tubes for artists and sold commercial canvas and wooden stretchers. There was an array of paint brushes with animal hair bristles from which to choose. Large flats were useful for laying in large amounts of color quickly and evenly. A bright brush was a flat brush with shorter bristles, making it ideal for applying broad strokes with a controlled edge. At the other end of the continuum of brushes were the rounds. This brush had a round head with hairs tapering to a fine point at the end. This brush came in various sizes suited for precise strokes and detail work.

In between flats and rounds were filberts. The filbert had an ovoid tip resembling a hazelnut. Extremely versatile, the filbert could be used as a flat to make broad strokes or as a round for more detailed work or for the making of a transition between places on the canvas.[4]

Carpenter learned to use a large wooden palette to organize his color schematics. The palette would generally go clockwise in succession with cool colors like vermilion and lapis blue followed by warm browns, umbers, and raw sienna, and then yellow oxide and green oxide on to warmer colors of yellow and cadmium red. Rarely would there be oranges; a mix of yellow and red produced an orange-like color. There was a lead white to use, but a titanium white worked best as a mixing white to get tints of color. For shading, mars black had three times the tinting strength. Besides the mixing white, two small mixing tins of medium would be needed. A medium mix consisted of turpentine, walnut oil and linseed oil or both, or even sunflower oil. Carpenter learned that the medium would help the paint, once mixed, to flow better and to mix to the correct consistency. He found he preferred to start a portrait with a neutral gray-green background and then to rough in the face *alla prima* directly with color, since colors are more easily perceived next to neutral hues.[5]

Properly trained by fine mentors in the use of the artist's tools, Carpenter returned to Homer in 1845. Before he turned sixteen, he opened a studio in the village. It was in Mechanics Hall on Main Street, south of the Green. For the first few weeks, Carpenter boarded at home on the farm. Then Asaph insisted his son had to live entirely by his chosen profession. Like an itinerant artist, Carpenter went from door to door in the village, offering to do portraits in exchange for meals. A clerk in a village store agreed to sit for his portrait; for this service Carpenter was given enough cloth for a pair of trousers. A second portraiture earned him a pair of boots.[6]

Frank Carpenter was very much the proverbial starving artist. The Barber family of Homer came to his rescue. Across the street from Jedediah's stately mansion was the Sherman Block, where Sherman nails, known for the letter "S" on their heads, were manufactured. On the second floor of this establishment[7] was a small room for rent for one dollar per week. Under Paris Barber's wing, Carpenter took it as a studio. Folks thought it likely that Paris paid the rent until the artist gained his financial footing, just as he outfitted the studio with chairs and other furnishings from the Barber household.[8] It was Paris who went about drumming up business for Carpenter and encouraged him to promote himself by displaying his handicraft at the 1846 County Fair. The most prominent exhibits were Paris' bulls and yearly steers *and* Frank's portraits.[9]

Next came the fledgling artist's first cash commission. The Honorable

6. Honing His Craft

Henry S. Randall of Cortland asked him to do drawings of a Merino ewe and a Merino ram. Pleased with the results, Randall included the illustrations, as engraved by William Howland, in his well-known book on *Sheep Husbandry*[10] and Carpenter received ten dollars. Soon afterward, Randall had Carpenter paint his portrait and that of his wife.[11]

The same year, 1846, was the twenty-fifth anniversary of Homer's academy,[12] a milestone that prompted Paris to have Homer's first resident artist make the next significant move in his career. Paris suggested that Frank do the trustee paintings. These are nine portraits in oil of the surviving members of the Cortland Academy's first Board of Trustees, along with two other portraits—one of Principal Woolworth and one of Father Keep. Paris, himself, set about to raise the necessary funds. He did so enthusiastically because he envisioned the trustee portraits being the nucleus of a free picture gallery to be housed in an octagonal edifice near the Episcopal Church on the north side of the Green. He prepared sketches of this building which he hoped could showcase Carpenter's portraits of Homer's early founders along with other works of art. Its location on the Green would make art accessible to the students of the academy. No art loving student should ever again have to begin his career up in a hayloft.[13]

This was a breathtaking undertaking for the frugal villagers of Homer to finance and for an inexperienced artist to bring to fruition. The art gallery Paris Barber planned for the north end of the Green never materialized, but over the next four years (1846 to 1850) Carpenter completed eleven portraits. Fittingly, today, at the opposite end of the Green, stands the stately Homer Center for the Arts—once a Baptist house of worship—built in the Richardson style of architecture. In the fall of 2006, the Center for the Arts was the first to exhibit Carpenter's Homer portraits in one gallery.

Samuel B. Woolworth, the distinguished principal, sat for his likeness to be rendered on canvas by Carpenter, not knowing that upon his departure from the position in 1851, he would go on to become principal at the Albany State Normal School and secretary of the New York State Board of Regents.[14] In the 1870s Frank had the aged educator pose for a second portrait.[15]

For the portrait of John Keep, who was in Oberlin, Carpenter had to resort to copying the minister's image from a daguerreotype. Father Keep had officiated at the wedding of Frank's parents in 1826,[16] but Frank was too young to know the man except by reputation. Keep left Homer three years after Carpenter was born. While the preacher had successfully argued in Homer for reforms like temperance and then co-education at the academy, his words from the pulpit condemning the practice of slavery did not sit well with the social club that gathered around the stove at the rear of the Great Western. Uncle Jed and the farmers who raised hogs in the area did not wish to risk losing the slave state of Maryland as a profitable market for pork. Asaph and Almira Carpenter were among Keep's closest supporters, but economic conservatism in Homer trumped political liberalism, and a consensus among all parties was reached in 1833 that it was time for a change in ministers.[17]

Thus, that is how John Keep came to live out his days as God's obedient servant in Ohio. There his calling was to help found Oberlin College, the first college in America to accept blacks and women.[18] From its inception, there was no doubt that Oberlin would be co-educational, but the vote on admitting blacks was close. Not without much prayer, it fell to Father Keep to break the tie and to cast the deciding vote. As of 1835, students were to be regularly admitted "irrespective of color." Keep served faithfully as a college trustee and fundraiser until his death in 1870. Because it was perceived to be a hotbed of abolitionism, Oberlin became known as "the town that started the Civil War."[19] Admittedly, Keep was a bit of a vocal firebrand, but Scripture compelled him: "Who is weak, and I am not weak? Who is offended and I burn not?" He continued, through the institutions of religion and education, to shape public opinion about the rights of the most marginalized in American society.

In 1901, when the Homer Congregationalists celebrated the centennial anniversary of their church on the Green, the Rev. Theodore T. Munger returned and spoke of Keep and his influence. He said: "I do not hesitate to pronounce him not only the greatest of your pastors, but the most effective citizen the town has known." Munger clearly vindicated Father Keep when he publicly recognized him for

> his ability to measure the questions that were coming to the front in both church and state, his clear insight into their meaning and their drift, and his courage and wisdom in maintaining them alone and under an opposition which led to ostracism.... As I look back upon him, I think he was at least half a century ahead of his day.[20]

Those with clearly altruistic vision usually are vindicated by history.

Six of the original eighteen Cortland Academy trustees whose names appear on the charter and indenture of February 1819 survived into the 1840s to live in Homer and to sit for their portraits by Frank Carpenter: Rufus Boies, treasurer of the county's Agricultural Society; David Coye, first sheriff; Dr.

Opposite: The Trustee Paintings: (1) David Coye, (2) Principal Samuel Buell Woolworth, (3) the Rev. John Keep, (4) Dr. John Miller, (5) John Osborn, (6) the Rev. Alfred Bennett, (7) Noah R. Smith, (8) Townsend Ross, (9) Rufus Boies, (10) Dr. Caleb Green, (11) Trustee president Jedediah Barber (courtesy Homer Central School, Homer, New York).

John Miller, respected physician who once dined with President John Adams, General George Washington, and venerable signer of the Declaration of Independence, Dr. Benjamin Rush; Townsend Ross, lawyer and first postmaster of Homer; Noah R. Smith, Homer sheriff; and William Stoddard's grandfather, John Osborn.[21]

In addition, two trustees were painted whose names did not appear on the academy's founding documents: the Rev. Alfred Bennett, early pastor of the Baptist Church, and Dr. Caleb Green, a young physician who had just set up practice in Homer.[22] Bennett's portrait was the earliest of the trustee paintings, having been done in Carpenter's first studio in Mechanic's Hall in 1846, and it was a bit larger than the others.[23] Dr. Green, incidentally, was the physician tending to Carpenter's ill son Bertie when the artist returned to Homer in 1863 for one of his summer visits.[24]

Rounding out the eleven dignitaries, quite fittingly, was Paris Barber's father, Jedediah. The influential merchant had taken the place of one of the original trustees, Judge Chauncey Keep, upon his resignation on March 12, 1819. The civic-minded Barber served as trustee of the academy for the next fifty years. At the time he sat for his portrait, he was the president of the trustees, a position he held for thirty-three years (1836 to 1869).[25]

On January 9, 1854, two and a half years after Frank Carpenter left Homer, the eleven trustee paintings were formally donated to the academy during a meeting of its Board of Trustees. The board accepted the paintings, thanked their donors, and stipulated that they be framed at a cost "not to exceed five dollars each." The amount of $61.51 was paid to a Thomas Holbrook "for framing and varnishing."[26]

The Carpenter paintings within the village of Homer comprise the largest collection of Carpenter portraits anywhere, and within that, the Homer School's paintings are the largest single collection of his portraits in existence. They have been the legal property of the academy and each of its succeeding institutional entities. Until the middle of the twentieth century, they proudly adorned the walls of the school library. Amazingly, these paintings survived four school fires—1869, 1893, 1904, and 1945—and a fire that broke out in the 1890 House Museum in Cortland, New York, on August 19, 1999, when the paintings graced the walls there.[27] Presently the Homer Central School District is the proud custodian of the Carpenter collection, a group of portraits that Frank Carpenter did as a teenaged artist, not knowing, as he rendered them, that they were helping him to hone his craft for more significant portraiture twenty years to come.

7

The Lemon Tree Comes into Bloom

Nothing succeeds like success, and with each portrait's completion, Carpenter's self-confidence grew and his skill improved. Clearly, all through the late 1840s, Carpenter thrived with Paris Barber as his benefactor. In 1847, Carpenter enrolled for a term at Principal Woolworth's academy, where his classmates included Jedediah Barber II and, once again, Theodore T. Munger.[1] Paris encouraged Frank to seek more education, and paying the young man's tuition would be in keeping with his strong Christian character.

To further Carpenter's learning, Paris decided, in 1847, to take him on a trip to New York City. Together, they went through the Gallery of Fine Arts and the Governor's Room at City Hall. The latter housed full-length portraits of the state's governors and other historical figures rendered in the epic style. This expensive and well-timed visit to the nation's cultural center was later described by Carpenter as "one of the most marked and enjoyable events of my early life."[2] Being mostly familiar with black and white engraved prints and the small, drab, colorless illustrations in circulation in the America of his childhood, Carpenter's first exposure to large-scale, colored, dramatic paintings in New York City had a memorable impact on him. It would be comparable to someone in the present day, who has only seen black-and-white television, suddenly coming across a large flat screen color television in wide screen format. The impression made would be stunning!

This time spent with Paris was part of the incubation of Frank Carpenter the artist. Art appreciation in mid–nineteenth century America deemed the ability to depict national events on an epic scale or to render portraits of heroic figures as the highest form of art. Art was valued for the patriotic emotions it could evoke. To be sure, genre painters existed along with landscapists, such as the Hudson River school's Thomas Cole, but they were not as highly esteemed as portraitists. Since colonial time the portrait painter in America had been in demand. Before photography, an oil painting on board or canvas satisfied several needs. It could stroke the ego of the subject, signify the wealth or status in society of the one depicted, serve as a memento of an absent individual, or provide the subject some degree of immortality. Wedding portraits were the bread and butter of many an itinerant artist. Paris opened Frank to the realization that portrait-making was a noble profession and that he could produce art equal in worthiness to what they had seen in New York. His poor brothers might remain on the farm if they chose, concluded Frank, but for him portraiture would be his life's passion.[3]

In 1848, the eighteen-year-old artist joined the Homer Congregational Church and was busily painting the local people. For both of these, he had Paris Barber to thank. So, Carpenter expressed his gratitude in the best way he knew. He did a portrait of his benefactor. What was captured on canvas was a thirty-six-year-old with an extremely high forehead, dark hair, and rather piercing eyes, wearing a light colored vest, dark coat, and a dark cravat tied around the white wing collar so typical of the fashion of the day.[4]

And Carpenter did not stop there. All through the early 1850s, he painted eleven portraits of the Jedediah Barber family, including two more of the venerable, white-haired merchant. The third one, and arguably the most finished one, was completed in 1852 as a companion piece for the same sized portrait (36 in. × 29 in.) Carpenter did of Jedediah's wife, Matilda.[5] Today, five of the Barber portraits are displayed in the Phillips Free Library, opposite the Green on Main Street in Homer. These are the excellent likenesses of Jedediah; George J.J. Barber; his wife, Catherine Reid; and their children, Jedediah II and Mary Louise.[6] For his efforts on George's portrait, Carpenter received thirty dollars on May 1, 1852.[7]

Soon Carpenter's reputation for portraiture was spreading beyond Homer. In 1848, at Paris' urging, he submitted the painting of an ideal female head to the American Art Union in New York City. Out of four hundred paintings received by the Union, only twelve were selected for purchase. One of those was Carpenter's. He received fifty dollars, which was a very remarkable sum in that day. Frank Carpenter had made an artistic and financial coup.[8]

The time had come for him to make a move. New York City, the center of all things cultural then and now, beckoned him. So, in the spring of 1851, Carpenter moved to the city and set up a studio suitable for the commissioned work he hoped would be coming his way. The next August the twenty-one-year-old married fifteen-year-old Augusta Prentiss, a daughter of a female music teacher at the academy in Homer.[9] Carpenter referred to his wife affectionately as "Gus." He and Gus had two children, Florence Trumbull (perhaps named after the American artist John Trumbull) and Herbert (called "Bertie") Sanford (perhaps after Sanford Thayer).[10] A third child, a son named Elliott or "Ellie," perhaps after Charles Loring Elliott, died in infancy.[11] When the first-born, Florence, arrived on March 10, 1854, the delivery was attended by Carpenter's long time friend and the former student of Homer's Dr. Caleb Green, the accomplished Dr. Stephen Smith.[12]

In the summer before their own wedding, on July 2, the Carpenters had attended the marriage of Paris Barber to Lydia Jane Eno. The remarried Paris and his new wife moved into the family mansion on Main Street, Homer.[13] Seven years and three children later, they finally moved into their own residence. The move was delayed because disaster struck twice. In 1854, the railroad from Syracuse to Binghamton, that Jedediah worked so hard to get built through Homer, failed. The company's stock dropped to fifteen cents on the dollar. As one of its directors, Jedediah lost over ten thousand dollars, and his three sons' investments were not spared. Then, on May 10, 1856, the Great Western Store, after forty-three years of serving the public, burned to the ground. It was a fifty thousand dollar loss. Only a portion of the inventory was insured. Had Father Keep been present, he would have reminded them that "the rain falls on the just and the unjust." But the indomitable Barbers rebuilt on the same spot—the Barber Block and the Barber Bank building north of it—and the Paris Barber family finally moved out of the mansion in 1857 and into their own residence around the corner on Clinton Street. This was one of six houses in the village then occupied by Barbers.[14]

In New York, Carpenter experienced a slow start. Upon his arrival in the city, he determined to set and attain a higher artistic standard for himself.[15] Yet, he was also concerned that his new studio might find commissions initially slow in coming in. Would it be good to just sit idle? His biographer explained the approach used during his first ten months when commissions were sparse:

> One of his earliest resolves was to keep at work at something; and if he had no paying sitters, he would prevail on friends or acquaintances to sit, executing their pictures with as much conscientious study and effort as if they had every one been Presidents. This was sound business practice as well as sound art practice, because his skill increased just as much as if his time were full; and when the next commission did come, he was sure to paint better than ever before.[16]

A Homer newspaper in August of 1851 predicted a promising career ahead for him,[17] and the next winter, just after William Stoddard participated in the well-publicized Jerry Rescue in Syracuse, Carpenter found himself engaged in rendering a full-length portrait of Mr. David Leavitt, president of the American Exchange Bank of New York City. The 8½ by 5½ foot painting, his first attempt at full-length portraiture, went on exhibit at the city's National Academy of Design to much acclaim. On the basis of this piece and the praise it drew, Carpenter was made an associate of the academy at the unheard of young age of twenty-one.[18] "The youngest person ever admitted to membership in the National Academy of Design" was reported to have "mixed his colors with his heart."[19]

When the heart of America was captivated by Jenny Lind, "The Swedish Nightingale," on a tour in America arranged by P.T. Barnum, the much celebrated opera star and philanthropist came to epitomize for Americans feminine grace and virtue. Carpenter, in 1852, captured these ideals in an exquisite rendering of Lind on canvas.[20]

In the autumn of 1852, with his reputation growing, Carpenter was commissioned to do another full-length portrait. This was of the president of the United States—Millard Fillmore[21]—native son of Summerhill, New York, just west of Homer. For his efforts, Carpenter received a very flattering written testimonial from the president, emphasizing that "it is the best likeness which has been taken of me."[22] Before his painting career came to a close, Carpenter painted four other U.S. presidents from life: John Tyler, James A. Garfield, Franklin Pierce, and Abraham Lincoln. President Pierce was so impressed with his portrait that he engaged Carpenter to do a portrait of his deceased son, Benjamin. He called him "Benny." This was a difficult task for Carpenter. All he had to work with was a defective daguerreotype and the descriptions of friends who had known the eleven-year-old Benny before he perished in a tragic train derailment. But Carpenter's efforts were successful. President Pierce invited Carpenter to stay at the Executive Mansion—what is now called the White House—while he finished up two portraits of New York's Governor William L. Marcy, one of Attorney-General Caleb Cushing, and a profile painting of the president.[23] Pierce wrote a letter of introduction for Carpenter in 1855 in which he described him as "an artist of rare genius and merit, and in all respects a most noteworthy and estimable gentleman."[24]

Such successful ventures contributed to his fame as an outstanding professional, and word also spread that his genial manner made sitting for him an enjoyable experience. When Fillmore was once asked if his sittings for Mr. Carpenter were tedious, he responded, "Oh, no madam; it is the pleasantest hour in the day."[25] Presidential commendations like that caused requests for Carpenter's artistic skills to come pouring in.

Carpenter was also consulted for his opinion of fellow artists. In 1853, when asked for "a list of the names of the most promising, as well as most eminent, painters in this country," Carpenter responded in writing.[26] He listed portrait painters first, with Charles L[oring] Elliott, of course, heading

7. The Lemon Tree Comes into Bloom

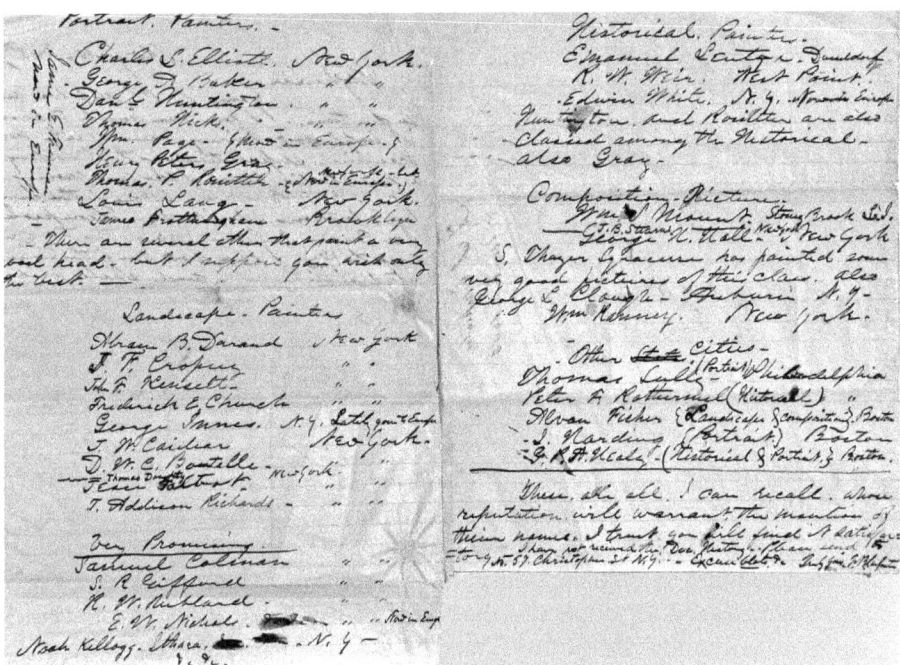

Portion of Carpenter's letter indicating his studio is located over an ice cream saloon in New York. He provides his opinion of the best artists of the day (courtesy David Quinlan).

the list of ten he considered to be "only the best." Next, he submitted the names of ten landscape painters, with Abram [he meant Asher] B. Durand and J[asper] F[rancis] Cropsey, both of the Hudson River school, at the top. Changing his mind on the order of ranking, he glued another piece of paper over the landscapists' names with a revised listing and the addition of the name Noah Kellogg of Ithaca, New York, to the list of five very promising artists. Six made it to his list of historical painters. At the top was Emanuel Leutze, best remembered for his *Washington Crossing the Delaware* that he had just completed three years earlier. For composition pictures, William S[idney] Mount was first, and George L[afayette] Clough of Auburn, New York, was fifth of the six. Above him, Carpenter wrote "S[anford] Thayer [of] Syracuse has painted some very good pictures of this class." The last category, other cities, included the names of Sully, Rothermel, Fisher, Narding, and Healy. Humbly, Carpenter did not indicate where he ranked himself in the listed notables, but he was going to leave his mark among his contemporaries.

To that end, he journeyed to Washington and boarded at Mrs. Duvall's at 331 Pennsylvania Avenue for most of 1855. For $14 per week, he had a room he could use as a studio.[27] A list of all the individuals who sat for portraits reads like a *Who's Who* in pre–Civil War America. There were Senators Cass, Chase, Houston, Seward, Webster, and Sumner.[28] Notable clergy of the day who sat for Carpenter included Henry Ward Beecher, brother of Harriet Beecher Stowe of *Uncle Tom's Cabin* fame, and the Rev. Drs. Samuel H. Cox, David Dudley Field, Horace Bushnell, and Leonard Bacon.

John C. Frémont, presidential candidate in 1856, was another subject. Later, in the 1890s, Carpenter told a reporter:

> I went to Frémont's house on 9th Street [in New York] for the sittings. He was young and vigorous then, but parted his hair in the middle and wore a beard which was not considered good taste at the period.... Frémont got numerous letters from persons all over the country advising him to cut his beard.[29]

As one who approached the world visually and surveyed all with a deep intensity, Carpenter seemed to be attributing Frémont's election defeat to his beard.

Even Carpenter's early mentor, Charles Loring Elliott, sat for him and introduced him to William Sidney Mount. Mount was an interesting artist from Long Island. He originated the idea of painting realistic scenes of ordinary American life. He sat for Carpenter, and during the nine days that he did so, a friendship developed that lasted until Mount's death in 1868.[30] Mount's views on painting scenes realistically must have resonated with Carpenter, an artist who strove to be faithful in his artistic renderings.

Carpenter found his work could net him a lucrative income, but he did not allow his work to be primarily driven by money. In an interview with a news reporter, he offered this advice to artists:

> Always make the most out of a subject without regard to pay for it, which should never be secondary; or in other words never paint a picture solely for the dollars and cents it would yield him in return, but, on the other hand, if there was anything in the subject he could be advantaged by studying, spare no pains in the endeavor to reproduce it.[31]

While Carpenter found ready hospitality at the literary salon of Alice and Phoebe Carey[32] and became fast friends with many of the movers and shakers of mid–nineteenth century America who posed for him, the artist did not forget his roots. On September 23, 1851, he wrote a letter to Mr. Dalrymple, a dentist in Homer. He wished to ascertain how receptive some of the leading men in Homer might be to a proposal conceived collaboratively with his life-long friend, Fessenden N. Otis. The plan called for painting *A View of Homer* from up on East Hill for the purpose of engraving and publishing.[33] Otis did the painting, and a lithograph was made of it by Endicott and Company of New York City. From that a photo-mural was later made in

1946 by Drix Duryea, Inc., of New York for a wall of the lobby of the Homer National Bank. Today, it is most apropos that the 22 ft. by 7 ft. mural depicting the village of Homer in 1852 graces the south wall of the Homer History Center at Key Bank adjacent to the Green.[34]

During his illustrious career, Carpenter frequently took the eight hour train ride from New York to Homer to visit family and friends. Most of his summers were spent at the Carpenter farm, which stayed in the family until it was offered for sale in 1915.[35] With his young son, Bertie, Carpenter enjoyed swimming in the Tioughnioga River and fishing in nearby Little York Lake on hot and humid August days. He and Gus cele-

Rare photograph of Sanford Thayer and Francis Carpenter, believed to have been taken in Homer by Luther Barker (courtesy Cortland County Historical Society; photograph by David Quinlan).

brated their wedding anniversaries at Glen Haven, at the southern tip of Skaneateles Lake, in the company of family and close friends that included Theodore Munger and Calvin Woolworth.[36] Coming to Homer from Syracuse, Sanford Thayer once spent a day with his former pupil, and the two "went to the village and sat for pictures at Luther Barker's."[37] In August of 1876, when Carpenter returned for his "usual summer vacation," he took the room over the drugstore and bookshop business of Atwater & Kellogg in the Barber Block where, managing to combine business with pleasure, he finished some work.[38] This was only five years after Mark Twain, sponsored by the Homer Literary Society, had given a talk at the Keator Opera House on the floor above Carpenter's summer rental — a talk that the audience found humorous but a tad "too racy" for their tastes.[39]

Besides the portraits of his parents, Carpenter did portraits of other family members. He painted Gus in 1851 and 1875. He painted his sister Helen and his daughter Florence. A portrait of his son Bertie was done when the lad was three years old. Friends he painted included the Rev. Thomas E. Fessenden of the Congregational Church and his supportive neighbors, Sylvester and Frances Nash. Frances showed interest because she had been a teacher of painting at the academy before her marriage in 1837. Judge Henry Stevens, uncle to Cortland's Henry S. Randall, had his portrait done,[40] as did Carpenter's boyhood friends Calvin C. Woolworth and Martius Lynde, both of whom had also taken up residence in Brooklyn.[41]

When William Stoddard's friend, the Homer native son Andrew D. White, became the first president of Cornell University in Ithaca, New York— a land-grant college under the Morrill Act signed into law by President Lincoln— it was another native son of Homer, Frank Carpenter, who was present for the university's opening in 1868. It was Carpenter that White commissioned to do the portraits of four distinguished intellects of the era: Louis Agassiz, Goldwyn Smith, James Russell Lowell, and George William Curtis.[42] Ezra Cornell posed, too, but the finished product was deemed to be not one of Carpenter's best paintings.[43] Cornell professor George L. Burr, who once attended the academy on Homer's Green, wrote in 1937 that he had last seen the portrait hanging in Sage Library in the early 1890s. He said, too, that members of the family, not satisfied with it, commissioned a Canadian artist named Forbes to do a portrait from photographs.[44] Carpenter did more than one portrait of Ezra Cornell, and one, bigger than life size and in dire need of restoration, now hangs in a stairwell of the university's law school library. The subject is standing and his hand rests on a docu-

Relief woodcut print of Francis Bicknell Carpenter in the 1850s (courtesy Phillips Free Library, Homer, New York).

ment bearing his time-honored wish of 1868: "I would found an institution where any person can find instruction in any study." In the painting, Carpenter included a bust of Benjamin Franklin, who, among his many accomplishments, was known for experimentation with electricity. This was, at the time, a recognizable symbolic allusion to Cornell's connection to Samuel F.B. Morse's electric telegraph from which the philanthropic Cornell derived his fortune as a contractor for the erection of telegraph lines.[45]

Occasionally Carpenter had visitors from Homer show up at his studio in Brooklyn. One of the visitors, in 1852, was Paris Barber. Paris brought his nine-year-old son, Samuel, to see the sights of the metropolis. They stayed at his father-in-law's house on Fifth Avenue and called on the great Daniel Webster at the Astor House on Broadway. Then, the boy was taken to see City Hall, the Battery Park, immigrants arriving from Europe at Castle Garden, a museum, and the ferry to Brooklyn. After all that excitement, the lad, as noted by his bemused father, found the long visit at his father's friend's studio to be terribly boring.[46]

It is doubtful that most people found the studio to be boring, for the studio was "hung around with statesmen and men of power."[47] Clearly, to the observant, if one of political or social prominence wanted his portrait painted, Francis B. Carpenter was considered *the one* to do it. The New York *Evening Express*, in a style of art criticism characteristic of the era, informed its readers that "Carpenter's portraits are remarkable chiefly for their subtle *mentality* [emphasis in the original]; for their faithful rendering of the inward life and disposition."[48] With free advertising like that, Carpenter had no shortage of notable clients. Before his career was over, the likes of Horace Greeley, the outspoken anti-slavery leader and the founder of the New York *Tribune*, sat for him to do a life-size 7' × 5' signed portrait.[49] The great American showman P.T. Barnum sat for Carpenter in 1871.[50] Five years later, Carpenter painted the American opera singer Emma Abbott in her most famous role as Margarita in *Faust*, and at the same time he honored her by publishing an account of her career, *The New Prima Donna: The True Story of Emma Abbott*.[51]

Frank Carpenter had a gift; he knew how to celebrate the famous. Though occasionally someone like General William Tecumseh Sherman refused to sit for a portrait, stating "I want no painter, photographer, or poet," there was always someone more gracious who agreed with the sentiments expressed to Carpenter by the poet John Greenleaf Whittier: "I know of no one I would sooner sit to a picture than thyself."[52]

Though Carpenter was none too keen about identifying his work with his signature, he did develop a style of portraiture with characteristics that made it recognizable. He painted his subjects' eyes with crescent shaped pupils, giving the eyes a certain marbled appearance. Women were frequently adorned with white lace at the neck or across the bodice, as was the fashion of the day, and the lace in Carpenter's portraits was marvelously realistic. Even as a young artist, Carpenter paid impossibly close attention to detail, and the task of applying white paint was painstaking and tedious in the rendering of lace that is light and ephemeral in quality. Perhaps this is the reason he once wrote in his diary, "Do not like to paint ladies." He may not have enjoyed painting hands either, since the hands of his subjects always have the same stylized fingers and nails and are certainly not his strong suit.[53]

Frequently Carpenter resorted to using the same type of background in his portraits. A comparison of the portrait of Anna Jones in the Cortland County Historical Society with the portrait of Mary Pierce in Homer's Phillips Free Library reveals similar backdrops—the Hudson River Valley and stylized sailboats with the type of sail and rigging of that day—both appearing over the shoulder of the subject. In both portraits he made use of the same type of yellow vine-like flowers. The use of heightened reds in draperies and sashes to attract the viewer's eye was typical of Carpenter, as well.[54]

8

An Ambition Rising Fast

By the late 1850s, as the United States was moving steadily toward an irrepressible conflict, life for both Frank Carpenter and William Stoddard was far from boring. While Carpenter was making a name for himself in the art world, the adventurous Stoddard was heading out West to find his niche. Stoddard went from Syracuse to Buffalo first and then by a lake steamer to Detroit. From Detroit, he went to Chicago where he worked in the summer of 1857 for twenty dollars a week as the literary editor of *The Chicago Daily Ledger*—until it went bankrupt soon after. From there, he ventured to Tolono, in Central Illinois, determined to try his hand at prairie farming or raising corn. Enduring the rigors of frontier life brought him some satisfaction. He developed a reputation as a "good shot" with a gun, something he had been working toward since his boyhood days in Homer and Syracuse. Successfully hunting deer, wild geese, rabbit, and grouse gave him a sense of self-reliance and the admiration of newfound friends and neighbors.[1]

Of interest to Stoddard, a Baptist by upbringing, was his discovery that his prairie friends of Champaign County, with a population of 2,000,[2] represented quite a diversity of religious beliefs. "Old Man Lemon" was a Universalist. The Williamses were Methodists. The McCarthys were Roman Catholic. "Old Man Southwick" was an "Infidel" and apparently downright proud of it. As for talkative "Old Man Howe," he "said that for his part he was an Auctioneer."[3] On the prairie, where survival could be challenging, one's religious affiliation was not perceived as being as important as one's willingness to roll up one's sleeves and work hard.

During his short time as a prairie farmer, Stoddard learned a bit about the perversities of prairie politics. A referendum was required to determine whether the community of Arcola or the community of Tuscola was to be the new county seat. A goodly number of interested voters turned out. Arcola was defeated because miraculously "Tuscola alone sent to the state capital a poll book which contained nearly 4,700 names, or more than three times the adult male population of the new county."[4]

Frontiersman Stoddard experienced the rough and tumble aspects of prairie life in more than politics. He was singed once in a wind-driven prairie fire,[5] and one November day he found himself caught in a blue norther, a sudden blast of dry, wind-driven polar air. Had he not been spotted and saved by his neighbors, the Williamses, Stoddard would have frozen to death where he had fallen unconscious from the cold.[6] Fortunately, he was spared. Finally, after experiencing a bout of "winter fever," he felt so physically weakened that he abandoned any further effort at prairie farming.[7] It was not his calling.

Instead, in the spring of 1858, Stoddard went to the Illinois community of West Urbana — now Champaign — in Champaign County to try his hand at journalism. He had learned that a local, crusty, forty-one-year-old self-made doctor of homeopathic medicine named John Walker Scroggs had purchased a defunct agricultural weekly journal for eight hundred dollars with the intent of turning it into a going concern. "Doc" Scroggs' *Central Illinois Gazette* was devoted to publishing his favorite isms and to denigrating men he did not like. The former included abolitionism and temperance; the latter included allopathic physicians and members of the clergy, both of which he denounced in colorful terms. Consequently, he was not the most popular editor in the region, and neither was his weekly. Furthermore, he seemed to manifest no understanding of grammar and nearly none in regard to spelling. In short, to keep the business going, the eccentric editor needed help.[8]

In 1858, Stoddard approached Scroggs with an offer to manage the journalistic operation for him and to make the paper pay for itself. All he asked was to receive by the end of the week a new suit of clothes and payment for board in a good boarding-house. Scroggs accepted his proposal: "Done! Take right hold. Take the whole damn thing and run it! I'm going out to see a patient." He headed out and then turned back to inquire for the first time, "What's your name?" and if Stoddard knew anybody in the village. He then disappeared and did not come back until the end of the day.

Grumbling among the printers commenced immediately as Stoddard made changes. A few were let go and the others had their wages reduced. A way to save the paper a dollar and a half per column per week in typesetting was found. With a less contentious, more fair-handed reporting and a new assistant editor, the *Central Illinois Gazette* became a money-maker. The nominal editor accumulated funds sufficient to build a new office building, with the first stone foundation ever seen in West Urbana. By the following year, the paper had a circulation of more than two thousand.[9]

8. An Ambition Rising Fast

Eighteen fifty-eight was an eventful year for Stoddard. He survived a near fatal bout with typhoid, and from back East he received a diploma from the University of Rochester. A bachelor of arts, *cum laude*, was granted *in abstentia*, "on account of standing and scholarship." Sharing his trials and tribulations in correspondence with friends in Rochester apparently netted him this unexpected recognition.[10]

In the fall, Stoddard's sister Kate arrived unexpectedly. Kate was seeking refuge from troubles with her father and her new step-mother in Syracuse. She would always be searching for that feeling of familial unity the Stoddards once had and lost. William had no means of supporting her, but he was able to find her employment as a teacher in a local primary school for an annual salary of forty dollars.[11] Kate, like her brother, found her new life challenging. She worked hard but later recalled feeling that she "was a very poor teacher, knowing very little and not knowing *how* [emphasis is hers] to impart what [she] did know."[12]

William O. Stoddard, May 4, 1859 (author collection).

William, on the other hand, continued to work hard at his new tasks and the *Gazette* prospered. He said that he now "really felt at home" and that his ambition "was rising fast."[13] He determined that he and the *Gazette* should venture into politics, even though Scroggs, a vehement abolitionist, considered his assistant to be merely lukewarm in his anti-slavery sentiments.[14] Unfazed by Scroggs' assessment, Stoddard joined a new political party — the Republican Party. He attended party conventions and made speeches in Champaign County, drawing attention to himself and to the weekly paper. Calling his assistant an "aristocrat," the jealous Scroggs assailed Stoddard's ambition: "It's in you, as big as a horse. Why, any man can see it in you — across the street!"[15]

One man, filled with ambition himself, spotted the same trait in Stoddard and decided to pay a visit to the office of the *Gazette*. The man was Abraham Lincoln. The forty-nine-year-old lawyer from Springfield, Illinois, had failed in his ambitious bid to unseat Stephen A. Douglas in the U.S. Senate but had made a name for himself during the debates. Undeterred, Lincoln had his eye on higher political position and was always surveying the landscape for potential supporters.

9

"Something in This Man's Face and Manner"

On April 27, 1859, Stoddard was in the *Gazette*'s printing room, shirt sleeves rolled up, composing, with hands covered with black ink and streaks of darkness across his brow. Scroggs entered and announced, "Old Abe is here and he wants to see you!"[1] Conscious of not looking exactly presentable for distinguished company, the printer washed his hands, smoothed his shirt, and went to greet the future president whom he had met face to face only once before. Stoddard had heard much about Lincoln since then and considered him to be an up-and-coming figure in the Republican Party, and he thought back now to the first time they had met in 1857. Stoddard had entered the only drug store in Urbana and came across a group of circuit court lawyers and a judge gathered around the store's black stove. They were deeply engaged in a discussion of English literature of the Elizabethan era. One man had just concluded a recitation of poetic verse from Ben Jonson, when a very tall man in a black stovepipe hat broke in with, "You are wrong there, Judge. That isn't from Jonson; it's from Sir John Suckling." The judge acknowledged his error before this lanky, disheveled fellow who did not have the appearance of an erudite scholar. Stoddard inserted himself into this intellectual discussion and learned that this man who spoke with literary authority was the circuit-riding lawyer Abe Lincoln.[2]

Now, Mr. Lincoln had come to see Stoddard, and Scroggs was more than a little miffed. After all, wasn't *he* the owner of the *Gazette*? Mr. Lincoln greeted Stoddard cordially, as if they had known each other for some time, and launched immediately into the reason for his visit. He was trying to assess the direction of political views in the nation, in the state of Illinois, and, in particular, in Champaign County. He had been told that William Stoddard knew the different voting precincts and their leading men, but Stoddard was amazed at how much information Lincoln already knew. Scroggs did not hang around, since the conversation proceeded without him. He went off "to see a patient." At some point the conversation included the subject of likely candidates for the presidency in 1860. They discussed the merits of William H. Seward of New York, Salmon P. Chase of Ohio, and Edward Bates of Missouri. At the end of the lengthy conversation, when Lincoln departed, Stoddard had no idea "that so unimportant an interview was to have any permanent effect" upon his life, but he had to admit that Mr. Lincoln was unusually interesting.[3]

Physically, Lincoln was not much to look at. His eyes were set deep into his clean-shaven, brown, furrowed face. A shock of unkempt black hair crowned his head. His clothes were wrinkled and revealed an indifference to sartorial matters. With arms folded behind his back or just hanging at his sides, he walked with an unusual gait, as if "his legs seemed to drag from the knees down, like those of a laborer going home after a hard day's work."[4] Despite Lincoln's awkward appearance, Stoddard said, "There was something in this man's face and manner that attracted me unusually."[5] Stoddard also observed how Lincoln carried papers around in his black stovepipe hat, like a portable office filing cabinet.[6] The lawyer knew exactly what document had to be extracted for any occasion, much as the man carried a plethora of humorous jokes and anecdotes around in his head and knew exactly which ones to pull forth to fit any circumstance.[7]

Lincoln's sense of humor served him well. As a lawyer, he once defended a client on trial for assault and battery. He told the jury that the case reminded him of a man who once killed a farmer's angry dog with a pitchfork. "Why did you kill my dog?" demanded the irate farmer. "Why did your dog come after me?" questioned the man. "Well, why didn't you come after him with the other end?" asked the farmer. "Why didn't he come after me with *his* other end?" countered the man. The much bemused jury found Lincoln's client not guilty.[8]

It was Lincoln's personality, his use of humor, and his ability to articulate views on complex matters like slavery that led Stoddard to conclude that Lincoln the lawyer was presidential material. When Stoddard informed Scroggs that the *Gazette* was going to endorse Lincoln for president, cantankerous Scroggs bellowed: "Oh, Hell! He'd never do for president. He might do for a nominee for vice president, perhaps, with Seward or some such man." By rights, Scroggs thought his assistant, born and raised in Central New York State, should have been a Seward supporter just as he had been a supporter of New York's Millard Fillmore.[9]

William Seward from Auburn, New York, a former governor and then a

U.S. senator, maintained that slavery was legal under the Constitution but was morally wrong. He proclaimed in 1850, with a finger pointed heavenward, that "there is a higher law than the Constitution." Yet, Seward was not an abolitionist, at least publicly. For political and legal reasons, he subscribed to the view that slavery would and should succumb in time to the forces of history without resorting to coercion or war.[10] Interestingly, after the Civil War, it was Frank Carpenter who provided evidence that Seward evolved into a closeted abolitionist. Carpenter wrote this of Seward's clandestine activities:

Abraham Lincoln in Illinois (courtesy Library of Congress).

Among the visitors in the evening was Mr. Wormley, the well known colored landlord of Washington. Greeting him cordially and introducing him to his other guests, Mr. Seward said: "Wormley and I went into the emancipation business a year and a half before Mr. Lincoln did, down on the James River. How was it Wormley — how many slaves did we take off on our steamer?" "Eighteen," replied Mr. Wormley.[11]

Abraham Lincoln was not an abolitionist either, at first. Some say he never was and that the Emancipation Proclamation was issued more for political reasons, but as early as the late 1850s, Lincoln was addressing slavery as a malignancy that had to be permitted to exist where it was, in the South, but not allowed to metastasize out West.[12] In 1859, Seward, overly confident that the Republican Party would nominate him to run for president, departed for an extended tour of Europe.[13] During the better-known Seward's trip abroad, the lesser-known Lincoln went to work, diligently lining up support in case Seward failed to win on the first ballot.[14]

Before this, Stoddard had gone to work, too. After his long talk with Lincoln, in the May 4, 1859, issue of the *Central Illinois Gazette*, Stoddard brought forward Lincoln's name. It was not in an editorial but in the Personal column (see Appendix A). He advocated Lincoln for the presidency and claimed: "No man in the West at the present time occupies a more enviable position before the people or stands a better chance for obtaining a high position among those to whose guidance our ship of state is to be entrusted."[15] This was the very argument that Lincoln's supporters in the East used to deprive Seward of the Republican nomination: that only a nominee from the West could win the executive office for the party.[16]

Eight months later, Stoddard ran an editorial, "Who Shall Be President?" (See Appendix B) "We in Illinois know him well...," wrote Stoddard, "a man of the people ... whose enlarged and liberal mind descends to no narrow view, but sees both sides of every great question." Stressing the importance of Pennsylvania and Illinois as key states in the election and presenting Lincoln as a moderate, Stoddard claimed that only Lincoln could consolidate the party vote in Illinois or "carry the great Mississippi Valley."[17] On December 21, 1859, Lincoln's name appeared at the head of the editorial columns of the *Gazette* and remained there until after the election. In January, February, and May of 1860 the *Gazette* ran pieces touting the fitness of Lincoln and the political necessity of electing a western man.[18]

Stoddard always believed or wanted to believe that he was the first to editorially nominate Lincoln for president. The New York *Times* ran an article on the day after his death that twice cited him as the first journalist to mention Lincoln as a possible presidential contender.[19] However, Jeriah Bonham had done so two years earlier on November 4, 1858, in the Lacon, Illinois, *Gazette*.[20] This was followed by the *Times* of Olney, Illinois, on November 19, 1858, and by the Chicago *Press and Tribune*, which published on December 16, 1858, a reprint of an editorial that first ran in the Reading, Pennsylvania, *Berks and Schuylkill Journal*.[21]

10

A Request "Bold, Even to Presumption"

Although Stoddard was not the first to editorially endorse Lincoln, he can be credited with arranging to have his editorial widely circulated. It appeared in *The Century* of New York and in two hundred other journals across the nation and in the West in particular.[1] This, along with his attendance at the convention at Springfield and his active campaigning in Champaign County, gained him recognition which did not go unnoticed by Lincoln.[2]

Back East in Homer, the Barber family was much inclined to have William Seward of nearby Auburn, New York, in the Executive Mansion, and not some unknown from out West. Paris, especially, was convinced that Seward's higher law speech meant the senator was an ardent abolitionist and had to be elected.[3] Paris' brother, George, served on the State Republican Committee and told the family about Lincoln's electrifying speech at Cooper Union. Presented in New York on February 27, 1860, the speech opposed the expansion of slavery out West and effectively deprived Seward of support even in his home state.[4]

At noon on May 16, 1860, the Republican National Convention convened on Lincoln's home turf, Chicago, Illinois. Delegates to the recently built convention hall, the Wigwam, were ready to adopt a platform and to name a presidential candidate. The central plank was opposition to the extension of slavery, but to appeal to a broader political base other issues were addressed: a protective tariff, support for the improvement of harbors and rivers, protection for naturalized citizens, a homestead act for agrarian interests, and a transcontinental railroad. Seward was confident he would walk away with the candidacy but was stunned when he learned he did not win the required simple majority of votes on the first ballot. The second ballot placed Lincoln only three and a half votes away from Seward's total of 184 and a half votes. Tension mounted as the third ballot was taken. Lincoln's total reached 231 and a half votes. He only needed one and a half votes for victory. When Ohio announced its switch of four votes for Salmon P. Chase to Abraham Lincoln, the Wigwam went wild. Soon, delegates, even those from Seward's New York, arose to make the vote for Lincoln unanimous.[5]

Seward received the devastating news at his home in Auburn, New York. Sitting with friends in his garden, he was handed the telegram by a rider from the telegraph office. It contained the results of the third ballot, which Seward conveyed to all in three words: "Abraham Lincoln nominated." He and his hometown felt crushed. As flags were rolled up and the celebratory cannons were sadly rolled away, Seward put up a brave front. Hiding anger, hurt, and humiliation, one week later, Seward publicly pledged his support of the Lincoln-Hamlin ticket and urged his supporters to do the same in November.[6]

On Election Day, 1860, Paris Barber and a large number of men from Homer cast their votes. They voted for Lincoln.[7] In New York City, Frank Carpenter wrote a simple phrase in his diary for Tuesday, November 6: "Voted for Lincoln and Hamlin."[8]

In Springfield, Lincoln was not planning to vote, thinking it improper for a presidential candidate to vote for his own electors. His law partner, William Herndon, convinced him that the candidates for the lesser offices would, at least, appreciate his vote. At 3 P.M., he went to the courthouse to do his civic duty. His appearance attracted a wildly enthusiastic crowd. By 9 P.M., Lincoln and some friends were collected at the telegraph office to receive the returns. By 10 P.M., the news indicated he had carried the Northwest, Indiana, New England, and the important state of Pennsylvania. At midnight, he partook of a victory supper served by the local Republican ladies, but he felt celebration was premature. An official victory depended upon New York State. Without those 35 electoral votes, the total he had amassed so far, 145 electoral votes, would leave him 7 shy of the constitutionally required majority. The Democratic Party's control of the New York City precincts could still deny him the presidency. It might be enough to offset the rest of the state, which traditionally voted Republican. A little after midnight, the telegraph started tapping again. New York State voted for Lincoln. To the ringing of church bells, a jubilant Lincoln hurried home to proclaim the good news: "Mary, Mary, we are elected!"[9]

Stoddard was delighted, too, with the election results. With only 40 percent of the popular vote but more than enough of the electoral votes,[10] the "Rail-splitter" from Illinois became president-elect — a fact that the Southern states had said would cause them to secede from the Union.[11]

10. A Request "Bold, Even to Presumption"   65

In his memoirs, Stoddard claimed he never entertained "any idea whatever of obtaining any other advantage from my political labors."[12] Yet, soon after the election, Stoddard journeyed to Springfield to attend a congratulation levee at the State House. The receiving line was filled with eager office-seekers, and when Stoddard came to take Lincoln's hand in congratulations, he claimed Lincoln asked him if he would like to come to Washington and take a clerkship "or something." Then and there, supposedly, Stoddard came up with the idea of responding, "Mr. Lincoln, the only thing that would tempt me to go to Washington is a place on your personal staff." Lincoln, supposedly, instructed him to write a letter to that effect and then to wait for further word. This Stoddard did. One month later, in December 1860, Stoddard claims, he received a lengthy letter from Lincoln instructing him to settle his affairs in Illinois and come to the nation's capital to await his arrival.[13]

If there was any such invitation, it has not survived. What has survived is an interesting letter Stoddard penned to Lincoln's law partner, William H. Herndon, on December 27, 1860, revealing Stoddard's anxiety about not hearing from Lincoln. He wrote that his request for a position was "bold, even to presumption," and wanted to know "what the indications are" of receiving an appointment as "private secretary." He further stated that he had had two friends from New York State submit letters of endorsement. Audaciously, Stoddard indicated that he would not object if Herndon suggested to Lincoln that he "begin 'on trial,' as the Dutchman took his wife." In desperation, he concluded how highly gratifying it would be to receive double the income he was then earning "editing a country weekly."[14]

Whatever impression one may form of Stoddard

Portion of Stoddard's letter to William Herndon (courtesy Library of Congress, Lincoln Papers).

from his memoirs, the recollections of an elderly man given to understandable lapses of memory and embellishments of an account meant for his children's enjoyment, one ought to recognize that tendencies to self-promotion at moments of opportunity mark ambition in a man. A certain amount of drive, or ambition, is good in a man, and this was a quality that was instilled in both Stoddard and Carpenter from their early days in Central New York State.

Stoddard acted upon his ambition, much to the chagrin of Scroggs, and pulled up stakes to go to Washington. His sister and brother went back East, too. Kate went back to friends, and Harry, who had followed Kate out West to their brother's home in Illinois, returned to Syracuse to a clerk position in the Bank of Syracuse with old friends, the Whites. William, too, returned to Syracuse for a short visit and then continued on to Washington by rail through Philadelphia and Baltimore.[15]

Arriving in Washington in the first week of February 1861, Stoddard found the city to be "little more than a great, straggling village."[16] Pennsylvania Avenue was a broad boulevard of mud and ruts. Hogs roamed at will and wallowed here and there in the streets. People tossed slops and refuse in the gutters. Dead domestic animals and sewage were deposited into the murky canal behind a row of dingy buildings along the south side of the avenue. The stench was revolting. Then, just a few blocks from the Executive Mansion was a pathetic crime-ridden neighborhood of saloons and brothels. Stoddard also observed that many of the government buildings were under construction. Blocks of stone were awaiting placement into a memorial to the nation's first president. The grounds of the Capitol Building were littered with work sheds, keystones, and blocks of marble. Looking up, he could not help but notice scaffolding over the center of the edifice where a great dome was meant to go. Was this not appropriate? Was this not symbolic of the moment? An incomplete architectural seat of government represented an incomplete nation.[17] But the work went on, as did the cause of emancipation.

11

Foiling the Plot to Kill "Nuts"

Because of its location along the Potomac River, the nation's capital was essentially a Southern town. The slave state of Maryland was to the north and east; the slave state of Virginia was to the south and west. With the secession of South Carolina from the Union on December 20, 1860, Washington was filled with and surrounded by potential enemies. More than once, Stoddard heard the ominous statement: "The damned abolitionist has been elected but he will never be president."[1] The *Washington Star* of January 2, 1861, revealed that Lincoln and Vice President-elect Hannibal Hamlin had "received anonymous letters threatening violent opposition to their inauguration."[2]

On February 11, 1861, two days after the formation of the Confederate States of America in Montgomery, Alabama, President-elect Abraham Lincoln, no longer clean-shaven but sporting a beard, stood on the back of a railroad car and bid farewell to Springfield, where he had lived for seventeen years. Standing in an early morning downpour, the crowd of well-wishers heard him say, "I now leave, not knowing when, or whether ever, I may return, with a task before me greater than that which rested upon Washington." At eight o'clock A.M. the train departed with Lincoln. His wife, Mary Todd Lincoln, and their three boys, Robert, William (called "Willie"), and Thomas (called "Tad") would join him in Indianapolis. A fourth son, Edward Baker Lincoln, had died at age three and was buried in Springfield. Now, Lincoln headed east, on a seventeen-hundred-mile route that was to pass through Syracuse, Albany, New York, Philadelphia, and Baltimore, to become president of a nation on the verge of civil war.[3]

At this juncture of the story, a third native son of Homer makes his entrance. His role is pivotal to the rest of the story. Without him, there would be no connection between Lincoln and Homer's Frank Carpenter and William Stoddard. Indeed, without this third gentleman, there would have been no President Lincoln and no fulfillment of the American abolition movement.

The third gentleman was the mysterious Eli DeVoe of Summit, New Jersey. Eli was the son of John and Helena Godwin DeVoe, early settlers of New York's Military Tract. Eli was born in Homer, New York, in a log cabin in 1809, the same year that Lincoln was born in a log cabin in Kentucky to Tom and Nancy Hanks Lincoln.[4] One infant son was destined to be a president, and one, born to members of the Congregationalist fold in Homer, was destined to save a president.

In response to rampant rumors that an attack would be made upon Lincoln along the published route to Washington, detective Allen Pinkerton made investigations in Baltimore, Maryland. The place was a veritable caldron seething with anti-Lincoln sentiments. Through the spouting off of an Italian barber at the Barnum City Hotel, Pinkerton and his men learned that there was, indeed, a plot to assassinate the president-elect prior to his inauguration. The railway system was configured in such a way that all southbound trains required a transfer to be made in Baltimore. The Northern railway ended at Calvert Street and the railway to Washington started at Camden Street. A one-mile distance between these two stations had to be traversed by carriage, making for a likely place to target Lincoln. An orchestrated disturbance could distract the police long enough for the conspirators to gain access to Lincoln and kill him.[5]

Unknown to Pinkerton, the New York City superintendent of police, John Kennedy, had already sent detectives into Baltimore. Two detectives sent by Kennedy were Eli DeVoe and Tom Sampson. Both had been in the employ of George Washington Matsell, the chief of police for the New York Police Department until Matsell was forced to resign in 1857 to make way for a commission enacted to oversee law enforcement in the city. Matsell's detectives were known as Matsell's Shadows.[6]

Eli DeVoe's birthsite marker near Atwater Cemetery, Homer, New York (courtesy David Quinlan).

Sampson had an outstanding performance record. He was one of the first seven New York City patrolmen to be inducted into the department's Legion of Honor on May 26, 1855, in front of City Hall. Sampson, of the 18th Patrol District, was cited as a hero by Mayor Fernando Wood:

> This officer has distinguished himself upon various occasions, particularly in saving life. He has saved four lives within five years. In August, 1854, he rushed into a house on fire in Seventeenth Street, near Sixth Avenue, and rescued a child, while no other man was found brave enough to undertake it. A distracted mother stood weeping and imploring some bold spirit to restore her child; all refused and skulked away, when this intrepid policeman dashed through the flames and soon placed the child in its mother's arms. On the 16th of May last he performed another feat almost equally commendable, in rescuing the child of Mr. J.H. Anderson from death, when thrown out of that gentleman's carriage on the Third Avenue, immediately under the wheels of a railroad car. In this effort he hazarded his own life, which was saved only by accident.[7]

In Baltimore, DeVoe, traveling under the name Davis, and Sampson, using the alias of Thompson, managed to shadow and infiltrate a subversive anti–Lincoln cell linked to the Knights of the Golden Circle. The Knights of the Golden Circle was a secret society originally founded to promote the interests of the Southern United States and to pave the way for the annexation of a "golden circle" of territories in Mexico, Central America, and the Caribbean to be included in the United States as slave states. Members in the North during the Civil War were known as Copperheads.[8] President-elect Lincoln was perceived by this subversive element as an abolitionist threatening their goals, and DeVoe and Sampson informed Superintendent Kennedy that there was a plot brewing in Baltimore to kill Lincoln. Kennedy informed Baltimore police chief George Kane, but Kane responded that additional police officers would not be needed along the rail route into and through the city. So Kennedy telegraphed his men's recently uncovered plot to Frederick Seward, son of New York's Senator Seward. The senator was to be Lincoln's secretary of state and Frederick was to be the assistant secretary of state in charge of consular service. Superintendent Kennedy then made an effort to rush men to bolster the ranks of Baltimore police.[9]

Allen Pinkerton, meanwhile, sent word to General Winfield Scott in Washington that there was reason to believe a group planned to detonate an explosive device on February 23, 1861, on the Gunpowder River Bridge and, during the impending confusion, kill Lincoln. The railroad officials were notified. Because two sources, Pinkerton and DeVoe, independently corroborated assassination plots, Lincoln agreed to participate in a plan to thwart them. Until Frederick personally presented Lincoln with DeVoe's information, confirming fears generated by Pinkerton, Lincoln had expressed a reluctance to change plans that called for a stop and public appearance in Baltimore.[10]

After a flag-raising ceremony in Philadelphia, word was put out that the president-elect had taken ill. In Harrisburg, on February 23, Lincoln, bareheaded, a soft felt hat in his pocket, exited from the rear of the hotel while a Lincoln double was seen quickly entering a carriage at the front of the hotel. Mary Todd Lincoln must have been full of terror. Ahead was the potentially perilous passage through the streets of Baltimore. High-strung by nature and much afflicted by stress-caused migraine headaches, Mary had to muster all the courage she possessed to go into harm's way with her children, separated from her husband, and all because of reports from perfect strangers.[11]

Accompanied by his physically imposing friend and self-appointed bodyguard, Ward Hill Lamon, Lincoln took a carriage to the railroad station. There an unlighted single car and engine awaited them in the night's darkness. Only railway officials and detectives were on board. After the train left Harrisburg, one of Pinkerton's operatives, using the crude, agreed upon code word for Lincoln, wired his boss this message: "Nuts left at six — Everything as you directed — all is right."[12] Then, the telegraph lines were shut down; no messages were to be sent from the city that night. A few minutes later, Lincoln was back in Philadelphia, where the night train was being held for an "important package." Detective Pinkerton and Ward Hill Lamon escorted Lincoln onto the rear car of the train. When the superintendent of the Philadelphia, Wilmington & Delaware Railroad handed the conductor "a bundle of old newspapers which were tied up," the train departed.[13]

The train reached Washington at about six o'clock in the morning, February 24. Senator Seward had a carriage waiting, with Illinois congressman Elihu B. Washburne as the only welcoming party. Lincoln, unrecognized by anyone else, was whisked off to the refuge of Willard's Hotel. Pinkerton quickly wired his operatives that their mission had succeeded: "Plums arrived here with Nuts this morning — all right."[14] Mary Lincoln and the boys passed through Baltimore without incident, which unleashed an angry exchange of letters between the police chiefs, Kane and Kennedy.[15]

Because their plot had been detected and had to be aborted, the assassination conspirators sought to ferret out the informant in their midst. Suspicions had been aroused when a letter was discovered. Mrs. DeVoe indiscreetly mailed a letter to her husband. It was addressed to his assumed name, but it bore a New York postmark. This did not dovetail with DeVoe's claim to be from Mobile, Alabama. Realizing the grave danger they were in, DeVoe and Sampson donned disguises and made a hasty retreat, leaving behind their baggage at the hotel. Followed to Washington by members of the subversive gang, DeVoe and Sampson experienced two close, life-threatening calls, but they escaped further harm through the assistance of a fellow detective who had shadowed them at Pinkerton's order.[16]

With the outbreak of the Civil War, DeVoe entered the United States' first secret service, organized by Pinkerton, and served through the war. Later, DeVoe was present at the arrest of Mary Surratt and Lewis Thornton Powell (aka Lewis Paine or Lewis Payne) in 1865 for being accomplices in John Wilkes Booth's successful assassination of President Lincoln. Powell had, also, just failed in his attempt to assassinate Secretary of State William Seward. For his efforts on this case, DeVoe was said to have received a large reward.[17]

Unlike Frank Carpenter and William Stoddard, who lived very public existences and left historians with a useful paper trail, Eli DeVoe's work was in the shadowy world of unrecorded secrets and covert operations. Hence, little is known about him, and for just

"Passage Through Baltimore" by Adalbert John Volck, March 23, 1861, contributed to the story that Lincoln disguised himself in a Scotch hat and military cloak (courtesy Harold Holzer).

cause. Not until after his death in 1874 was an article published describing his role in thwarting the plot to kill Lincoln.[18] Eli was the stereotypical unsung hero, working quietly and professionally behind the scenes and at great personal risk. It is known that at the close of the war he worked until his death as a messenger and private detective for the Ninth National Bank of New York, on Broadway near Walker Street. He personally received a costly gift from the famous banker Baron Rothschild of Paris as "a remembrance of skill, energy, perseverance" rendered in the line of service. Most likely, this was for the successful capture of Carpentier, Brelet, Parot, and other notorious defrauders who robbed the French Railway Company in France.[19]

In December of 1873, the sixty-four-year-old DeVoe was suffering from what was called rheumatism in his right leg. His physician advised him to remain indoors. In disregard of this injunction, he went out to trot a colt up and down the yard. In doing this, DeVoe fell. He injured the rheumatic leg so badly that he could barely manage to hobble into his house. The leg began to swell. In less than an hour the skin below the knee broke in several places. Several doctors were summoned, but he grew progressively worse because of a virulent bacterial infection. Amputation was called for. Though his weakened state lessened the likelihood of his surviving the procedure, it was regarded as the only possible option left to save his life. On January 25, 1874, Dr. James Wood amputated the leg above the knee, and DeVoe succumbed two hours later. His funeral was held at the family homestead overlooking a branch of the Passaic River, with many of his old friends of nearby Monmouth in attendance. He was buried in Monmouth, leaving behind the wife he had married in 1832, Abigail D. Spear, two children, and "considerable property."[20]

For service rendered to Lincoln, there is no doubt that Eli DeVoe deserves as much attention and praise as—if not more than—Carpenter and Stoddard. Perhaps, in the fullness of time, this courageous son of Homer will receive the recognition that is his due as one of the protectors of Lincoln. His covert operation led Lincoln to take action that resulted in the president beginning his administration with an unwanted public image of cowardliness. Yet, by saving the life of the future Great Emancipator, Eli DeVoe unknowingly moved the abolition movement forward and Lincoln toward a far different and longer-lasting presidential image.

12

On Loan to the White House

While Lincoln was saved from bodily harm by the fine detective work of DeVoe and Pinkerton, nothing could spare him from the derision of the secessionists when they learned of his seemingly cowardly entry into the nation's capital.[1] Though mocked by political cartoons, Lincoln stood on the U.S. Capitol's East Front on March 4, 1861, and, with his right hand on the Holy Bible, took the presidential oath of office, promising "to preserve, protect, and defend the Constitution." With those words he became the sixteenth president of the *dis*–United States of America. Seven states had seceded from the Union, but Virginia and Maryland were not among them. In the North there was fear that it would be only a matter of time before they increased the number to nine. The hills of both neighboring states were thick with pro-secession forces. During the inauguration, sharpshooters were placed along the roofs of nearby buildings because of the security threat.[2]

In his Inaugural Address Lincoln spoke directly to the rebel states: "In your hands, my dissatisfied fellow countrymen, and not in mine, is the momentous issue of civil war. The government will not assail you. You can have no conflict without being yourselves the aggressors." Stoddard was present[3] to witness the event and to hear the stirring, poetic conclusion:

> We must not be enemies. Though passion may have strained, it must not break our bonds of affection. The mystic chords of memory, stretching from every battle-field, and patriot grave, to every living heart and hearthstone, all over this broad land, will yet swell the chorus of the Union, when again touched, as surely they will be, by the better angels of our nature.[4]

The Democratic-controlled *Cortland Gazette* reported that Republican gentlemen from the Cortland-Homer area of New York State were attending the inauguration but, in reality, were in Washington to seek high office. The

Photograph taken by Alexander Gardner at Mathew Brady's Photographic Parlor on the day after Lincoln arrived in Washington (photograph was taken directly from glass plate #68 in the Frederick Hill Meserve Collection and was later acquired by the late Lincoln historian Richard F. Lufkin. Now part of author's collection).

new president had put together a cabinet, but *The Cortland Gazette* was unimpressed. Its editor reported that the cabinet "lacks unity of views" and added "we shall be surprised if this incongruous cabinet holds together a six months."[5]

Soon after the inauguration, Stoddard made his way to the Executive Mansion to see how the new administration could make use of his services. The main stairway leading up to the executive offices was clogged with office-seekers. It was sheer noise and confusion. Somehow he managed to leave a calling card with an usher. In a few days time, he received his commission. He was to be secretary to sign land patents at the Interior Department building. It was not the office in the Executive Mansion he wanted, but it would have to do. Because of an outdated Executive Mansion administrative budget, only one personal secretary to the president was permitted, at a salary of $2,500 per year, and that position was already filled by twenty-nine-year-old John G. Nicolay of Illinois. He and Stoddard were acquaintances from their days as journalists covering Illinois politics. As need dictated, the lawyerly Lincoln found a way to get additional aides. He simply appointed them to other government posts and had them assigned on loan to his staff. This was how it worked out for twenty-three-year-old John Milton Hay, also of Illinois, who served as another personal secretary on loan from the Interior Department. This, too, was how twenty-six-year-old William came to be an assistant personal secretary to President Lincoln with an annual salary of $1,500 and his very own brass key to allow himself entrance to the Executive Mansion at will.[6]

The executive workload began to increase on Friday, April 12, 1861. At 4:30 in the morning, forty-three Confederate guns opened fire on Fort Sumter at Charleston, South Carolina. The next day, the fort surrendered. The nation was at war![7]

Telegraph wires sent the news across the land, and it spread by word of mouth from there. In Cortland County, New York, the bad news arrived first on April 12 by wire to Sager's Drugstore near the northeast corner of Main and Court streets of the community of Cortland.[8] It did not take long for word to reach the nearby village of Homer. A group of men was gathered in the Homer post office, discussing the significance of this news, when Paris Barber ambled in. In dismay he heard one after another conclude, "There is nothing left to do now but fight." One youngster interjected his sentiments: "I'd like to smash Jeff Davis's skull with my axe!" Paris was horrified. It was one of his pupils from Sunday school. Paris, in vain, tried to present his case. Was it not God's desire that Mr. Lincoln and Mr. Davis meet and talk it over? With Mr. Seward present to tell of God's law, would not Mr. Davis be convinced, on Christian principles, to avoid war? When the first troops left Homer, the man named after a Trojan war hero was not among them. Nor did this peace-loving Christian accept an invitation from Jacob Schermerhorn to go with him to Virginia to bring spiritual encouragement to the men of Company D, 12th Regiment, in training there. Instead, he preferred to stay and promote the building of a much-needed new edifice for the Congregationalists. Jacob Schermerhorn agreed to chair the building committee. With his talent and treasure, in the midst of national turmoil, a brick structure was to rise. The church was to have a bell, a clock, and a tall spire pointed heavenward above the trees of Homer, like hands steepled together in fervent prayer to the God of Peace. Of course, poor Paris was again the object of ridicule. Even his own brother, Watts, scornfully asked, "What does Paris want done with his dog; he fights?"[9]

In Washington, William Stoddard, the secretary on loan to the president, did not waste any time in signing up for military duty. Aware that the city was under-garrisoned and woefully vulnerable to rebel attack, he went immediately to see the president and to ask his permission to enlist for three months in a unit known as the D.C. Rifles. Lincoln gave his consent.[10]

Fear of an imminent rebel invasion of the capital from across the Potomac in Virginia was palpable in the muddy streets of Washington. The D.C. Rifles were to help stand guard at key positions in the city until reinforcements arrived from the North. It might be on a bridge spanning the Potomac during a fierce rainstorm, or at night at the entrance to the Treasury Building, or out in the middle of the cobblestoned main street of Georgetown — anywhere and under any conditions to thwart secessionists until Lincoln's proclamation calling for 75,000 volunteers was heeded.[11]

The situation confronting the capital was grave. "Friday April 19 1861 is likely to become historic in the nation's annals," Nicolay wrote in his own memorandum of events. "The 6th Regiment Mass[achusetts] Volunteer Militia, in passing through the city of Baltimore, was assaulted by a mob, and finally in self-defense fired upon the mob in return."[12] In a letter to his fiancée, Therena Bates, Nicolay described the Baltimore incident "in which several were killed on both sides":

> It is I believe the first bloodshed in this civil war, and singularly enough is the anniversary of the first bloodshed [at Lexington] in the Revolution.... The secessionists may at any hour cut the telegraph wires, tear up the railroad track, or burn the bridges, and thus ... cut off all communication.... 1500 men are [rumored to be] gathered and under arms at Alexandria.... A vessel late this evening was seen landing men on the Maryland side of the [Potomac] river."[13]

An attack seemed imminent, but it did not come.

Participating with the D.C. Rifles in the night-time capture of a steamer full of armed secessionists at a Potomac pier, Stoddard wrote an embellished description of "the first naval victory ever won at sea by riflemen" in a letter to his brother Harry. To William's surprise, Harry had it published in the Syracuse newspapers.[14]

Reinforcements finally arrived. First to march into the city were the Pennsylvania Fifth Volunteers and then the New York Seventh Regiment. Harry arrived in Washington at the same time, seeking to join the D.C. Rifles, too. The ranks were full, but William finagled him in.[15]

Those who signed on for military glory soon had their first confrontation with deadly reality. Stoddard was an acquaintance of Colonel Ephraim Elmer Ellsworth, a close friend of the Lincoln family, and had been present once when the handsome twenty-four-year-old officer had accidentally thrust a carbine through a pane in an Executive Mansion window.[16] Ellsworth was born in New York State and once studied law under Lincoln and Herndon in Springfield. It was Ellsworth who accompanied the Lincolns by train to Washington and had raised a colorfully uniformed company of soldiers called the 11th New York Zouaves. On May 24, 1861, the day after news arrived of Virginia's secession, Ellsworth marched his Zouaves across the Potomac River into Alexandria, Virginia. There, the young colonel personally removed a Confederate flag from the rooftop of the Marshall House hotel which had been irritatingly visible from the Executive Mansion. On his way down the stairs with the rebel banner, Ellsworth was fatally shot by the proprietor of the hotel, James W. Jackson. The Lincolns were devastated. Their dashing friend and protector, an early Union casualty of the war, was given a funeral in the East Room.[17]

Colonel Ellsworth from a CDV in the author's collection.

The night before Ellsworth marched on Alexandria, he wrote to his dear fiancée, Carrie Spafford.

> My own darling Kitty,
>
> My regiment is ordered to cross the river & move on Alexandria within six hours. We may meet with a warm reception & my darling among so many careless fellows one is somewhat likely to be hit.
>
> If anything should happen — Darling just accept this assurance, the only thing I can leave you — the highest happiness I looked for on earth was a union with you.... God bless you as you deserve and grant you a happy & useful life & us a union hereafter.
>
> Truly your own,
> Elmer

Ellsworth had then put on his person a gold medallion bearing the inscription *Non Nobis, Sed Pro Patria,* or Not for us, but for our country. When he was fatally shot, a bullet drove the medallion deep into his flesh.[18] To avenge his death, a call went out to raise a regiment made up of one unmarried man from each town and ward in New York State. Thus, the 44th New York was popularly known as Ellsworth's Avengers.[19]

Before the war reached its conclusion, too many other hearts were broken and too many other calls for vengeance went forth on both sides, North and South. The war caused great upheaval in people's lives. The war made and unmade men. It opened ways and means for some, and it crushed and killed others.[20] It put men to the test. And each side claimed that God was on their side.

13

A Desk Near the President's Chamber

Understandably, the Stoddard brothers were all too eager to see the end of their three months of military service. At Rockville, Maryland, Harry suffered from sunstroke while on march and never fully regained his health.[1] He got a job at the Treasury Department, and his older brother returned to the Interior Department where a huge stack of land patents had accumulated. Each patent required him to sign President Lincoln's name. This he proceeded to do "at the rate of about nine hundred times per diem."[2] Shortly, he was summoned to the Executive Mansion and assigned a desk in the northeast room on the second floor near the president's spacious executive chamber — the room Lincoln called his workshop.

Besides signing land patents here, Stoddard was to assist Nicolay and Hay in their secretarial duties. The position on the presidential staff that he had hoped for was now his and remained so through Lincoln's first term of office. Other than document paper, the secretaries, for budgetary reasons, had to provide their own pens and stationery.[3] Their work environment was hectic. As Nicolay and Hay described it,

> At any hour of the day one might see at the outer door and on the staircase, one line going, one coming. In the anteroom and in the broad corridor adjoining the President's office there was a restless and persistent crowd, — ten, twenty, sometimes fifty, varying with the day and hour, — each one in pursuit of one of the many crumbs of official patronage. They walked the floor; they talked in groups; they acknowledged every arrival and blessed every departure; they wrangled with the door-keepers for the right of entrance; they intrigued with them surreptitious chances; they crowded forward to get even as much as an instant's glance through the half-opened door into the Executive chamber. They besieged

the Representatives and Senators who had privilege of precedence; they glared with envy at the Cabinet Ministers who, by right and usage, pushed through the throng and walked unquestioned through the doors.[4]

The burdens upon the president were staggering. Trying to be accessible to all who sought his ear, while waging a war to crush a rebellion, was starting to take its toll. His secretaries noted that "he was subjected to a mental strain and irritation that made him feel like a prisoner.... He said he felt like a man letting lodgings at one end of his house, while the other end was on fire."[5] Lincoln told paymaster Robert Wilson, an old friend in whom he felt he could confide, that he was so harassed by job applicants that "the only way he could escape from them would be to take a rope and hang himself on one of the trees in the south lawn."[6] The assistance of a third secretary on the second floor of the Executive Mansion was desperately needed.

As that secretary, Stoddard's main responsibility was to open the great quantity of mail that came to Mr. and Mrs. Lincoln each day and to determine what warranted their attention. By his estimate the mail bag averaged 250 pieces of mail per day. Copious amounts of hate mail addressed to the Lincolns, both Mr. and Mrs., were discarded. Mr. Lincoln had more than a fair share of scurrilous comments directed at his conduct of the war. One day a visitor waiting to see the president watched the assistant personal secretary discarding letter after letter into two waste baskets. Indignation over what he perceived to be a callous treatment of the president's mail gave rise to an expression of anger. Stoddard responded by handing the man "a number of the vilest scrawls that infamy could put on paper." As the man read, "his red face grew redder," and he gasped, "Young man! You are right! He ought not to see a line of that stuff! Burn it, sir! Burn it! What devils there are!" Communication arrived almost daily from "the Angel Gabriel," who claimed to be writing in blood, and William eventually concluded "that whenever any man went clean out of his head, he sat down and wrote to the President." By mail and in person, people were constantly prevailing upon the president for favors, job appointments, pardons or patents for their inventions. Too many of the inventions were ludicrous. One writer proposed forming a regiment of cross-eyed men that would use a cross-eyed gun he had invented. Other individuals lodged complaints of all kinds or offered unsolicited advice. Even threats of presidential assassination came across Stoddard's desk. Ultimately, Stoddard would earnestly attest, "I doubt if there was any spot in the United States in those days, outside of a battlefield that was more continually interesting than was the correspondence desk of the Executive Mansion."[7]

Stoddard kept many letters from reaching the over-worked president. It was a difficult decision to make. What was to be discarded, and what was to be passed along? One morning in 1863, a discarded letter was retrieved from

13. A Desk Near the President's Chamber

the waste basket and shown to Stoddard's sister Kate. The letter was written on a page torn from a book. It had been sealed in an envelope that had been stamped with the image of a soldier holding a flag. It had been written by a child.

> Mr. Linkum, we are very poor my father is a good man, he went to your war from Indyanny in the volenties and now they are going to shoot him because he came to see us. My mother cryes all the time for i am only 10 years old and there is three littler ones than me all night i said our father who art in heaven i don't know any other prayer. When i said give us today our daily bread i thought i would right to you and ask you to forgive and escoose our father and send him back to us for we want bread, we are so hungry and thine shall be the glory for ever and ever amen. mandy brooke

By the time the letter had arrived, the child's father had been executed for desertion. President Lincoln never saw the letter. Kate was deeply touched, to the point that she committed the letter to memory and commented on it and others like it two years later.

> From every state came some cry of pain; from little out-of-the-way villages and smaller hamlets, out of which had been sent the strong young men: the husbands, fathers, brothers, and lovers who were the pride and defenders of the home. The only ones in the wide world that belonged to and were waited for in those quiet homes. From these little villages and homes came many an appeal to the president for mercy and even for money for daily need.
> This poor child had trusted in President Lincoln's pardon, feeling as many did that the war was his, and that he controled [sic] all things and could annihilate time and distance. It was an impossible thing for him to have known or heard of or seen all and requests in letters that came to him.[8]

In addition, for awhile, the assistant secretary was to read the important newspapers of the day and to provide the president with a written daily digest, but this was abandoned as Lincoln had little time to devote to the condensations. Besides, Lincoln preferred what he called his "public-opinion baths." These were weekly receptions where he got to have direct contact with average Americans.[9]

One day, President Lincoln, knowing Stoddard to be a crack shot with a gun, requested his assistance in testing some new weaponry for average Americans to carry into battle. The new armament required presidential approval or rejection. Stoddard joined Lincoln on the Mall, the grassy slope between the mansion and the Potomac River. The area was littered with rubbish and building lumber, making a perfect spot for target practice. A hundred yards was marked off, and the two men took turns firing at a target. Lincoln kneeled down to get a better sight with his firearm, completely oblivious that military orders strictly forbade the firing of any guns within the limits of the city of Washington, D.C. Bam! Bam! The gunfire on the Mall drew the attention of a short corporal and four of his men who had been posted on guard duty nearby. They came running across the Mall, cursing and ordering a cessation of the shooting. The corporal came upon the kneeling figure, squinting over a breechloader, and shouted, "Stop that firing!" At that moment, the gun went off, and the commander in chief slowly stood up to his full six feet plus, turned around, and looked smilingly down upon the short corporal and his men. Stoddard noted: "All their lower jaws went down together but not one of them said another word right there." The contingent did an abrupt "bout face," and both the president and his assistant secretary had a good laugh as they heard the embarrassed men exclaiming, "We've been cussin' Old Abe himself!"[10]

Nicolay and Hay saw more of Lincoln than Stoddard did,[11] and both men were grateful that the prim and imperious Mrs. Lincoln preferred the diplomatic assistant secretary over them. There was no love lost between Mrs. Lincoln and the two personal secretaries, who, unlike Stoddard, were always present because they resided at the Executive Mansion. The first lady suffered, as did those around her, from her severe and unexpected mood swings. According to Lincoln's friend Oliver H. Browning, Mary was psychologically "always 'either in the garret or the cellar.'"[12] Nicolay, to the first lady and to everyone, could be brusque,[13] and behind her back, Hay called her "the Hell-Cat."[14]

Aside from minor personality clashes among themselves, the three members of the White House staff got along reasonably well.[15] Both Nicolay and Hay assigned "Stod" any of the more unpleasant tasks. This included the delicate and problematic responsibility of deciding who did and who did not get invited to receptions at the mansion.[16] Wielding such decision-making power made Stoddard well known in Washington social circles.

Along with this duty, Stoddard was to be in attendance upon Mrs. Lincoln at all of her private and public receptions in the Red Room and upon Mr. Lincoln at his weekly public receptions.[17] Being handsome in appearance, with a well-trimmed moustache over full lips, and diplomatic when needed, Stoddard was a good choice for handling introductions in receiving lines. He was, also, very supportive of the first lady. He seemed to understand that as one from the West, Mrs. Lincoln felt a need to prove to Washington society that she could fit in. He grasped full well how her inclination to wear expensive, colorful New York fashion, even when a costly war was raging, made her the object of scorn and gossip. A bevy of women from New England were received at the mansion one evening, and Stoddard reported his observations:

13. A Desk Near the President's Chamber

The tall, gray-haired, severe-faced lady, in very plain black silk, has two sons in the army. She may own streets in Boston, for all you know, but her dark eyes search the crimson silk and every other item of Mrs. Lincoln's outfit remorselessly, in spite of the warm, hearty cordiality of her greeting. Every woman who has yet arrived has come as a critic, and not one of them will be capable of doing kindly justice; and they will be authorities, hereafter, swelling a miserable tide of misunderstanding. Somehow or other, the best of women make too much of dress, and there is no more patriotism in their plainness than there is in the tint of this Red Room, which has not been changed because of the war.[18]

As for patriotism, because Mrs. Lincoln was from the border state of Kentucky and had relatives fighting on the secessionist side, she was the target of those who questioned her loyalty or simply disliked her and wanted an excuse to cast aspersions upon her. Years later, with biting humor, Stoddard mocked her assailants:

She has gone now, and we may as well linger a moment in the Red Room. It is not large, and it is made smaller by its massive furniture, its heavy curtains, its grand piano, and by the consciousness that it is in the middle corner, so to speak, of an unusually large house.

Put aside the curtains and look out of this window, across the White House grounds. You cannot see far, because of the trees and bushes; but, upon a careful study, you will understand, as you shove up the sash, that this is one of the most important windows in the United States. Mrs. Lincoln is in constant communication with the Confederate Government, betraying the war-plans of the Union generals, and this must be where she does it, for this is sacredly her own room. Even the President himself has never been seen here. The mails are not a channel for treachery, since every letter to Mrs. Lincoln is opened and read upstairs. The telegraphic wires are under War Office censorship, of a peculiarly rigid kind, and there is no private wire to the White House. The servants, downstairs, are known to be intensely loyal, and would neither carry nor bring communication of the Arnold-André kind. There is, therefore, but one entirely reasonable solution of the problem of how Mr. Jefferson Davis, or his next of kin, can receive army plans from Mrs. Lincoln, after she has obtained them from the President, and [General] Halleck, and [Secretary of War] Stanton, and [General] McClellan, and General Smith. The Confederate spies work their way through the lines easily enough, fort after fort, till they reach the Potomac down yonder. The Long Bridge is closed to them, and so is the Georgetown Bridge, but they cross at night in rowboats, or by swimming, and they come up through the grounds, like so many ghosts, and they put a ladder up to this window, and Mrs. Lincoln hands them out the plans.

Where do they get the ladder?

Well, now, you tell, if you know. They may borrow it of Jacob [of the Old Testament]. But there is no other way for the alleged treasonable communication to be carried on.[19]

Thus, like Frank Carpenter in New York, William Stoddard in Washington came into a position in which he made the acquaintance of influential individuals and their wives. There were senators, congressmen, cabinet members, journalists, editors, generals, high-ranking naval men, members of the diplomatic corps, and all sorts of celebrities—friends and foes of the Lincolns.[20] Not all were known for being virtuous. He quickly reached the conclusion that "a man may be able to carry the hundred and first ward of Babylon by an overwhelming majority, and yet not be just the person you would like to see dancing with your wife"[21]— a character assessment of some congressmen that has not been altered by time.

Friends of Stoddard from Homer passed through the Executive Mansion receiving line, too. Jacob M. Schermerhorn of The Hedges on South Main Street brought his daughter Anna and one of her girl friends to Washington. When they approached Mrs. Lincoln, Stoddard registered delight at the opportunity to welcome his former neighbor and the two young ladies. He invited his friends to wait until he completed his obligations and said he would then like to give them a tour of the mansion. It was an offer that was gladly accepted and long remembered for including a chance to meet the president. Anna would later recall how Lincoln's face was sincerely welcoming as he took her hands in his and stated, "It is always a pleasure to me to meet young people."[22]

Stoddard was well positioned in the Executive Mansion to observe its inner workings and to make political connections. He became as adept at "wire-pulling" as any Washington politician. He was able to secure the appointment of old "Doc" Scroggs as the postmaster of Champaign. Scroggs had actually come to Washington with hopes of obtaining an important post. Receiving none, he returned to Illinois claiming Stoddard had deprived him of patronage that was his due for having printed the nomination editorial. Later, when Stoddard learned that there was a fight over the Champaign post office between Scroggs and a rival editor named Crandall, he had a chance to insert his preference. He told the congressman of his home district that Crandall and his paper lived in Urbana while Scroggs and his paper resided in Champaign. Stoddard told the congressman, "Make it a question of locality and give it to Scroggs." Later, with tongue in cheek, Stoddard explained that this was how "the doctor got the post office instead of being tied down to a mere Comptrollership of the Treasury at Washington — or a place in the Cabinet."[23]

Through his favorable connection with Mrs. Lincoln, Stoddard was able to prevail upon the first lady to have his sister Kate assist at receptions.[24] Years later, Kate claimed to be unimpressed by the opportunity afforded her to stand near the Lincolns when they were receiving: "I think I cared very little

Photographs gifted to William O. Stoddard by the Lincolns and signed by him (author collection).

for such things— perhaps I did not know enough to feel honored. At least, I cared so little that I cannot remember the names of those I met. Though many names are now in our country's history."[25]

The assistant personal secretary was also in a position to enhance his limited income. From 1861 to 1864 he anonymously wrote newsletters for the *New York Examiner & Chronicle* about life in Washington. He used the pen name "Illinois." This had been at the invitation of the paper's owner, Stoddard's maternal uncle, Edward Bright. Bright had been the pastor of the Homer Baptist Church during Stoddard's childhood.[26]

More problematic was Stoddard's speculation in gold. As an inside judge of changing situations in Washington and aware of their effects on the gold market, the assistant secretary, not one averse to gambling, established an association with a New York banker named Edward Wolff[27] and made enough to alter his finances and his lifestyle. He gave up his residence in a boardinghouse in 1862 and leased a brownstone along the prestigious "morticians' row" of Louisiana Avenue for himself, Kate, Harry, and three friends who boarded there.[28] He paid off the debts he had accumulated back in Illinois and his father's debts in Syracuse.[29] He always maintained that Mr. and Mrs. Lincoln were aware of his speculations. Once, Mrs. Lincoln was reported to have been informed that her favorite secretary had cleared half a million dollars. Her response was, "Has he, indeed? I'm so glad to hear it. I wish he may make a million! I think a great deal of Mr. Stoddard. Glad of his good luck."[30]

Because of his position as an insider at the Executive Mansion, Stoddard's later writings and memoirs offer glimpses into the life of President Lincoln. Here was a president who allowed alcohol to be served at White House receptions, as was the custom, but he and Mrs. Lincoln never imbibed.[31] Here was a man, who in the dark days of the Battle of Chancellorsville in May 1863, "weary of delays and sore with defeats," spent a sleepless night pacing back and forth across the floor of the Executive Chamber with "sentry-like tread," in "a long wrestle with disaster."[32] Here was a man who sought relief from the burdens of his high office by taking in performances of Shakespeare's plays at Ford's Theater.[33] On two evenings, Kate Stoddard was invited by the Lincolns to join them at Ford's. During a scene from *The Merry Wives of Windsor*, Kate laughed with gusto. The president turned with a smile and rhetorically asked, "You enjoy it, don't you?" He certainly enjoyed those masterful insights into human nature that only the poetic Bard could offer, as he sat there relaxing in the very box where he was going to be martyred in a matter of months.[34]

14

The Sound of Breaking and Falling Chains

Within the Executive Mansion, William Stoddard not only observed history in the making but he participated in a singular way in the unfolding of history. A few days after the press was proclaiming a costly but effective Union military victory against General Robert E. Lee's army at Antietam Creek, Maryland (September 17, 1862), Stoddard found himself face to face with history, in direct service to President Lincoln. Seated at his desk one afternoon, Stoddard was engrossed in the letters of the day when John Hay came up to him with "a white sort of flush on his face." Placing a document upon the desk, Hay informed Stoddard that "the President wants you to make two copies of this right away. I must go back to him." As a nineteenth century Xerox machine, so to speak, Stoddard proceeded to comply with the presidential request. "Mechanically, in the ordinary course of business, as cool as a cucumber," he went about the task of manually duplicating the sentences upon the document. As he went from word to word, dotting his i's and making his distinctive umbrella-shaped T's, the significance of the document's content began to dawn upon him, and he later recalled "a queer kind of tremor shaking my nerves." For a moment, he stopped his copying. In his own words, this abolitionist said,

> Then I looked up from my work and listened, for far away, nearer, near, I could hear the sound of clanking iron, as of breaking and falling chains, and after that the shouts of a great multitude and the laughter and the songs of the newly free and the anger of fierce opposition, wrath, fury, dismay. For I was writing the first copies from Abraham Lincoln's own draft of the first Emancipation Proclamation.[1]

President Lincoln arrived at his position on the status of slavery in a slow and deliberate manner. It frustrated those who were impatient for quick action. When the popular General Frémont exceeded his authority in August of 1861 by issuing his own "emancipation proclamation" in Missouri without consulting the White House, Lincoln felt he had no choice but to ultimately revoke the proclamation and to relieve Frémont of his command. Northern abolitionists flooded the White House with letters of support for Frémont. The embarrassing situation simply focused national attention on the topic of abolition, for which there was no shortage of ideas offered on how best to go about it but with little thought about the possible consequences.[2] Some thought the president should promulgate a policy calling for the colonization of the slaves. Others thought a policy of gradual emancipation was best. Still others demanded immediate emancipation. Though he was a radical Congregationalist minister on the abolition issue, Illinois congressman Owen Lovejoy was politically savvy and understood Lincoln's need for a moderate approach. As Lovejoy told Carpenter, the president was "compelled to *feel* his way [Carpenter's emphasis]."[3] On June 12, 1862, Lovejoy delivered a speech in New York, in which he compared the president to a carriage driver: "If he does not drive as fast as I would, he is on the right road, and it is only a question of time."[4]

Initially, the president had contemplated adopting a program of gradual emancipation with compensation for the slaveholders. By July 13, 1862, the president decided to ease into the subject of emancipation with a couple of cabinet members. During a carriage ride with Secretary of State William Seward and Secretary of the Navy Gideon Welles the subject was broached. Welles recorded in his diary:

> It was on this occasion and on this ride that he first mentioned to Mr. Seward and myself the subject of emancipating the slaves by proclamation in case the Rebels did not cease to persist in their war on the Government and the Union, of which he saw no evidence. He dwelt earnestly on the gravity, importance, and delicacy of the movement, said he had given it much thought and had about come to the conclusion that it was a military necessity absolutely essential for the salvation of the Union, that we must free the slaves or be ourselves subdued.[5]

He had not acted sooner, though he had been pressured by Northern abolitionists to use the war with the Southern slave-owning states as an opportune moment to strike a blow against the South's peculiar institution. In the same summer, in a response to Horace Greeley, editor of the New York *Tribune*, Lincoln made his position quite clear:

> My paramount object in this struggle is to save the Union, and is not either to save or to destroy slavery. If I could save the Union without freeing any slave I would do it, and if I could save it by freeing all the slaves I would do it; and if I could save it by freeing some and leaving others alone I would also do that.[6]

14. The Sound of Breaking and Falling Chains

Lincoln considered these three options, and by midsummer of 1862 had determined to follow the third option, an emancipation policy that would apply only to states in rebellion against the United States. The policy would not apply to the so-called border states, those slave states, like Missouri and the state of his birth, Kentucky, which had not seceded from the Union but surely would if their slaves were set free.

On July 22, 1862, Lincoln called a cabinet meeting. Gathered around the table of council in his Executive Chamber, the cabinet members were informed by the president that he "had resolved upon this step, and had not called them together to ask their advice, but to lay the subject-matter of a proclamation before them; suggestions as to which would be in order after they had heard it read."[7] He then read it. The cabinet listened and responded. Secretary of the Treasury Salmon P. Chase, expressed his pleasure that there was to be no more inaction on the subject. He, also, wished that reference to the arming of the slaves contained stronger language. Postmaster General Montgomery Blair expressed fear that the policy "would cost the Administration the fall elections."[8] Secretary of State William H. Seward expressed his approval of the document but advised that the issuing of the document be postponed "until you can give it to the country supported by military success." Otherwise, he feared it might be viewed as "the last measure of an exhausted government" or "our last shriek on the retreat."[9] It was true that in spite of more than 660,000 soldiers in the field and a navy of 246 ships, 22,000 sailors, and 1,892 guns, no decisive harm had been done to the rebel states.[10] Lincoln accepted Seward's advice and agreed to set the proclamation aside and to wait patiently for a Union victory. He was aware that, in politics, timing is everything.

Away from the unhealthy heat and humidity of the capital, the Lincolns stayed at a large cottage near the Soldiers' Home, a presidential summer retreat some three miles north of the city. Here Lincoln followed the news of the war, commuted to work at the Executive Mansion by horse, and finished writing the second draft of the preliminary proclamation.[11] When the news of Antietam arrived, Lincoln decided the time had come to make the groundbreaking proclamation public.[12]

On September 20, 1862, the President gathered the cabinet again. Frequently he was known to begin cabinet meetings by reading from the humorous writings of Artemus Ward, the pen-name of Charles Farrar Browne, or from the writings of Petroleum V. Nasby, the pen-name of David Ross Locke, a political commentator, who, at the age of ten, had apprenticed for the *Democrat* of Cortland County.[13] On this day, Lincoln's choice was the folksy spelling and vernacular of Artemus Ward:

> In the Faul of 1856, I showed my show in Utky [Utica], a trooly grate sitty in the State of New York. 1 Day as I was givin a descripshun of my Beests and Snaiks

in my usual flowery stile what was my skorn & Disgust to see a big burly feller walk up to the cage containin my wax figgers of the Lord's Last Supper, and cease Judas Iscarrot by the feete and drag him out on the grond. He then commenced fur to pound him as hard as he cood.[14]

But in light of the 23,000 casualties sustained in fourteen hours of desperate combat at Antietam, the moment seemed too painful for levity in the judgment of the others assembled.[15] Perhaps they failed to grasp that a keen sense of humor was what kept Lincoln sane in the face of dire stress.

As the nervous smiles subsided, Lincoln, then, proceeded to read the proclamation. It decreed that, as of January 1, 1863, all persons held as slaves within any state that "shall then be in rebellion against the United States, shall be then, thenceforward, and forever free." The document went on to add that the military and navy would "*recognize* the freedom of such persons." At this juncture, Secretary of State Seward pressed for the insertion of the words "and *maintain*" after the word "*recognize.*" (All emphases are Perkins.') Lincoln indicated his doubt that the government could make good on such a promise, but Seward insisted, and Lincoln acquiesced to this one alteration to the document.[16]

As reported by Secretary of the Navy Welles, in the course of the discussion over the document, the president "remarked that he had made a vow, a covenant, that if God gave up the victory in the approaching battle, he would consider it an indication of Divine will, and that it was his duty to move forward in the cause of emancipation."[17] (For Welles' version of the Cabinet meeting see Appendix C.) Secretary of the Treasury Chase later confirmed hearing the president make the same statement at the meeting: "Mr. Lincoln replied: 'I made a solemn vow before God, that if General Lee was driven back from Pennsylvania, I would crown the result by the declaration of freedom to the slaves.'"[18] Apparently, Lincoln had entered into prayerful bargaining with the Almighty as all beleaguered believers have been known to do from time to time. The sign at Antietam Creek was enough for the president to hand the document to the secretary of state for publication the next day.

The Emancipation Proclamation (see Appendix D) is not Lincoln's best piece of writing. It is not comparable to his Gettysburg Address or his Second Inaugural Address. Not at all. Those documents contain memorable, almost poetic, prose. The Emancipation Proclamation is dry and boring to read; it is legalese. It is Lincoln as lawyer, not Lincoln as orator. Lincoln scholar Douglas L. Wilson has described it as containing "inexquisite language exquisitely suited to the occasion."[19] It is a carefully crafted legal document issued by him as commander in chief, since authorizing it as president could be construed as an impeachable violation of his promise "to preserve, protect, and defend" the Constitution of the United States—the supreme law of the land that protected a citizen's right to own property. Furthermore, as a military order, it avoided the need to go through Congress to be enacted. Skillfully, the document applied only to slaves in states still in rebellion as of January 1, 1863 (see Appendix E). Effectively, this gave the rebel states one hundred days' notice to return to the Union or risk forfeiting their slaves. Though white Southerners would refuse to recognize Lincoln's authority over them, what mattered would be the response of black Southerners. Once Union armies arrived upon Southern plantations with fixed bayonets, the document could be militarily enforced, the slaves would abandon their masters, and the economic basis of the South's resistance to federal authority would be broken. The Emancipation Proclamation would begin the process of opening the gates and ultimately freeing slaves everywhere in the United States. Furthermore, such a document would make it difficult for Great Britain to support the Confederacy, for Great Britain had already legally freed its slaves and would appear to be hypocritical if it insisted upon aiding a rebel government that would not abandon the practice of slavery. In short, the document reveals Lincoln's genius. It is not an act devoid of controversy, but it is a defining moment in American history. Next to the preservation of the Union, the abolition of slavery became the secondary reason for the North to fight the South. Among abolitionist clergy it was believed that God, in his infinite wisdom, had placed the right man at the right place at the right time. Others adamantly disagreed.

No other event during the Civil War generated as much mail for William Stoddard to handle. As he described it,

> There is no telling how many editors and how many other penmen within these past few days have undertaken to assure [the president] that this is a war for the Union only, and that they never gave him any authority to run it as an Abolition war. They never, never told him that he might set the Negroes free, and now that he has done so, or futilely pretended to do so, he is a more unconstitutional tyrant and a more odious dictator than ever he was before.[20]

One who would not have agreed with this description of President Lincoln was the stout black woman who for years had been living with and cooking for Jedediah Barber's extended family in Homer. The elderly Hannah, who had been employed by Jedediah since 1830, would repeatedly proclaim in 1867 from her four-poster deathbed set up in one of the Barbers' front parlors, "I have lived to see my people free."[21]

15

"Do You Think You Can Make a Handsome Picture of *Me*?"

Back in New York City, Frank Carpenter saw the proclamation as "an act unparalleled for moral grandeur in the history of mankind."[1] At first his artistic muse inspired him to symbolically envision Secession as a "beast," "offspring of the 'dragon' Slavery," being fatally pierced. He even saw the war as taking on apocalyptic proportions, equal to the battle between the Archangel Michael and Satan. In his opinion, "Surely Art should unite with Eloquence and Poetry to celebrate such a theme."[2]

On a Sabbath near the end of 1863, on his way home from church, the artist first pondered doing a portrait commemorating Lincoln and his cabinet at the moment when the proclamation was first read that would "give freedom to a race."[3] Carpenter began to imagine what the event looked like that would forever be associated with Lincoln as a moral act.

> I conceived of that band of men, upon whom the eyes of the world centered as never before upon ministers of state gathered in council, depressed, perhaps disheartened at the vain efforts of many months to restore the supremacy of the government. I saw, in thought, the head of the nation, bowed down with his weight of care and responsibility, solemnly announcing, as he unfolded the prepared draft of the Proclamation, that the time for the inauguration of this policy had arrived; I endeavored to imagine the conflicting emotions of satisfaction, doubt, and distrust with which such an announcement would be received by men of the varied characteristics of the assembled councilors.[4]

A design of Lincoln as lawgiver was slowly maturing and he determined to have his own name forever attached to this historic occasion.[5] All of his pre-

15. "Do You Think You Can Make a Handsome Picture of Me?"

vious portraiture work, especially of three sitting presidents, had primed him for this next step in his career.

Late one December night, Carpenter took an unframed photograph from some clutter in his room and on the blank side hastily did a preliminary sketch of the composition he had in mind.[6] Fixating on this tentative design, Carpenter made up his mind "to paint this picture now while all the actors in the scene are living and while they are still in the discharge of the duties of their several high offices." Furthermore, it was his desire that the painting should become "the standard authority for the portrait of each and all especially Mr. Lincoln." To accomplish this, Carpenter approached Samuel Sinclair, publisher of the New York *Tribune*, about the possibility of interesting two men in lobbying the president: Speaker of the House Schuyler Colfax, whose portrait by Carpenter had been exhibited that year at the National Academy of Design,[7] and Illinois congressman Owen Lovejoy. The next week, Sinclair and Colfax went to Lincoln and gained his consent. Through this "shrewd little piece of wire-pulling," Carpenter had Lincoln's permission, but the next matter was funding.[8] Such an ambitious artistic undertaking, involving not just one portrait but eight, would be time-consuming and financially more costly than he alone could afford. How was he to come by the money?[9]

As Carpenter described it, a "providential" meeting took place next.[10] On December 21, 1863, he crossed paths with Frederick A. Lane, a prosperous lawyer he had been acquainted with five years earlier when he had his studio in Brooklyn. He invited Lane up to see his studio on Broadway and told him of his proposed project. Convinced of Lincoln's promised cooperation, Lane responded, "Then you shall paint the picture. Take plenty of time. Make it the great work of your life; and draw upon me for whatever funds you will require to the end."[11]

On January 15, 1864, Congressman Lovejoy finally responded that he, too, had seen the president about Carpenter's proposal. His letter explained that Carpenter would "have to find bed and board at some other place," because "Mrs. Lincoln is expecting her son [Robert] home soon [from Harvard] with some friends, and that they will not be able to spare the room immediately opposite the President's study." Lovejoy assured Carpenter that the president "feels quite favorably disposed to the enterprise": "I think the coast is all clear to you any time you choose to come on now. You can make yourself immortal as soon as you choose."[12]

Assured of financial backing and Lincoln's cooperation, Carpenter, at the age of thirty-four, left for Washington on February 4, 1864. The next day, he visited the terminally-ill Congressman Lovejoy, who sat up in bed to pen a note of introduction to give to Lincoln,[13] and three days later he met with his own congressman, Thomas Treadwell Davis of Syracuse.[14]

Congressman Lovejoy was a well thought out choice for the source of an introductory note. He was a staunch abolitionist, and his brother was the late abolitionist editor and Presbyterian preacher Elijah Parish Lovejoy. Elijah's murder at the hands of a pro-slavery mob in Alton, Illinois, on the night of November 7, 1837, was the death of a martyr. Father Keep of Oberlin called it such in a sermon he delivered two months later in Lockport, New York. In no uncertain terms he proclaimed Elijah's death to be the justification for the nation's citizenry to come to the defense of the abolitionist cause. To do otherwise, he said, was an abandonment of "the principles in our bill of rights" and "the abandonment of these is a sure sacrifice of our Republic."[15] It was fitting that the murdered Lovejoy's brother should endorse Carpenter's proposal. Did not the Emancipation Proclamation represent the affirmation of the cause for which Lovejoy's brother was martyred? Would not a painting of the Great Emancipator by Carpenter bring legitimacy to the struggles of all the abolitionists of the past? And, furthermore, what if by some rare chance President Lincoln recalled the name of Carpenter out of all the correspondence he received in 1861 championing the errant General Frémont's edict of emancipation? The name of Lovejoy might be enough to remove any bad taste associated with the artist's name and to permit this once-in-a-lifetime opportunity he was seeking. An introduction to the president by a respected confidante to Lincoln[16] was crucial.

Owen Lovejoy died the next month of Bright's (kidney) disease, but his assistance to Carpenter earned the Lovejoy family, three years later, a portrait painted in verso on glass of the congressman by Carpenter. From Homer, New York, Carpenter sent Lovejoy's widow a letter informing her that the portrait had been shipped "as a small token of my appreciation of the great worth of your lamented husband and of his invaluable service to me in opening the way for the painting of my Emancipation picture." Some months after receiving the painting, Lovejoy's son, also named Owen, wrote a letter of thanks to Carpenter, which stated in part:

> Nothing could be more lifelife than the hair, forehead, eyes and in fact all the features.
> We did not think you would be so successful....
> We know the hand which painted the greatest Historical Subject of the century, and [father's] friend Mr. Lincoln's Portrait, did [father's] also.
> For the slight favor he did you, you have repaid his memory and family tenfold.
> And we shall ever bear you in grateful remembrance.[17]

According to William Stoddard, it was he who, at the White House, introduced Carpenter to President Lincoln.[18] If that were the case, why did Carpenter complain of "waiting in vain for two days" at the Executive Mansion in an attempt to gain physical access to the president?[19] Surely, Stoddard could have expedited matters.

Instead, Carpenter recalled that, on a Saturday afternoon, he went to a public reception at the Executive Mansion and waited in line for a chance to make his initial contact with Lincoln. Upon stepping into the Blue Room, Carpenter got his first glimpse of the gaunt, haggard-looking figure dressed in black, shaking hands and greeting people. For Carpenter, this was the figure who had earned the praise and blessings of a million freed men and women. Later, he wrote, "Never shall I forget the electric thrill which went through my whole being at this instant."[20] Carpenter found himself shaking "that honored hand" as his "name and profession were announced to [Lincoln] in a low tone by one of the assistant private secretaries, who stood by his side."[21] Though Carpenter never identified this "assistant private secretary" by name, it might very well have been William Stoddard, since making introductions at presidential receptions was one of Stoddard's responsibilities. So, in this sense, Stoddard may truthfully lay claim to having introduced Carpenter to Lincoln.[22]

Still grasping Carpenter's hand in his white-gloved hand, Lincoln seemed a bit puzzled at first as he sized up the slender man of medium height, with a graying moustache, "delicate features, abundant straight black hair, and dark gray eyes" and then said, "Oh yes; I know; this is the painter." Then, Lincoln asked, loudly and playfully, with a twinkle in his eye, "Do you think, Mr. Carpenter, that you can make a handsome picture of *me*?" He emphasized the last word. With others looking on, Carpenter felt put on the spot, but he managed to ask for a private interview after the reception. Lincoln acceded with the words "I reckon."[23]

As Carpenter discovered, Lincoln was well known for self-deprecating humor when it came to his personal appearance. Later, Carpenter would relate the following story, purported to be an actual incident, that Lincoln took great glee in telling his friends:

> In the days when I used to be "on the circuit," I was once accosted in the cars by a stranger, who said, "Excuse me, sir, but I have an article in my possession which belongs to you." "How is that?" I asked, considerably astonished. The stranger took a jack-knife from his pocket. "This knife," said he, "was placed in my hands some years ago, with the injunction that I was to keep it until I found a man *uglier* than myself. I have carried it from that time to this. Allow me *now* to say, sir, that I think *you* are fairly entitled to the property."[24]

At the agreed upon time, Carpenter met with Lincoln in the Executive Chamber. Seated in a chair next to Lincoln, he presented Owen Lovejoy's note of introduction. After reading it, Lincoln removed his reading glasses and, using a metaphorical expression taken from the oxen and pastures of

Homer and Springfield, he announced, "Well, Mr. Carpenter, we will turn you in loose here, and try to give you a good chance to work out your idea."[25]

Then, Lincoln launched into a detailed description of the history of "the adoption of the emancipation policy." He said, "It had got to be midsummer, 1862. Things had gone on from bad to worse, until I felt that we had reached the end of our rope on the plan of operations we had been pursuing; that we had about played our last card, and must change our tactics, or lose the game!" He recalled reading it to the cabinet for the first time in late summer of 1862, the wisdom of Seward's suggestion of a delayed public announcement, and the final meeting with the cabinet on September 20, 1862, when Seward edited the version Lincoln offered then. Carpenter took in all the details. As he formulated it in his artist's mind, the painting should depict the moment, just after Lincoln read the document, when Secretary Seward counseled delay in its announcement. This would also make Seward, his fellow Central New Yorker, part of the focal point of the painting, with the other cabinet members taking up places on either side of the president.[26]

Lincoln concluded his account for Carpenter by describing how he and the cabinet members were positioned at that first meeting in 1862: "As nearly as I remember, I sat near the head of the table; the Secretary of the Treasury and the Secretary of War were here, at my right hand; the others were grouped at the left." At this, Carpenter showed the pencil sketch he had already made. By reversing the picture and, thereby, placing Lincoln at the other end of the table, the sketch was pretty consistent with Lincoln's account.[27] Initially, Carpenter was given the library over the Blue Room in which to work, but shortly the state dining room became his studio for the next six months.

16

"Turned in Loose" for Six Months at the White House

In the truest sense of the words, Carpenter, for half a year, was "turned in loose" at the Executive Mansion. While he did not reside there,[1] he was permitted, like William Stoddard and the other personal secretaries employed there, to freely come and go no matter the hour. With sketch pad in hand, he even sat in the Executive Chamber while confidential business was transacted. At one such meeting, an individual showed discomfort at Carpenter's presence, and Lincoln responded, "Oh, you needn't mind him — he is but a painter."[2]

From February to July of 1864, at a time when fellow Homerite William Stoddard was on the staff at the Executive Mansion, Frank Carpenter worked diligently on his most ambitious artistic project. He was the closest thing America had to a court artist. Sometimes, he painted through the night by the light of the room's great gas-lit chandelier.[3] He arranged for individual sittings by the president and the cabinet members, when their schedules permitted, so as to make sketches of the faces he planned to incorporate into the aggregated composition. To get them to relax for these sittings, he engaged them in easy conversation, and they would share stories, opinions, and reminiscences. Once, when he had the luxury of a full two hours of Lincoln's time, the president read Shakespeare aloud and "repeated two exquisite poems"—"Oh! Why Should the Spirit of Mortal Be Proud" and "The Last Leaf on the Tree."[4]

Carpenter, however, found it necessary to make use of the technology of the era that was beginning to compete with painted portraiture. Photography was a useful way to capture the likenesses of individuals who were simply too busy with the affairs of state to sit for him. Carpenter also recognized the influential power of both the photographic and painted image. He was convinced, for example, that a photograph of Lincoln taken at the New York City studio of Mathew Brady on February 27, 1860 — the day Lincoln delivered his Cooper Institute speech — and widely circulated, as was the speech, during the presidential campaign "was the means of his election."[5] Lincoln, too, as a self-made man, most certainly was aware of the image-shaping power of the pen, the photograph, and the paint brush.

On February 9, 1864, Carpenter walked over a mile with Lincoln to Mathew Brady's Photographic Parlor on the corner of Pennsylvania Avenue and Seventh Street. There Carpenter had a photographic portrait of the president done by Anthony Berger.[6] Unbeknownst to any of them, the profile photo taken of the president would be the image used on the Lincoln penny, and another portrait would grace the five dollar bill.[7] On April 26, at the Brady studio, Carpenter had himself photographed in the pose he intended to use for Secretary Seward in the painting.[8] On another occasion at the Brady studio in Washington, Lincoln posed seated in a chair with his son Tad at his side looking at a book in his father's lap. Taken by Berger and destined to be another classic image of Lincoln, the photograph was composed by Frank Carpenter.[9]

Like Stoddard, Carpenter found being an insider at the Executive Mansion allowed him to exercise some degree of influence upon the chief magistrate. Case in point is the pull Carpenter had in helping his close friend and fellow artist William Sidney Mount. Mount's twenty-five-year-old nephew, William Shephard Mount, had gone in 1860 to live in Warren County, Mississippi. When the war broke out, he managed to stay out of the fray until he was "forced into the rebel army" in April 1862. Presented with an opportunity to leave the army in October of 1863, he crossed into the Federal lines near Vicksburg with the intent of giving himself up. There he was taken prisoner and sent off to the U.S. Military Prison at Alton, Illinois. By March of 1864, with all efforts to gain his son's release amounting to nothing, Shepard Alonzo Mount, a portrait painter himself, wrote to Carpenter to beseech his aid in the matter. With the letter and one from William Cullen Bryant, editor of the *New York Evening Post,* Carpenter presented the case to President Lincoln and spoke of the loyalty of the incarcerated soldier. He met with success, and a letter of unbridled gratitude was sent to him on March 28, 1864, from Shepard Alonzo Mount:

> My soul is lifted to Heaven in gratitude for the joyful tidings your letter brings me of my son's release from prison by the hand of Abraham Lincoln. God bless him, and those dearest to his heart, forever. He has raised me from the grave of

16. "Turned in Loose" for Six Months at the White House

Carpenter sat for this photograph by Anthony Berger in the very position he wished to portray Secretary of State Seward. The books on the floor and the chair to the right were used as models for the painting (courtesy Indiana State Museum, from the Lincoln Financial Foundation Collection)

despondency to a place among the living.... I had faith in his goodness and it has pleased God to show me it was well grounded.

My Dear Friend, I know it has given you great pleasure — as you assure me — to accomplish so much for me and mine. I said in my letter to my son yesterday, "All will be well when I shall hear from Mr. Carpenter." ... Oh! *liberty liberty*. I should like to look upon his face, when he shall be told it is his.... May he ever remember the noble hearts that plead for him, and the benevolent voice that ordered the prison doors to be opened.

Again and again, I have read your highly valued letter, which I shall preserve to the end of my life.... When you come to the final sitting [for your painting] — those last touches upon the head of President Lincoln, may some good Angel direct your hand, and touch your heart with unwonted fire of Genius.[10]

This was fine wirepulling by one who was "but a painter" in his first two months at the Executive Mansion.

Visitors at the mansion frequently dropped by the state dining room to see Carpenter at work. They wished to see how the great painting they had heard about was progressing. Some learned by word of mouth of the ambitious project Carpenter was undertaking; others read about it in *Frank Leslie's Illustrated Newspaper*.[11] Sometimes President Lincoln brought in the curious, and they engaged the painter in conversation.[12] Like Stoddard, Carpenter was in a unique position at the Executive Mansion to not only interact with President Lincoln but to observe him in interaction with governors, senators, diplomats, and ordinary citizens. Carpenter is reputed to have "introduced Lincoln to the suffragette Elizabeth Cady Stanton and her brother-in-law Samuel Wilkeson, Washington correspondent for the *New York Tribune*."[13] Like Stoddard, Carpenter made the acquaintance of some of the notable and not-so-notable personages of nineteenth century America and later wove their accounts of Lincoln into his own memoirs—recollections that are still used as valuable primary source material by historians.

Some visitors noted that Carpenter's painted version of the historic scene was "barren" and devoid of antique columns and tasseled draperies usually found in painted depictions of momentous events.[14] Edward Dalton Marchant of Philadelphia had already done a painted portrait of Lincoln with the Emancipation Proclamation in hand with symbolic broken chains at the feet of a statue of Lady Liberty.[15] Carpenter, however, was determined to avoid using any of these popular allegorical devices. He said he wished to "endeavor, as faithfully as possible, to represent the scene as it actually transpired; room, furniture, accessories, all were to be painted from the actualities."[16] He was so intent on accuracy that he took measurements. He went so far as to ask Lincoln the size of the sheet of paper used to write the proclamation, and Lincoln gave him a half sheet of foolscap. Later, in 1872, Carpenter signed and presented it to Theodore Munger's sister-in-law who resided in Homer.[17] In Carpenter's opinion, the scene he was painting was "second only in historical importance and interest to that of the Declaration of Independence" and, as such, should be rendered realistically. It is not realism by today's understanding, not with the figures of the Lincoln administration staring off into space and barely interacting, much like statues. Carpenter explained his understanding of realism this way: "I felt in this case, that I had no more right to depart from the facts, than the historian in his record."[18] His intent was to make the portraiture all important, to minimize background distractions, and to render *truth*fully the moment when the "salvation of the Republic" and "the freedom of a Race" hung in the balance.[19]

Truth is the operative word. Carpenter confronted both slavery and portraiture with a focus on truth. Here was a man imbued with a radical nineteenth century moral compass. He had been steeped in the influence of a theology merged with social activism. In Homer and then in Oberlin, Father Keep was part of a growing chorus in America advocating religion merged with reform — a liberation theology. Keep would stand in the pulpit with the Scriptures in one hand and a copy of William Lloyd Garrison's paper, *The Liberator*, in the other and preach truth:

> Truth is fallen in the street and equity cannot enter — the Lord saw it and it displeased Him. The superior is always reached by the blow that falls on the dependent. Touch a child and you reach the parent. Bind a citizen and you speak into the ear of the government under which he lives. Take from a single human being, whom God had made in his own image, any right which God has given him, and you make a direct encroachment upon the prerogative of God, and, by His own direction you are recorded in His Book as a robber.[20]

The message was clear. Those who bought and sold the image of the Blessed Savior were in sin, and the day was approaching when that sin needed to be expunged. Some firebrands were all too aware that such a moral imperative, taken to a level of polarizing fanaticism, would produce the likes of a John Brown rampaging through Bleeding Kansas in 1856 and raiding the arsenal at Harpers Ferry, Virginia, in 1859. It was hard to stem the tide once the days of compromising were past.

In terms of cause and effect, the human struggle for rights was traceable to the English Magna Carta of 1215 and to the Protestant Reformation initiated by Martin Luther in 1517. The concept of rights of Englishmen was transplanted from Europe to the New World by those seeking religious freedom. Flowing from the early New England Puritanism of Jonathan Edwards through the abolitionist Calvinism of Edwards' son, Jonathan, Jr., to humanitarian Congregationalists from Massachusetts and later the Yale theologian Theodore T. Munger, there was in the first half of the 1800s a rising call for moral truth. And this resonated with Carpenter.[21] "Execution of John Brown!" was the artist's sole diary entry for Friday, December 2, 1859.[22] Later, it was said that Carpenter possessed an "inability to distinguish between art and morals" and that his "subjects had to come up to his own high moral standards ... [or] he would not paint their portraits."[23]

Painting in the Executive Mansion in 1864, Carpenter saw no need to glorify the republican "moment of moral grandeur" that had sounded the death-knell of slavery. Rather, he would depict the momentous occasion, like all his portraiture, in an honest, straightforward manner. He would faithfully paint *truth*.

17

"It Is as Good as It Can Be Made"

With palette, paint, and brushes, Frank Carpenter labored on. May 4, 1864, was the day Gus, Bertie, and his mother-in-law came to see his handiwork for the first time, and two days later a Mr. and Mrs. Cook of Homer came to see him at work. On May 28, four men from Homer came to see how he was progressing. The four included the man who had once been unreservedly discomfited by Frank's career aspirations—the artist's father, the now proud sixty-four-year-old Asaph Carpenter.[1] He gloried in his son. The man from Homer, who had supported John Keep's vocal moral stance against slavery, had a son painting the scene of moral victory.

In early June, Horace Greeley called upon Carpenter at the Executive Mansion, and Carpenter later recalled their conversation:

> Very near-sighted, his comments upon my work, then about half completed, were not particularly gratifying. He thought the steel likenesses in his book, "The American Conflict," were much better. I called his attention, among other points, to a newspaper introduced in the foreground of the picture, "symbolizing," I said, "the agency of the 'Press' in bringing about *Emancipation* [Carpenter's emphasis];"—stating, at the same time, that this accessory was studied from a copy of the "Tribune." Upon this his face relaxed;—"I would not object," said he, "to your putting in my letter to the President on that subject."[2]

Not wishing to alienate the other newspapers, Carpenter did not paint in the *Tribune*'s head but only its form, hoping that Greeley, whom he admired, would appreciate the compliment being extended. Before the editor departed, Carpenter arranged for him to meet with the president, though Lincoln was none too pleased at the time about editor Greeley's lack of support for his renomination.[3]

By July 22, 1864, Carpenter thought the painting was complete enough to receive criticism from the painting's subjects. On this date, exactly two years after the first reading of the proclamation before the cabinet, President Lincoln and the cabinet assembled in the state dining room to view Carpenter's work.[4] They saw themselves arranged on canvas as a veritable object lesson of the political spectrum, according to their espoused views on emancipation. Liberals were painted to the left of Lincoln and conservatives to the right. Secretary of War Edwin M. Stanton, whom Carpenter had usually found to be "taciturn" at his sittings,[5] sat grimly on the far left, sporting his eyeglasses and distinctive two-tone beard. Next, Salmon P. Chase, secretary of the treasury, was depicted with arms folded, standing behind a seated Lincoln. This was an appropriate stance, considering Chase's tendency to self-aggrandizing machinations behind Lincoln's back.[6] Seated to the right of Stanton, with his left leg crossed over his right, was the president. In his lap, he held a copy of the proclamation he had just finished reading. His face, with the iconic wart, wore "a characteristic expression of patience, melancholy, kindness and perhaps a faint touch of humor."[7] Depicted looking intently at Seward, Lincoln shared the focal point of the painting with the secretary of state. Seward, at the forefront, seated in front of the table, with legs crossed, was painted in profile. Calmly facing Lincoln, Seward rested his right hand upon the table and his forefinger was raised to emphasize the need for delay in issuing the proclamation until there was a military success. On the table, between Lincoln and Seward, was a parchment copy of the United States Constitution. Painted immediately to the right of Lincoln was Secretary of the Navy Gideon Welles, looking ever so much like Father Christmas with his full white beard, though the newspapers referred to him as "Father Neptune." Standing to the right was Caleb B. Smith, secretary of the interior. His portrait was, arguably, the weakest. Carpenter had little to work from because Smith had died in January of 1864, before Carpenter had come to Washington to do the painting.[8] The last figure standing to the right was that of Postmaster General Montgomery Blair, who was known for his hot-tempered stance against radical Republicans.[9] Finally, on the far right, seated at the opposite end of the table from Lincoln, Carpenter had depicted the attorney general, Missouri's Edward Bates, the first cabinet member to come from west of the Mississippi River. Bates, who believed that freed blacks should be deported to Africa, frequently clashed with Lincoln about slavery.[10]

A letter written by a jealous Chase was critical of the place of prominence given to Seward in Carpenter's painting.[11] Seward, himself, had not waited for the completion of the painting to register his criticism. He did not object to the place of prominence given him by a fellow New Yorker. Rather, during one of his sittings, he challenged Carpenter's decision to do a painting that focused upon slavery's demise as the central act of Lincoln's administration. Seward maintained that the preservation of the Union was a vastly greater accomplishment. "If I am to be remembered by posterity," he explained, "let it not be as having loved predominantly white men or black men, but as one who loved his country."[12]

Carpenter respectfully disagreed. He claimed that the Declaration of Independence was "the *assertion* that all men were created free" and that "Mr. Lincoln's Emancipation Proclamation was the *demonstration* of this great truth ... the sign and seal of the consummation."[13] Later, Carpenter cited Lincoln's own words: "In our case, the moment came when I felt that slavery must die that the nation might live!"[14] Then, in February of 1865, after the passage of the Thirteenth Amendment, which ended slavery, Carpenter visited President Lincoln and expressed his pride in having been the first to paint a picture commemorating the act of emancipation. He told Lincoln he thought the act was "the most sublime moral event in our history." To this, Lincoln responded, "Yes, as affairs have turned, *it is the central act of my administration, and the great event of the nineteenth century* [Carpenter's emphasis]."[15]

After the cabinet members viewed Carpenter's work, a free public exhibition of the painting was permitted for two days in the East Room. Several thousand came to see it.[16] Viewers were first drawn to Seward's figure in the forefront of the painting and their eyes followed his pointing finger to the figure of the president. From Lincoln, the viewer next notices the figure of Chase, then Stanton, back around Seward's body to the unoccupied chair, then to Blair and Smith, and finally to the illuminated face of Welles—essentially a counterclockwise movement of the eye in an elliptical pattern around the canvas.[17]

One cannot help but notice an empty chair in the forefront. Why is there an empty chair? What is its meaning? The answer remains sealed in mystery. One theory is that the chair was Carpenter's way of acknowledging Anna Ella Carroll of Maryland as "the great unrecognized member of the Cabinet." President Lincoln did accept counsel from Carroll on constitutional matters and secretly sent her, accompanied by an army officer, to report on the war on the western front and to devise military strategies which contributed to the demise of the Confederacy. Because of this, it has been conjectured that the chair is hers—a chair for an influential presidential advisor who was a female, no less, in the male dominated world of national government. This theory is given credence by the folder of maps and notes near the chair similar to those carried by Carroll.[18] What undermines this explanation is the doubt that Carpenter, whose painting extols the Emancipation Proclamation, would have symbolically recognized a woman who owned slaves—and admittedly did free them—but did not support wholesale emancipation and spoke out against the Emancipation Proclamation. Another possibility is the theory of the artist's conceit. With a red sash placed across the chair by Carpenter in a later, retouched version, the eye is drawn to what might be considered the painter's chair. For six months, Francis B. Carpenter had a front row seat to history; he had access to the Executive Chamber and to the Lincoln administration — to the set and the actors involved in the moment of "sublime moral grandeur." By capturing the set and the actors on canvas as Trumbull did in the *Declaration of Independence*, Carpenter may have thus represented his place in history through this device, although he was not actually present at the event. Or, is it possible that Carpenter, by painting the empty chair, is making a statement to the viewer of his painting? Is he saying to viewers of the work — then, today, and forevermore — here, pull up a chair, be present at the corner of this table, and fully appreciate the significance of this historic event. Take it in with your eyes and enter into dialogue with the participants and with me, the artist. Do you not agree that a few mere mortals, in a radical moment of "sublime moral grandeur," moved "We, the People" closer to "a more perfect Union"?

Among the throng in the East Room studying Carpenter's work was the journalist Noah Brooks. He studied the painting and entered into a public dialogue. He reported seeing a "rawness, lack of finish, and commonplaceness, such as might be expected in the work of a young artist who has grappled with a subject so difficult." Expecting a colorful allegorical rendition, perhaps, of such a momentous event, Brooks registered his disappointment in finding not American deities but merely a stiffly posed "group of men, wearing the somber-hued garments of American gentlemen."[19]

Mrs. Lincoln, on the other hand, registered her approval of what she saw. Knowing all too well how contentious and competitive the members of her husband's cabinet could be, with tongue-in-cheek and to Lincoln's delight, she nicknamed the painting "The Happy Family."[20] Perhaps the most glowing commentary was offered by the *New York Times*: "It is, by all odds, next to Trumbull's Picture of the 'Declaration of Independence' ... the best work of this class that has been painted in America."[21]

On the last afternoon, before the painting was to be removed, Lincoln stopped by with Carpenter for one last look. Of all the critics of this piece, the one whose opinion mattered most to Carpenter was the president. Just as Lincoln had carefully crafted the written proclamation in exact legal terms to make sure Chief Justice Roger B. Taney of the slave state of Maryland would not have recourse to reverse the order, Carpenter was equally anxious to have gotten the painting of the proclamation visually exact for posterity. What would the president think of his work?

Lincoln took a seat and "gazed silently at it." After awhile, Carpenter asked the president if he had any final criticism or suggestions to offer. "There

Francis Bicknell Carpenter with autograph on reverse (courtesy Harvard University Fine Arts Library; photograph by Alexander Gardner, Washington, D.C. [1864]).

is little to find fault with," Lincoln replied. "The portraiture is the main thing, and that seems to me absolutely perfect." Carpenter drew Lincoln's attention to the maps, the books, the portrait done by Thomas Sully of President Andrew Jackson who had opposed states' rights and the concept of nullification in 1828 through 1832, and various other accessories in the painting. He elicited comment from the president. Lincoln requested a change in coloring of the book shown leaning against a chair leg. The book, William Whiting's *War Powers of the President* (1862), was a book Lincoln had utilized in preparing the Emancipation Proclamation, but the coloration made it appear to be a law book. Carpenter agreed to fix it. When asked if there were any other changes he would like to see made, Lincoln said there were none, and he repeated the same thing he had said upon perusing Carpenter's first sketch: "It is as good as it can be made."[22]

Carpenter's portrait of Lincoln was not the last painting of the president to be done from life. Fifty-year-old Matthew Henry Wilson did an oil on board life portrait for his friend Gideon Welles in February of 1865, but Lincoln did not critique the finished product as favorably as he did Carpenter's. Carpenter relished the opportunity to later record Lincoln's response to Welles' observation that Wilson had rendered "a successful likeness": "'Yes,' returned the President, hesitantly; and then came a story of a western friend whose wife pronounced her husband's portrait, painted secretly for a birthday present, 'horridly like;' 'and that,' said he, 'seems to me a just criticism of *this!*'"[23]

Pleased with Lincoln's compliment of his own work, Carpenter then took the opportunity to thank the president for the kindness he had received for six months. As he did so, Lincoln's gaze continued to be fixed upon the painting. Perhaps, the man who did not want to pass through this life unremembered[24] was grasping that, in the event depicted in oil on canvas, he had attained his ambition. As Carpenter concluded his expression of gratitude, Lincoln turned and said, "Carpenter, I believe I am about as glad over the success of this work as you are." With these words and a final handshake, president and painter parted company.[25]

A few days before Lincoln's second inauguration, the painting was placed on temporary exhibition in the Rotunda of the Capitol. This was where Carpenter had hoped it would be permanently placed, along with paintings already there of a similarly immense scale.[26] As the painting was being raised to a spot over a door leading to the Senate Chamber, a group watched. When it reached its destination, a sunbeam broke through from the recently completed great dome and illuminated Lincoln's head, while the rest of the painting was in darkness. A policeman, noticing the singular effect, exclaimed to the group, "Look! That is as it should be. God bless him; may the sun shine upon his head forever."[27] No one in the group or the policeman or the artist of the painting knew that the illuminated head in the painting was going to be that of an early martyr in what would be called the civil rights movement.

From Washington, the painting went on a successful public tour across the North, including stops in New York, Boston, Chicago, and Milwaukee.[28] The exhibitions netted Carpenter a weekly royalty of fifty dollars. An attempt at safely transporting the painting was accomplished "by means of joints in the frame at top and bottom, which allow[ed] the picture to fold over upon itself from each end...." Creasing of the canvas was prevented by the use of a softly covered roller placed within the canvas at each folding place. Reduced to a manageable size and secured by screws, the painting was ready for transport.[29] Nevertheless, upon arrival at New York, some minor damages were discovered, and Carpenter, the perfectionist, worked on it for thirty-six straight hours to get it ready for the opening of the exhibition.[30] By the end of 1864 he would be able to look back with satisfaction and state "It has been the most memorable year in my professional life!"[31]

18

Last Days in the Service of Lincoln

William Stoddard, at the executive mail table, dealt with the expected controversy unleashed by President Lincoln's signing of the Emancipation Proclamation on New Year's Day 1863 (see Appendix D). Then, he observed President Lincoln's anguish over the debacle at Chancellorsville in May. News of Lee's rout at Gettysburg, Pennsylvania, and of Grant's successful siege of Vicksburg on the Mississippi in early July was welcome relief.[1] The good news arrived during a Fourth of July celebration in Washington that Stoddard had been appointed to organize. He arranged for the Marine Band to perform as regiment upon regiment in Union blue and Zouave red marched smartly down Pennsylvania Avenue. Stoddard, easily putting humility aside, claimed it to be "the grandest Fourth o' July procession that had been seen in Washington since the city was founded."[2] Best of all for the secretary, he had correctly anticipated the military turning-point and "went wildly short of gold in New York" just before the price of gold tumbled.[3]

On the heels of this excitement, Stoddard became ill with Potomac River malaria. He applied for some time away from his job at the Executive Mansion and decided to head for some rest at the seashore. He traveled with his brother, Harry, who was going to Syracuse. When their train arrived in New York City, the Stoddard brothers found the streets filled with anarchy and confusion. Rioters were outraged over the military draft being instituted that meant they had to fight now to free blacks, not just to save the Union. Impoverished working-class New Yorkers and Irish Catholic immigrants were angered by the conscription law permitting the affluent to avoid the draft by paying three hundred dollars and securing a substitute. Resentment brought terror to the sweltering summer streets of Manhattan. The criminal element of the city took advantage of the situation, and looting, murder, and mayhem occurred for several days in mid–July. Although ill, Stoddard volunteered to help the military defend the Sub-Treasury and the Customhouse from any mob attacks.[4]

On July 13, 1863, Frank Carpenter and a younger brother also found themselves caught up in the thick of the rioting. Frank was anxiously headed for his residence in a horse-pulled freight wagon with his twenty-seven-year-old brother, William Wallace Carpenter. A private in the 157th Regiment, William, known as Will, had been caught in a crossfire of rebel bullets and struck on the first day of intense fighting at Gettysburg, July 1. He was in serious need of surgery. He was suffering from a broken leg sustained from a bullet taken just above his left knee. While another brother, Daniel Webster Carpenter, was among the few in the 76th Regiment who survived the first day of the three day battle at Gettysburg, Will ended up in a deplorable condition. Daily rains pelted the ground that served as the poorly sheltered army field hospital. Will received no medical attention for ten days due to the sheer overwhelming numbers of wounded requiring attention. Extremely distraught over the prospects of needing an amputation of his leg and witnessing "things that would make you crawl all over," Will wrote letters to Frank in New York and to family in Homer imploring them to hurry to his aid.[5]

On Sunday, July 12, Frank Carpenter arrived at Gettysburg accompanied by his childhood chum, Dr. Fessenden N. Otis. The overpowering stench of death greeted them, and Frank noted that "the town and country was one continued battleground."[6] When they came upon Will, they found his leg had been set by a doctor. He was being cared for by an amiable, wounded member of his company, twenty-two-year-old Wesley Huffman of Preble, a community north of Homer, New York. Daniel Carpenter had tried to find his wounded brother but had not been able to, and each was worried sick about the well being of the other.[7]

The next day, with great difficulty, Frank arranged for Will to be transported by train to Philadelphia and then by express to New York. An intimidating crowd briefly blocked their progress through the streets of Manhattan. The rioters were not reacting kindly to anyone in "good clothes" or Union blue.[8] Troops surviving Gettysburg were dispatched to New York to help quell the violence, which was directed, for the most part, at blacks and the hated Republican elite of the city and their supporters. Even a hospital on Forty-First Street, where 250 wounded Union soldiers were being treated, was threatened by a mob seeking to burn it to the ground.[9]

With the help of his life-long friend, Dr. Stephen Smith, Frank was able to get Will admitted to Central Park Hospital, where surgery was done immediately to remove bone fragments from the injured leg. For two days Will rallied. Then, on Friday, July 17, Frank was summoned by Dr. Smith to the hospital. Gangrene from the wound left unattended for too long at Gettysburg had spread through Will's body. Will was dying. Overwhelmed, Frank and Gus raced by carriage to the hospital through dangerous streets. Frank recorded in his diary: "[Will] lived about an hour and a half afterward, realized his situation and gave minute details about his affairs. Our hearts are almost broken."[10]

Taking Will's remains by an overnight train, Frank and Gus reached Homer at 8:30 on the morning of July 18. The next day, Sunday, a funeral took place at 12:30 P.M. at the Carpenter homestead followed by a 2 P.M. service at the Congregational Church.[11] This was one of the first funerals to be conducted at the newly built church on the Green. The church had just been dedicated ten days before, just five days after the end of the decisive battle at Gettysburg. Father Keep accepted the invitation to return to Homer for the dedication but, apparently still fearful of the old firebrand they dismissed in 1833, the dedication committee chose not to allow him to give the sermon. Instead, he was kept safely "confined to the prayer of dedication."[12]

On Thursday, July 23, 1863, needing a burial plot for Will, the Carpenters selected a "beautifully located" family lot in Homer's new cemetery. This cemetery, known as Glenwood, was another beautification project headed up by the civic-minded Paris Barber. Barber had designed the cemetery on the hillside of his farm located west of the village.[13] Private William Carpenter was buried there on the afternoon of Sunday, July 26. It was the same day as the funerals of Captain George A. Adams and Private Morris I. Shattuck of William's regiment. Frank recorded in his diary that the day was "a solemn time for Homer."[14] Twenty-six days later, on the anniversary of Will's enlistment, another Carpenter brother, Clement DeWitt — known as Witt — was drafted.[15]

Four years later, in the summer of 1868, when the darker days had passed, Frank painted a 16-by-13-inch oval portrait on canvas of his brother, Will, from a photograph and memory.[16] There is an aura of softness to this portrait, which makes Will's countenance appear to be truly coming forth from the haze of memory. The portrait, one of two done of him by his brother, is now owned by the Homer Congregational Church, where, at the time of his death, William Wallace Carpenter was the Sunday school superintendent. His last written words were directed to the children: "Tell the children of the Sabbath School to meet me in heaven."[17]

When the violence in the streets of New York subsided, an exhausted William Stoddard headed for Syracuse with his brother. Twenty-four years later, back in New York, Stoddard wrote *The Volcano under the City*, an account of the frenzied "upsurging of the criminal classes of the great city" and the near fatal beating sustained by Superintendent of Police Kennedy during the infamous Draft Riots.[18] Using New York City Police Department records, Stoddard helped to document the complex political, class, ethnic, and religious conflicts that contributed to the wanton mob brutality that he and Carpenter witnessed and managed to escape. Neither knew, at the time, that the other was caught up in the riots.

On the way from New York to Syracuse, a weary Stoddard stopped at Homer "and spent days in looking around upon the old, familiar places." He visited the Osborn homestead, looking in upon the room where he had been born almost twenty-eight years earlier. He returned to the millponds where he had learned to fish and to swim. It was refreshing to the body and the spirit to return to the river, the woods, the pastures, and the orchards of Homer again, and to gaze upon the verdant, gently rolling hills. Perhaps he was prompted to recall Psalm 121: "I will lift up mine eyes unto the hills, from whence cometh my help. My help cometh from the LORD, which made heaven and earth." Upon walking to the Homer Common, Stoddard found it changed. It was no longer the barely grassy space for pasturing sheep and oxen, as in his childhood. Now an attractive, tree-studded park was in front of the academy and the churches.[19]

Portrait of William Wallace Carpenter, painted by Frances Carpenter about 1875 (courtesy Homer Congregational Church, Homer, New York).

Homer's own Paris Barber, at the start of the war, had been a prime mover behind this change. Though some farmers had grumbled about replanting trees where once woods, at great effort, had been cleared for grazing, Paris persevered. An impending war mattered not; he was determined to see an attractive park spread before the churches and the academy. On February 15, 1861, when a beleaguered Lincoln was making his inaugural train trip to Washington, Paris, it is believed, was the one who crafted a poem, "The Homer Festival," to inspire supporters of the landscaping project. Its final verse revealed the author to be a man of vision.

Homer's park, churches and academy, *New Historical Atlas of Cortland County, New York, Illustrated* (Philadelphia: Everts, Ensign & Everts, 1876).

> In future years when we are gone,
>   Fair children in our groves
> Shall sport upon their greenest lawn
>   Or tell their gentle loves.
> I see in after time these bowers.
>   Sweet voices from their glades
> Do bless the names who sowed the flowers,
>   And set these classic shades.[20]

Stoddard found that the population of the village had grown. More houses had been built along streets west of Main Street, and those under construction had decorative gingerbread along the rooflines and expansive porches in front. The businesses of Main Street were now mostly concentrated northeast of the Green, and another unmistakable sign of progress was the illumination of the streets and dwellings with gas. It was becoming a beautiful little village with streets lined with trees and gaslights, just as Paris Barber imagined it. Just the summer before, the Syracuse *Journal* had provided an enthusiastic description of Homer during the academy's traditional and much expanded annual exhibition:

> The central week of all the year in this fair village of Homer is now drawing to its close. It has been a week of the highest literary and social enjoyment to the many friends of Cortland Academy, whose history has been closely linked for

more than half a century with the growth and prosperity of our churches, our families and our daily avocations. We have had whatever is needed for the refined festivities of the week. We have had cloudless skies and moonlight nights; gardens gay with flowers; streets alive with holiday faces; college boys come back to renew school-day friendships; serenades, vocal and instrumental; hospitality, hearty, refined and enjoyable; essays in racy prose and liquid verse; orators from the school, the college and the church; pleasant talks over mammoth strawberries, and no end of fun for the young, and comfort for "children of larger growth."[21]

How peaceful is the scene presented. Who would have thought that furious battles were being fought at the time and that young men were dying? Who would believe that coffins would soon be transported to grief-stricken families?

Stoddard walked up Cayuga Street to see another of Barber's projects, Glenwood Cemetery.[22] Part of the new rural cemetery movement, Glenwood was more than a graveyard; it was a landscaped, aesthetically pleasing space in which the living could meditate. It was where one could be refreshed in a natural, park-like environment with a gurgling brook making its way down the center of the area. Barber's design called for a flower-lined pool and an ornamental gateway at the entrance. The remains in the cemetery behind the Congregational Church were to be disinterred and respectfully moved to the new site on West Hill.[23] Glenwood would be a suitable place, too, for the community to memorialize their war dead. A section would be set aside for the fallen of the Grand Army of the Republic.

Renewed in spirit by his Homer visit, Stoddard took the train to Syracuse. While only in Syracuse for a couple of days, he found it necessary to bail his father out of one of his all-too-frequent financial difficulties. After paying his father's "considerable" debt, Stoddard headed to New London, Connecticut. He visited his paternal grandparents and enjoyed the restorative powers of the salty air. He enjoyed fishing in the cove, with noisy seagulls darting overhead, as much as he enjoyed the stories he heard at the family farmhouse about the days before the Revolutionary War.[24]

After two months of vacation, a reinvigorated Stoddard returned to his post in Washington, only to be informed that Nicolay and Hay were going to take some vacation time. The assistant secretary found himself having to stand in for Nicolay as "big Private Secretary." He admitted, from the experience, that for this job Nicolay, indeed, "was much better qualified."[25]

Large numbers of blacks streamed into Washington after the Emancipation Proclamation had been signed. Apparently they thought they were safer the nearer they were to the government and "Massa Lincum." A refugee camp, of sorts, was set up a little over a mile north of the city limits to provide shelter and army rations. The numbers swelled by Thanksgiving Day in

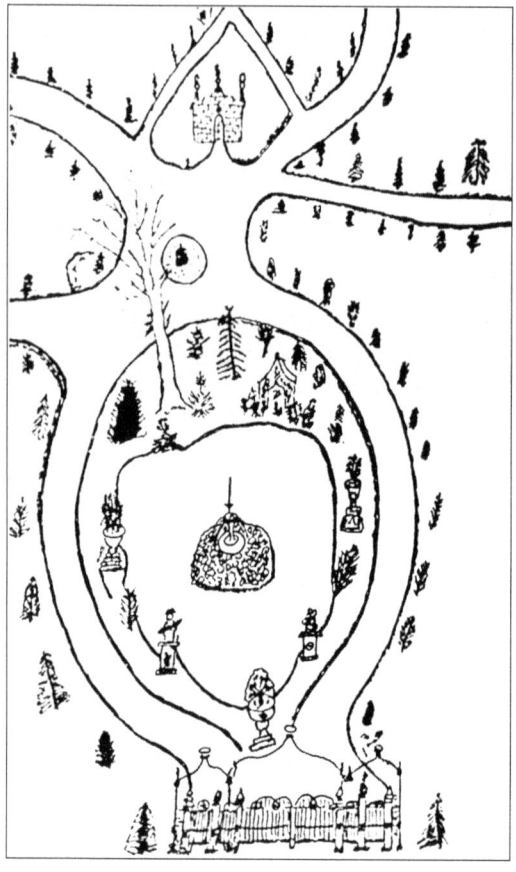

Paris Barber's sketch for Homer's Glenwood Cemetery in biography of Paris by Herbert Barber Howe, 1968 (courtesy Cortland County Historical Society).

response to the news that some charitable abolitionists were planning to host a Thanksgiving dinner. Stoddard was given one day's notice that he was to give the main speech for the occasion. With a "wonderful sea of black faces" before him, Stoddard stirringly addressed not his audience's past, but their future. He asked them if, having received freedom, they could now see their way to fight for it. "Other men are shedding blood for you; are you ready to give life and blood of your own? Will you fight, if called upon?" The question was met with "a great tumult" of voices demanding guns and bayonets. "We'll show you, Massa! We's ready!"[26]

For Stoddard, the autumn and winter of 1863 brought receptions, dinners, parties, army news, and daily meetings—which involved, according to him, "a kaleidoscope full of statesmen, generals, rascals, battles, dissipations, hard works." Then he came down with typhoid fever. After several weeks, he mustered enough strength to return to his desk. He returned to learn that General Ulysses S. Grant, after his successes in the West, was now in charge of the Army of the Potomac. Lincoln spent most of the war urging Union generals to action. He was once so frustrated he caustically asked, "If General McClellan does not want to use the army, I would like to borrow it for a time."[27] A much relieved commander in chief told Stoddard,

> Grant is the first General I've had! He's a General! You know how it's been with all the rest.... They all wanted me to be the General. Now, it isn't so with Grant. He hasn't told me what his plans are. I don't know and I don't want to know. I'm glad to find a man who can go ahead without me."[28]

18. Last Days in the Service of Lincoln

After experiencing a relapse of typhoid fever, Stoddard gained Lincoln's consent to spend the summer of 1864 as his emissary, inspecting federal armies in the South and out West as far as St. Louis, Memphis, and Little Rock.[29] When he returned to submit his report to the president, Stoddard asked to be appointed marshal of the Eastern District of Arkansas. For this post he was commissioned on September 24, 1864, his twenty-ninth birthday, but his name was not formally sent to the Senate for confirmation until January 27, 1865.[30]

Over his sister Kate's objections that his health was not up to the resentments and difficulties awaiting him in this former rebel state, Stoddard prepared to leave Washington that fall.[31] Harry, who had just been jilted by his fiancée in Syracuse, was to join him in Arkansas.[32] John Hay told Stoddard that news of his impending departure had caused Nicolay to exclaim with dismay: "John! What'll we do with the Madame after Stod goes? Heaven! You and I can't manage her."[33]

Unknown to Stoddard, the conversation with the president on his day of departure would be the last time he would ever hear words spoken by Abraham Lincoln. Lincoln wished him good health and success in his new career. He told Stoddard that the war would be over soon and asked him to do all in his power "to get the ballot into the hands of the freedmen" in Arkansas. "We must make voters of them before we take away the troops. The ballot will be their only protection after the bayonet is gone, and they will be sure to need all they can get. I can see just how it will be." Stoddard assured Lincoln he would care for the future of the blacks of Arkansas, and, once again, he headed out West.[34]

19

Assassination and the Iconic Image of Lincoln

On April 18, 1865, William and Harry were in the Statehouse in Little Rock. They had heard frightful news from Washington that an attempt had been made upon the life of Secretary of State Seward, but the next news, brought by an agitated army captain, struck like a bolt of lightning: "Marshal Stoddard, President Lincoln is assassinated!" The president had been shot on April 14 and had succumbed the next morning at 7:22 A.M. William was shocked. He stumbled out the door. He was further shocked to find men crying openly in the formerly rebel street — men who grasped "that in the murder of Abraham Lincoln the really best friend and protector of the future interests of the defeated South had been taken away." William Stoddard had personally lost a friend and a statesman he was proud to have served.[1] Writing four days later to John Hay, Stoddard reflected upon their mutual loss: "Men who had never seen him wept when the news came. How shall we say our sorrow, — who knew him as he really was?"[2]

Frank Carpenter was in New York when news came to him of Lincoln's assassination. In his diary he wrote, "God have mercy upon the nation." Two days later he wrote, "Got out the original study of Mr. Lincoln and had a good cry over it."[3] The funeral train bearing the coffin of the assassinated president back to Springfield stopped in New York, and Carpenter went to City Hall to pass by the open casket and pay his respects. Near the casket, Carpenter's original study of Lincoln was displayed. The next day, he witnessed "the great funeral procession in honor of the universally lamented President," and wrote in his diary: "New York never saw such a day."[4] Sixteen horses pulled a wagon bearing the presidential casket up Broadway to 14th Street. At Union Square, it went west to Fifth Avenue and then north on the great boulevard to 34th Street, and from there to the Hudson River Railway Depot, at the corner of 30th Street & 10th Avenue. Thousands of mourners lined the streets and all along the tracks to Springfield.

The next month, Carpenter wrote to Mrs. Owen Lovejoy: "The death of our beloved President overwhelmed me, as it did all those who were permitted to come so near him, with sorrow, such as was never before experienced upon the death of anyone not of the family circle. It seemed too awful to be true!"[5]

Carpenter's *Emancipation Proclamation* painting was on exhibit in Pittsburgh when word arrived of the conspiracy against the government, including the failed attempt on Seward's life and the murder of Lincoln just a few days after General Lee had surrendered. The public's interest in seeing the painting intensified. At one point, the doors to the exhibit had to be closed, because the crowd pressing forward was becoming unmanageable.[6]

In Washington, D.C., Secretary of State Seward was confined to his bed, suffering from the multiple knife wounds murderously inflicted upon him by Lewis Thornton Powell. News of Lincoln's death was withheld from the secretary. In his critical state, his doctor felt telling him about the assassination would cause a shock too great for him to bear. Nevertheless, Seward arrived at the tragic truth. On the day after Lincoln died at the Peterson boarding house across the street from Ford's Theater, Seward asked that his bed be moved around so he might have a view out his bedroom window. As he surveyed the spring foliage emerging upon the tops of the trees in the park across the street, he noticed the American flag on the roof of the War Department building. It was at half-mast. He studied it briefly and then blurted out to an attendant: "The President is dead!" No amount of denial could convince him otherwise. "If he had been alive," the secretary reasoned, "he would have been the first to call on me; but he has not been here, nor has he sent to know how I am; and there is the flag at half-mast." The man who had entered into Lincoln's administration in 1861 as the president's political rival had, in time, come to see Lincoln as a dear friend and respected statesman. He felt the loss deeply. Later, Carpenter would write that Seward's "inductive reason had discerned the truth, and in silence the great tears coursed down his gashed cheeks, as it sank into his heart."[7]

In Homer, New York, Paris Barber was just leaving the office of the Homer *Republican* newspaper in Mechanics Hall when a boy came rushing in, shouting, "Lincoln's dead, telegraph says so." Paris was shaken to his very core. How could this be? Lincoln, with a stroke of his pen, had resolved the moral issue of slavery. To this act Paris had given his full endorsement, and now its author had been martyred, one of the last casualties of the cruel war that had just ended. Paris was not alone in asking: How could God permit this? With his faith rattled and tears streaming down his face, Paris drove home to share the nightmarish news with his family. Neighbors soon came by. For the better part of an hour they sat with the Barbers in their living room, grieving in silence.[8] Indeed, the entire nation was thrown into an unprecedented period of mourning. By his assassination Lincoln was immediately elevated from the position of a mere mortal to that of a secular saint, and interest in having a print of the martyred president increased immediately.[9]

Before Lincoln's assassination, Carpenter had hoped the United States government would show a willingness to purchase the *Emancipation Proclamation* painting, but that willingness had not materialized. Fortuitously, Carpenter had been shrewd enough to make plans for another way to make money from the painting. Soon after completing the painting, he arranged with New York publisher Derby & Miller to produce a print of the painting for public sale.[10] Alexander Hay Ritchie, a well-known engraver in New York, was contracted to reproduce the painting as a steel engraving for $6,000.[11]

Carpenter started working on a smaller version of the painting — twenty-one by thirty-three inches — for Ritchie's use. He brought the painting with him during a vacation visit to Homer. On Saturday, August 19, 1865, needing "material assistance," he "went to the village and got a group of men together like [in his] Emancipation picture" and had the photographer Luther Barker make him an ambrotype. Homer's very tall butcher, Burdett Newton, was asked to sit at a table as Lincoln. Lewis Henry posed for Stanton; "old Mr. Gardner" for Welles; Ki Munger for Seward; Mr. Hicok for Blair; Mr. Wardell for Smith; and Judge Reed for Bates. A visitor from New York named Mr. Gillett was commandeered to stand in as Chase.[12]

From this small painting, Ritchie produced a high quality print. Though a fire on Broadway in New York consumed Carpenter's small painting, the steel plate was spared,[13] and Noah Brooks predicted that the engraving would be "prized in every liberty-loving household as a work of art ... a perpetual remembrance of the noblest event in American history."[14] Carpenter gave copies to each cabinet member depicted in the painting. An autographed copy was given to his parents as a Christmas present.[15]

By modern standards, Carpenter was good at marketing the print and contributing to the iconic image the world has of Lincoln as the Great Emancipator.[16] He sent a two-page letter to John Nicolay on September 12, 1864, asking Nicolay to obtain a letter from Lincoln expressing the favorable opinion he had already shared with Carpenter in person about the painting. Carpenter stated that, ostensibly, this would be a prized document he could show to friends and an heirloom for his children. Yet, on the second page of the letter, Carpenter went on to state that he had enclosed a note for the president, asking him to head up a list of subscribers for the forthcoming print by Ritchie of the scene which was the first "in the art history of our country ... to represent a historical scene *literally* from the life!" Boldly, Carpenter indicated that he would like a reply from the president "stating that 'he has much pleasure in replying to my request' (or something to this effect)," which "can properly be followed by any comments upon the painting, he may choose to make." Carpenter pressed further, telling Nicolay that he would like the president to subscribe for two or three copies of the print, which would be signed artist's proofs — one for himself, one for Robert, and one for Tad, "who may each have a house of his own, one of these days? ... provided that he can *conscientiously* endorse my work." Mapping it all out for Nicolay, Carpenter concluded with this postscript: "You are at liberty to lay this note before the President. Of course, it is understood that the 'proofs' are to be *presented* to him. F.B.C." (Emphases are Carpenter's.)[17]

An accommodating Lincoln signed on as the first subscriber, thereby giving his public endorsement and playing along with Carpenter's masterful marketing ploy. Other prominent persons, including those depicted in the painting, added their autographs to the pre-publication sales book, thereby adding further enticement for customers to put down fifty dollars for a proof copy. Carpenter asked the members of the cabinet to offer comments about the painting. Bates wrote favorably of the portraitures but not of the event depicted: "The execution seems to me excellent — far better than the theme, the historic incident." He explained that those assembled had no opportunity for "deliberation upon the principles involved in the Freedom Proclamation" crafted by Lincoln "and therefore ... no claim to the dignity of a grand idea."[18]

Unfortunately, Lincoln did not live to see his copy. His assassination, however, contributed all the more to a public clamor for images of him, and after 1865, Carpenter had no dearth of competitors. The market for prints of Lincoln was flooded by images of the Great Emancipator rendered by other printmakers. Yet, the Ritchie print was an overwhelming success — again, in no small way, because of Carpenter's marketing strategies. The appearance of his published memoirs, *Six Months at the White House with Abraham Lincoln: The Story of a Picture*, in 1866, boosted print sales. Equally helpful was the placement of advertisements on page one of the *New York Times* and within his best-selling book. The clever use of glowing reviews by the very men depicted in the print proved to be tantalizing advertising.[19] Seward wrote, "I think all the likenesses in your elaborate picture are admirable, except one, concerning which I am incompetent to discern."[20] Stanton thanked Carpenter for his artist's proof and added: "The work is in every respect, that I am capable of judging, entirely satisfactory and worthy of national admiration — as a fitting commemoration of Mr. Lincoln's great deed."[21]

Around May 7, 1865, at the ripe, old age of eighty-four, Father Keep felt compelled to send Carpenter a piece of heartfelt praise from Oberlin. Addressed to "my dear boy," the letter contained these complimentary and prophetic words: "I have been much gratified by the sight and study of your splendid and very popular painting of President Lincoln and his Cabinet. Now it is sure that your name as an artist will hold a high position in all future history of your country."[22]

Besides artist's proofs for fifty dollars, india proofs were available for twenty-five dollars and plain prints for ten dollars. A thousand orders were placed within two months, representing $40,000. By the 1880s, Derby & Miller boasted to have made 30,000 prints from the original steel plate before it wore out. When Mrs. Lincoln, the president's widow, received a print, she acknowledged it on June 3, 1866, and included this endorsement: "I have always regarded the original painting, as very perfect, and the engraving, appears to me quite equal to it."[23]

20

Lobbying for Carpenter and the Painting

From 1865 to the early autumn of 1866, the original *Emancipation Proclamation* painting remained stored in Carpenter's studio at 653 Broadway in New York.[1] Then, he took it to Homer for an awe-inspiring exhibition at the recently rebuilt Barber Hall and later at the Cortland Agricultural Fair.[2] By then the painting was hardly the original. Carpenter had still been working on it. According to Homer lore, a tall Homer resident, C.O. Newton, of Newton Water Works fame, posed for Carpenter while changes were made on the canvas and, for this favor, Newton was gifted with an oil painting of Lincoln.[3]

In a technical sense, the painting Lincoln saw before his death was not the same painting the people of Homer saw after his death. Carpenter's constant, if not obsessive, revising did not improve his handiwork; it lessened it.[4] Fortunately, the Ritchie print, which is closer to Carpenter's original and best imagery, is the vehicle by which the image of the un-retouched painting entered countless American homes and businesses and enjoyed such mass appeal.

In a letter dated January 22, 1866, John Nicolay suggested to Carpenter that the painting with "the rare accuracy of the individual portraits" and "the historical fidelity of the scene" needed a permanent repository. He urged Carpenter to bring before Congress a proposal for purchasing the painting on behalf of the nation.[5] Carpenter expended great effort in this regard for the next seven years, but Congress showed no willingness to appropriate the huge amount the painter was asking for the picture—$25,000. The hard times of the Panic of 1873 did not help. At this point, Carpenter needed some assistance; he needed some respectable individual to lobby in Washington on his behalf.⁶ He turned to his old friend Will Stoddard to help him obtain the recognition and remuneration he felt he deserved.

With the end of the war, Stoddard had stayed on in Arkansas, toying with the notion of becoming one of the state's senators, but malaria and the "bloody flux" (dysentery) altered his political aspirations. Saddled with debt and poor health, he went back North. In Washington, he went to the Executive Mansion. In spite of a presidential assassination, he found the place still easily accessible. Amazingly, his old latchkey let him in for one final look.⁷

From there, it was on to New York to launch a new career, using his one marketable skill — writing.⁸ Never known to be at a loss for words, he wrote for newspapers and pulp fiction publishers and made a living. In 1870, he married Susan Eagleson Cooper, a schoolteacher who was ten years his junior. The effects of the severe economic depression of the 1870s forced him to take another government job — as chief clerk of the Bureau of Engineering in the Dock Department of the City of New York.⁹

In 1873 Carpenter asked Stoddard to meet him at a loft he had rented in the city. According to Stoddard, when he arrived at the loft, he found the great canvas and Carpenter at work upon it, making final touches. "Well, what do you think of the improvements?" asked Carpenter. Stoddard's worst fears had materialized: "Yes, the picture is all there, but where is Lincoln? You have gone to work and painted him out." From smoothing and regulating, it was no longer the image of the Lincoln they both had known. Stoddard insisted that Carpenter mount his stepladder at once and undo what he had done. He told him what was needed: "A darkness under the simpering eyes. A renewing of the wrinkle in the forehead. A reproduction of the furrow under the lower lip. A readjustment of the chin. Putting back the lost wart on the right cheek." Even Chase and Seward needed attention, and a softening of old, cantankerous Stanton was just unacceptable.¹⁰ While Carpenter sought *truth* in his painting, he sometimes did not know when to set the brush and palette down. Fortunately for posterity, Stoddard did know, and Carpenter heeded the advice.

With the retrieval of Lincoln's lost face, the canvas was ready for exhibition in Washington. Stoddard agreed to go along to testify before the Joint Committee of the Library on February 24, 1873. He presented, on behalf of "his warm personal friend of long standing," reasons why the painting "should become the property of the nation."¹¹ (See Appendix G.) It was to no avail. The Republican controlled House and Senate would not budge.¹² So, Stoddard decided to pay a visit to President Grant. At the Executive Mansion, he faced three disappointments. The locks had been changed; his latchkey was reduced to a souvenir. Much of the furniture from the Lincoln years, including his desk, Lincoln's desk, and the cabinet table, had been carted away for sale at some second-hand furniture shop. And President Grant agreed to go see the painting on the next day but was unable to keep the appointment.[13]

Four more years passed, but Carpenter did not relent. By 1877, with Stoddard's help, he had worked out an arrangement with the wealthy, widowed New York philanthropist Mrs. Elizabeth Thompson, in whose home on East 10th Street the Frank Carpenter family had once lived. Thompson said "she could not consent to *cheapen* [his emphasis] the Emancipation painting by taking it at a less sum than ... asked the Government." She agreed to buy the painting for $25,000, and would, in turn, donate the painting to Congress to hang in the Capitol, if the national legislature could be persuaded to accept the gift.[14]

Once again, Stoddard came to Carpenter's rescue. Over luncheon at Mouquin's on Sixth Avenue, Stoddard agreed to go to Washington to do some behind-the-scenes lobbying.[15] At that time, Rutherford B. Hayes occupied the White House, and the Senate was strongly Republican. However, in the House of Representatives, ex–Union general James A. Garfield was the leader of the Republican side of the aisle, while the Democratic side was managed by the ex–vice president of the Confederacy, Alexander Stephens of Georgia. How was a joint resolution to be secured between the politicians of the party of Lincoln and the politicians from the "dead Confederacy"? How could one hope to gain support for a painted memorial to the Great Emancipator from the likes of Stephens, the rebel leader and slave owner who had been confined to prison for two years after the war?[16]

Stoddard managed to pull it off. He skillfully convinced each side of the merits of a joint resolution. He got Stephens to commit to seconding the resolution if Garfield offered it, and Garfield to commit to offering it if Stephens agreed not to oppose it. Surprisingly, it was Stephens who was more supportive of the resolution. Stoddard found that Stephens "genuinely approved of that measure and believed the removal of slavery a good thing for the people whom he represented." Remarkably, Stephens even spoke favorably of the service rendered by President Lincoln and expressed a desire to see the "removal of all remaining sectional bitternesses and a restoration of a complete Union."[17]

General Garfield kept his word and offered the joint resolution and, to the amazement of many, it was met with a vigorous second by the former Confederate leader. The measure passed in the House by all but one vote. That vote was from a Texas representative.[18]

The Republican Senate was expected to pass it, but Senator Timothy Howe, a Democrat from Wisconsin, attempted to obstruct it in his role as chairman of the Senate Library Committee. Stoddard convinced him that it would not look so good for the *Emancipation Proclamation* to be honored by a Rebel House but not by a Republican Senate. How would the party of Lincoln be viewed? With this political hurdle removed, the measure passed the Senate with only one opposing vote. That was cast by Republican senator George Franklin Edmunds of Vermont. Stoddard sarcastically referred to Edmunds as "a tenderfoot art critic and ... a personal friend of Caleb B. Smith, whom Frank had murdered in the picture." Stoddard had lobbied masterfully, and now the way was clear for Congress to be presented his friend's painting in February 1878.[19]

21

A Dream Fulfilled and Dark Days

The official presentation of the *Emancipation Proclamation* painting took place on the sixty-ninth anniversary of Lincoln's birth. A joint session of Congress convened in the House for a public ceremony. This was "the first major Lincoln commemoration in which both Northerners and Southerners took part."[1] For Frank Carpenter, it was a dream fulfilled — the apex of his ambition. Stoddard said, "It was really something tremendous."[2] The public galleries were packed — but blacks were restricted to a separate gallery, a clear indication that Lincoln's ideal of equality of rights had yet to be attained. The painting, in a gilt frame with the seal of the United States and rising suns in each corner, hung magnificently behind the speaker's chair.[3]

By now, more tampering with the painting had occurred. The quill pen, which originally was near Seward's hand, was *in* Lincoln's right hand, and the document was *in* Lincoln's outstretched hand. Right up to the last moment changes were made. General Benjamin Butler told Carpenter that Confederate general David E. Twiggs' sword of surrender had been sent from New Orleans to Lincoln in 1862. So, Carpenter dashed over to the Treasury Department to see it and make a drawing. Then, on the eve of the unveiling, Carpenter worked to insert a faithful rendition of the symbol of Confederate submission in place of the sword of General Emerson Opdyke he had just painted in the week before.[4]

The next day, February 12, 1878, the dignitaries presented to Congress included Mrs. Thompson, Nicolay, Stoddard, and Carpenter. The New York *Times* reported that Carpenter looked "pale" and "nervous." Ironically, none of the men depicted in his painting were present. With the exception of Montgomery Blair, everyone was dead — and Gideon Welles had just died the day

Carpenter's final version now displayed in Senate stairwell of U.S. Capitol (U.S. Senate collection).

before. A recess was called to allow those present a closer look at the gift[5] and an opportunity to personally meet and thank the "handsome and dignified" Mrs. Thompson.[6] Once again, it fell to the former White House staff member to make the introductions— this time Stoddard was assisted by Congressman Banks. The Associated Press incorrectly reported Stoddard to be the former private secretary of President Lincoln, which may have been done intentionally by Lawrence Gobright, head of their Washington Bureau. Gobright's reporting during the war had not made him a favorite of Nicolay, and Gobright did not hold Nicolay in high regard.[7]

The "jewel of the whole affair," according to Stoddard, was the speeches made by Garfield and Stephens.[8] Diplomatically, both men took the occasion to say that Lincoln's primary goal in the war had been to preserve the Union, not to free the slaves— the position Seward had championed but not the view held by Carpenter. For Stoddard, the most remarkable sight of all was seeing the former vice president of the Confederacy eulogizing Lincoln. Publisher J.C. Derby concurred. He described the acceptance of "a painting commemorating the downfall of slavery" by the ex–Rebel to be a "sublime sight."[9] February 15 was for Frank Carpenter "another memorable day." The painting was installed in a staircase in the eastern wing of the House of Representatives, the place he said he had "desired for the last 14 years."[10]

Having accomplished their mission, Carpenter and Stoddard returned to New York. Stoddard expected to receive a bigger portion of Carpenter's $25,000 than he did, but, in appreciation for his help, Carpenter did a life-size portrait of Stoddard, a portrait of Stoddard's wife, Susie, and one of his daughter, Sadie.[11] In 1884, in a letter, Carpenter expressed gratitude to his friend Stoddard. He admitted that without him the opportunity presented in 1878 would have been missed and that he would still be the owner of the painting.[12]

Today, the painting, with wart and all, now hangs in the west stairway of the Senate chamber[13] — "the only nineteenth-century history painting of Abraham Lincoln in the United States Capitol."[14] Never one to miss a chance for taking credit, Stoddard commented, "There is the picture to this day, and I am glad that it fell to my hand to have so much to do with its placing on the wall of the Capitol."[15] Actually, three men from Homer made the national treasure possible. Eli DeVoe saved the one destined to be the Great Emancipator, and with William Stoddard's persuasion, Frank Carpenter's image of the Great Emancipator became a revered artifact of the nation's abolitionist movement.

Carpenter was also appreciative of another Homerite — the first one, after Fessenden Nott Otis, to take an active interest in and encourage his artistic talent — Paris Barber. In 1876 the nation was one hundred years old, and Paris was preparing for the Centennial Exposition at Philadelphia. He planned to construct "King Corn," a colossal human figure made entirely of corn stalks, corn silk, and corn husks and tassels. Its base was to be made of agricultural products of all the states. Carpenter had been consulted all along on the design, and when Paris' health did not permit him to travel to Ithaca to seek support for the project from Cornell University, Carpenter went in his place. The university offered approval but no financial support. It was a disappointment. But it did not matter, for the project died in May of 1876 with the death of Paris, just two weeks after his father, Jedediah, died on April 19.[16] Paris was delighted that a few years earlier his father had finally joined the rest of the Barber family as a member of the church on the Green.

Carpenter returned for the funeral at the Congregational Church where, earlier, Paris had accepted the post of deacon.[17] After Paris was laid to rest in Glenwood Cemetery, Carpenter walked slowly back down Cayuga Street accompanied by Joseph R. Dixon, editor of the *Cortland County Republican*. They reminisced about Paris's "beauty-loving soul" and his being "generous to a fault." When they reached the Homer Green, the artist pointed. "There are the trees planted by the Deacon and the Church made worshipful by his floral arrangements and over yonder he planned a community art gallery." Sadly, Dixon concluded, "We laughed at him because he seemed a stranger to our ways. We failed to appreciate the high plane on which he lived."[18] Carpenter, however, never failed to appreciate. Gratefully, he recalled the 1847 trip he and Paris took to New York and summed up his benefactor this way: "He had so much of the artistic instinct himself, that he could enter perfectly into the aim and ambition of my life."[19]

At the end of the 1860s, when alumni and friends of the academy gathered on the Green to celebrate the school's semi-centennial, the man selected to deliver the main oration was Andrew Dickson White. Among those in attendance was Carpenter.[20] As he sat in a pew in the Congregational Church listening to the speakers, it is likely that he reflected upon his own early education in Homer and the influences that later moved him to rise to the task of doing the *Proclamation* painting. Besides the impetus received from Paris Barber, there had been other influences. Father Keep had left his mark. After his departure from Homer, a few Congregationalists, like Simeon S. Bradford, defiantly picked up the anti-slavery banner and held anti-slavery meetings, such as the one once "held in the schoolhouse near Factory Hill on Monday evening at early candle-light."[21] Carpenter had heard the angry clamor generated by such meetings and heard his parents wonder aloud in dismay about the moral character of their church brethren. Could they not see the righteousness of abolitionism, as Father Keep had? Were they not as moved as Carpenter was in his boyhood by the stirring sentiments in the song *The Old Granite State*?

> We're the friends of emancipation,
> And we sing the proclamation,
> Till it echoes through the nation
> From the Old Granite State.[22]

And then there was his brother, Will, whose life had been sacrificed on the altar of freedom at Gettysburg. Not granting freedom to those in bondage would have meant Will's death had been in vain. Lincoln's struggle for emancipation had been felt personally by Carpenter, and the artist, as social critic, had felt an obligation to document in paint Lincoln's ideals "wrought out of the strife of a living humanity."[23] Given these intensely personal experiences, he felt compelled to "sing the proclamation" and to embrace the personal fame that came with it.

22

Carpenter's Last Three Decades

By the 1870s, Carpenter was receiving much public attention for his paintings. He never was one to object to fame, but public attention of another kind worked against him. In the 1870s, Carpenter was involved in the Beecher-Tilton Scandal because of his friendship with both the plaintiff and the defendant. Theodore Tilton was a well-known newspaper editor and the one to whom Carpenter had written thirteen days after Lincoln's assassination: "It has been the business of my life as you know to study the human face and I say now as I have said repeatedly to my friends, Mr. Lincoln had the saddest face I ever painted."[1] Henry Ward Beecher was the famous moral and spiritual preacher, and brother of Harriet Beecher Stowe, of Plymouth Church, Brooklyn.[2] Tilton and Beecher had been friends and working associates, but in July of 1874, Tilton charged Beecher with adultery with Mrs. Tilton. A trial ensued in January 1875, which was second only to John Brown's trial for the raid on Harpers Ferry in 1859 as *the* trial of the nineteenth century. Public attention was riveted upon the courtroom drama as it unfolded and was reported in the press.[3]

Because he knew both Tilton and Beecher, Carpenter was expected to testify. That never came to pass. Instead, a print made from a photograph of Carpenter's face was splashed across the front of the Friday, June 11, 1875, edition of *The Daily Graphic* of New York. The lurid headline read "Carpenter's Secret," and below that the reader's eye fell on "The Whole Story Out at Last," "Important Statement by Frank B. Carpenter," and "Beecher Contradicted on Material Points." The published interview was lengthy and Carpenter obliged the reporter by revealing conversations that had occurred in his studio.[4] If Carpenter's clientele dropped off after this published interview,

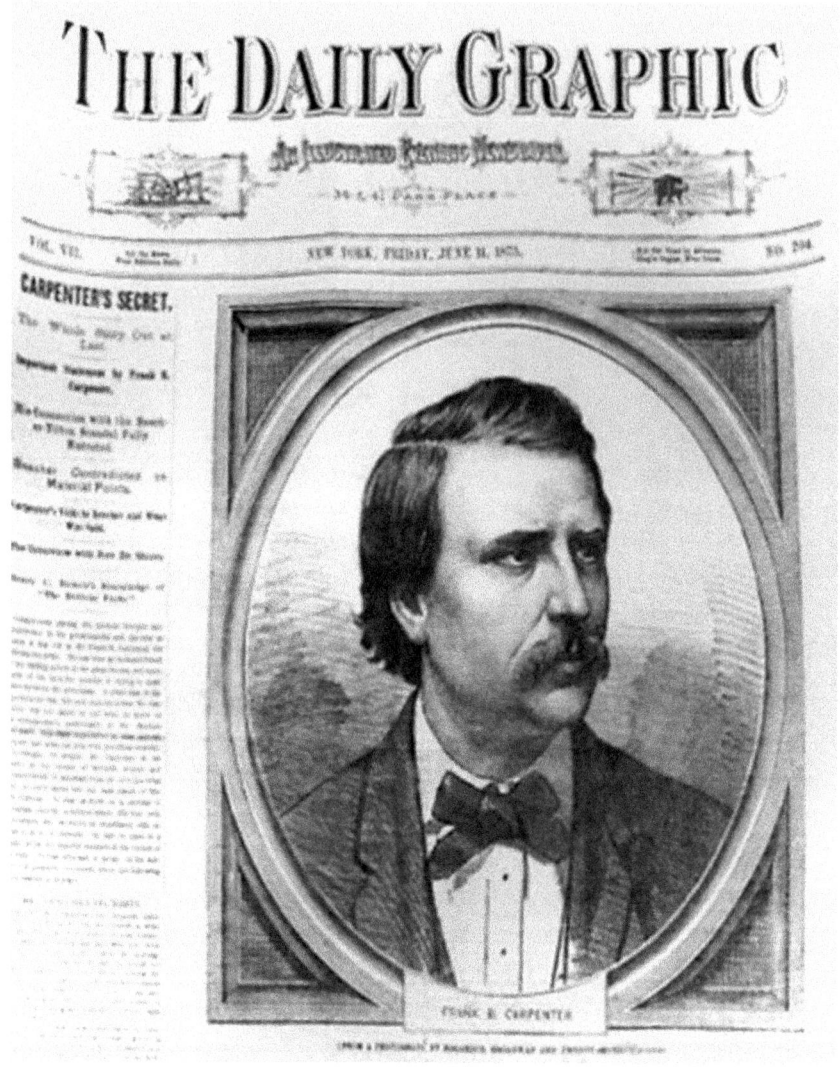

The Daily Graphic, dated Friday, June 11, 1875, with the lurid headline of "Carpenter's Secret" discovered in attic of Phillips Free Library in Homer, New York, and photographed by David Quinlan (courtesy Gail Servies and library trustees).

it was, in no small part, out of concern for a possible breach of confidence by this gregarious artist that might transpire after sitting for a portrait by him. Who would want to risk that? The trial ended with a hung jury; nine voted to acquit, three to condemn.[5] And another question was raised: If a man of the Reverend Beecher's high social prominence and accomplishment could not be trusted, who could be trusted? Carpenter was personally shaken by how both of his friends had come to ruination.

One client Carpenter may have lost because of fallout from the trial was Frederick Douglass, a friend of President Lincoln. According to the *Dryden Herald* of Dryden, New York, in the spring of 1876, Carpenter was engaged to paint the famous black abolitionist's portrait for Harvard University, but there is no record that it was ever completed. Carpenter had known Douglass for years. The abolitionist had come to Homer in 1851 to speak out against slavery, but "that meeting was quickly brought to an end by the throwing of rotten eggs" by those not in sympathy at that time with the position taken by the speaker.[6]

Famous individuals still sat for portraits by Carpenter, and newspapers continued to provide coverage. In August of 1879, the New York *Daily Tribune* reported on a Carpenter portrait presented to the Georgia Legislature. The paper described the subject as "sitting in a graceful and thoughtful attitude beside a table." It, also, in an odd way, reported that "the pose of the figure is ... unconscious." The "unconscious" figure was that of Crawford W. Long, the doctor who discovered surgical anesthesia.[7]

Carpenter found himself involved in another litigation in 1888. William Ivins of the International Chemical Company was charged with defrauding one Mrs. Stone of $2,000. Because Carpenter was the secretary of the company, he was called as a witness in the Stone-Ivins trial.[8] While on the stand he became rather defensive of his reputation when questioned by a juror. "But you are a painter," persisted the juror. Carpenter emphatically countered, "No sir, I am an artist."[9]

Another side to the multi-faceted Carpenter was his attraction to the occult. Though his diary reveals an active and sincere religious life, with constant attendance at prayer meetings and frequent critiques of Sunday sermons, there is evidence that, on occasion, he dabbled in Spiritualism. He went with one Mrs. Newton on December 22, 1870, to see a clairvoyant named Mrs. Manchester. He came away unsatisfied. Another meeting with a medium was mentioned in a letter of February 27, 1889, addressed to Steele MacKaye, the celebrated actor, dramatist, and founder of the first school of acting in the United States, the Lyceum Theatre School.[10] Perhaps Carpenter sought to make contact with his late brother, Will; his sister Helen, who died on his forty-first birthday; his mentor, Sanford Thayer, who died in 1880; or with his parents who died in 1882 and 1885.[11]

Spiritualism originated in the 1840s in upstate New York. Rampant with fraud, Spiritualism accelerated in interest after the Civil War. Understandably, Spiritualism's belief in the ability to contact the spirits of the deceased through a human medium was extremely appealing to the countless number of

Americans suffering with grief over the loss of loved ones in the long and brutal war. Legitimacy was lent to the Spiritualism movement by the fact that its ranks of adherents were filled with well-meaning citizens—even abolitionists, proponents of women's rights, and members of mainstream Protestant congregations. The middle and upper classes were mainly drawn to the movement, and it was especially attractive to women.[12] Mary Todd Lincoln was afflicted with unbearable grief over the loss of her son Willie. He died in the Executive Mansion of typhoid fever, and she invited mediums there for séances. Even her husband, the president, was known to attend, albeit reluctantly.[13] Thus, in the context of the times, to be fair, it was not something unusual for Carpenter to have been curious and to have investigated what a clairvoyant or medium had to offer. Even Stoddard, in his college days at Rochester, had gone with curious friends to see "the performances" of Spiritualists.[14]

After the Civil War, Carpenter's reputation as a painter endured mainly because of his portraits of Lincoln and their popularity as prints. Prints were a common way for artists to get their names and images into public circulation. Sometimes a piece of art was done with the intention of mass producing it as a print. *The Lincoln Family*, showing the presidential family as it was in 1861, before eleven-year-old Willie's death, was done in black and white by Carpenter to facilitate the work of Auburn, New York's native son, the engraver, John Chester Buttre of New York.[15] Since Carpenter never met Willie, he had to do the boy's likeness from a photograph of Willie and Tad provided by Mrs. Lincoln.[16] He completed this project while vacationing in Homer in 1865. The same day he posed for his own picture with Theodore Munger, Carpenter had a Homer lad, young Henry Wheadon, pose as Willie Lincoln. With the aid of this ambrotype, he finished the drawing in Homer on August 17, 1865.[17]

Carpenter did several portrait studies of Lincoln, but the best known is the one done for the *Emancipation Proclamation*—the one for which Lincoln was reported to have said, "I feel that there is more of me in this portrait than in any representation which has been made."[18] From this portrait, Frederick W. Halpin, the talented engraver, rendered a line-and-stipple adaptation.[19] This amazingly life-like print carried the signatures of both Halpin and Carpenter. From Paris, John Hay had written to Carpenter in early 1866 to inquire as to the progress of the engraving which he said would "give the world the final idea of what Lincoln was." Hay opined that portraits of Lincoln sold in the shops of Paris were "mere caricatures" whereas he anticipated Carpenter's study would be superior: "No man had your opportunities; it is only natural that none should have had your success."[20] On December 4, 1866, Gideon Welles wrote to congratulate Carpenter and Halpin on their successful engraving. "I am better pleased with it," he wrote, "and with the likenesses than with any engraved portrait I have seen of Mr. Lincoln."[21] Only the day before, Schuyler Colfax had written a letter to Carpenter on official stationery of the 39th Congress. He stated that he had just seen the Halpin engraving of Lincoln and offered his critique: "It is a very striking portrait of him but I am not surprised at its fidelity ... your daily study and the frequent sittings he gave you. Mr. L. always spoke of your portrait as the best ever taken of him."[22] It made a suitable item to give as a gift. Even the artist gave this print as a Christmas gift to seven friends in Homer in 1894.[23]

The only other attempt Carpenter made at painting a historic event on a grand scale was what he called his *Arbitration Picture*. He started it in 1871 and completed it in 1891. This is the painting showing the American and British signers of the May 8, 1871, Treaty of Washington gathered around a table in the manner of the men in the *Emancipation Proclamation* painting. A photograph was taken of Carpenter at work upon this huge painting commemorating the end of three months of negotiations over the *Alabama* claims.[24] To mark the successful completion of this project, a dinner in Carpenter's honor was held at Sherry's, an elite New York restaurant. The toastmaster for this special occasion was none other than Andrew D. White. Among the twenty-seven guests were New York senator Frank Hiscock of Tully, New York, Dr. Stephen Smith, Calvin C. Woolworth, and the Rev. Theodore T. Munger.[25] In 1892, the *Arbitration Picture* was presented by Mrs. William W. Carson of Newburg, New York, to Queen Victoria and accepted through Robert Todd Lincoln, who was then the American minister to the British Court. For a while, it hung in St. George's Hall, the Royal Banqueting Room, at Windsor Castle.[26] No one knows its whereabouts today.[27]

As Carpenter aged, the quality of his paintings noticeably declined.[28] Not only did he continue to have a problem with knowing when to stop working on a piece, but he resorted to the less expensive use of bitumen, or coal oil, in his paints. This was an unfortunate miscalculation on his part because it tended to muddle or darken the paintings, and they cracked and degenerated more quickly.[29] However, though a veteran painter, he still showed an interest in continuing to learn about his craft. One day he met a friend and showed him what he was carrying under his arm. It was a book by John Gadsby Chapman (1870): *The American drawing-book: a manual for the amateur, and basis of study for the professional artist: especially adapted to the use of public and private schools, as well as home instruction.* He explained that he bought it "with the intention of studying it thoroughly."[30]

The success Carpenter enjoyed in his later years was due less to his artistic prowess than to his marketing skills. His *Emancipation Proclamation* painting became quite popular in 1879 when the engraving by Ritchie was offered as a premium to new subscribers to the newspaper *The Independent*.[31] Then, in 1895, Carpenter shrewdly copyrighted and self-published a reprint of his *Emancipation Proclamation* painting. This time it included a reproduction of Lincoln's handwritten draft of the historic document.[32]

Five years later, on Wednesday afternoon of the twenty-third of May 1900, Francis B. Carpenter passed from this world. Funeral services were held two days later in the chapel of the Presbyterian Hospital in New York City where he died. Distinguished alumni of the Homer Academy were present, including the presiding clergyman, the Rev. Dr. Theodore T. Munger. Among the twelve pallbearers were childhood friend Calvin Woolworth and the first president of the American Public Health Association, Dr. Stephen Smith. Carpenter was buried in the upper southwest corner of Glenwood Cemetery in the Carpenter family plot. It is on a tree-studded hillside overlooking the Village of Homer below. His obituary in the *Times* of May 24, 1900, made what has become an all too common mistake of referring to his greatest work as being the *signing* rather than the first *reading* of the Emancipation Proclamation.[33] No doubt, the final version, showing Lincoln with pen in hand, contributes to that mistaken notion, as well.

Since Carpenter's death, reproductions of his most famous painting have been included in periodicals, history textbooks, and scholarly works, especially those dealing with Lincoln. The painting has not always been credited to him.

Today, Carpenter's paintings, which regrettably he did not always sign, are scattered all over America. Besides three institutions in Homer, the Cortland County Historical Society of nearby Cortland, New York, is home to several of Carpenter's paintings. Some are in private residences where the owners may not even be aware they own a work by the Lincoln portraitist. There is no telling how many have made their way into attics, basements, garage sales or the curb-side trash.

Starting in the 1930s, Mary Bartlett Cowdrey of New Jersey hoped to search out and catalogue all of Francis B. Carpenter's paintings. She estimated them to be in excess of 400 in number. The task proved to be daunting and was never completed. When she quit the project, she had amassed information on portraits of over 228 individuals and could account for over 33 portraits or sketches in oil of Lincoln alone.[34] At present, the Smithsonian American Art Museum in Washington, D.C., maintains an Art Inventories Catalog, which includes a lengthy list of portraits attributed to Carpenter and their last known locations. The portrait of John Miller from the Homer School's collection of the Trustees Paintings was added to the catalog in 2007 through the good efforts of a Homer Board of Education member, David Quinlan. In late summer of 2010, Quinlan and the author came across two more Carpenter portraits in a private collection in Central New York. These were the images of Homer's Gideon Hobart and his wife, Electa Wadsworth Hobart. Painted in 1867 and signed on the back by Carpenter, the pair of portraits needed to be registered with the Smithsonian.

23

"To Portray *the Man* as He Was Revealed to Me"

While there were better painters in the nineteenth century than Francis B. Carpenter, he best provided the iconic image of Lincoln that has endured in the American mind.[1] That is the image of the Great Emancipator with heavy-lidded, blueish-gray eyes "always in deep shadow" and looking "remarkably pensive and tender, often inexpressively sad, as if the reservoir of tears lay very near the surface."[2] In addition, the only artist involved with President Lincoln to provide posterity an extended memoir is Frank Carpenter.[3] Thus, not only did Carpenter contribute by paint to the world's understanding of Lincoln, he contributed by print, though a reporter once surmised that upon his death Carpenter took with him "more Civil War history than he ever told."[4]

Unlike William Stoddard, Carpenter never wrote an autobiography. He could have easily done so because he kept letters and a diary from 1851 until his death. Sadly, his biographers and historians are stymied in their research because, as Mary Bartlett Cowdrey found, "Carpenter's wife, who lived until 1926 (dying at the age of 90), destroyed most of the letters and more than half of the Diary." Cowdrey conjectured that "Carpenter's widow was anxious to cover up Carpenter's connection with the Beecher-Tilton scandal and the fact that he was in continual financial difficulties."[5] The documents may have been destroyed out of embarrassment or to protect Carpenter's reputation or for some other reason, but at least his recollections of Lincoln have survived.

Carpenter's reminiscences of Lincoln were first published in a series of articles for the New York *Independent* and then in an afterword — pages 725 to 766 — to Henry J. Raymond's *The Life, Public Services and State Papers of*

Abraham Lincoln, published in New York in 1865. Again, like some of his artwork, some of Carpenter's literary work was done while summering in Homer. His diary entry for August 20, 1865, reads: "Commenced my 'No. VII' [installment] for the 'Independent' this evening, under the tree in the southeast corner of the orchard."[6] His own book, *Six Months at the White House,* completed on the first anniversary of Lincoln's death[7] and published by Hurd and Houghton in 1866, was a best-seller. In its preface, Carpenter wrote (and the emphasis is his), "My aim has been throughout these pages to portray *the man* as he was revealed to me, without any attempt at idealization."[8] Carpenter gave readers of that era exactly what they craved. The public, upon Lincoln's death, wanted personal anecdotes of the man more than critical assessments of his statesmanship. This was true for more than just Americans. According to John Hay's letter from Paris in 1866 to Carpenter, "There is a great deal of interest exhibited in Europe in regard to [Lincoln's] life and character."[9]

In the strong demand for reminiscences about Lincoln, some information coming from individuals other than Carpenter suffered from muddled memories and outright fabrication but ended up in later years as part of Lincoln lore. Two examples were delightful tales involving Carpenter. The first merits being presented in its entirety:

> During the Lincoln administration Kate Chase was the belle of Washington. She was the daughter of Salmon P. Chase of Lincoln's cabinet and very important to her father's political life.
> According to the *American Statesman Series,* Kate Chase was "young, remarkably beautiful, regal and captivating. She made it her business in life to establish cordial relations with her father's political friends and she was a gracious hostess for the hospitality which her father enjoyed giving."
> "Ambassadors, senators and politicians were eager for her goodwill and willing to promise her aid, and Mrs. Lincoln had battles royal with her, coming, as she said, to the receptions at the White House as a guest and holding court on her own account." Mrs. Lincoln was inclined to be jealous and it is not surprising that she envied this fascinating girl.
> President Lincoln, on the other hand, was a great admirer of Kate Chase. When she married the brilliant Senator [William] Sprague of Rhode Island in 1863, Lincoln promised to attend her wedding. Mrs. Lincoln willed otherwise. She locked the president in his room and hid his evening clothes.
> At this time, Frank B. Carpenter, the artist (born in Homer, N.Y.) was residing at the White House, painting the picture of "Lincoln and His Cabinet and the First Reading of the Emancipation Proclamation." Lincoln attracted the attention of Carpenter and got him to find his clothes and put them over the transom of his door. Lincoln in this way was able to dress himself properly and later made his exit by the window and attended the wedding.

It is true that the vivacious Kate Chase, whom Mrs. Lincoln regarded with an unhidden disdain, married in November of 1863. President Lincoln attended the wedding and the reception; his wife's absence was noted by the press.[10] Perhaps there was jocular speculation among Washington society as to what lengths Mrs. Lincoln might go to prevent the president from attending, which gave rise to this amusing tale of his temporary imprisonment. Any accomplice, real or imaginary, required to fetch the president's clothes, was confused with Carpenter. It could not have been Carpenter. The artist did not arrive at the White House to do the painting until February 1864, and he did not reside there. The image conjured of the president making an exit via the window is the type, however, that would surely have drawn a chuckle from Lincoln.

The tale appears in a typed, four-page, undated manuscript[11] archived at the Phillips Free Library in Homer, New York, and is attributed to the former Miss Mary Hunt of Hunt's Corners, New York, "who heard it from the lips of a man who had received the story directly from Frank Carpenter." To say the least, the authenticity of an event passed along by oral tradition is highly suspect.

So, too, is this second piece of lore from the same four-page typed document. It is said to be offered by a Mr. H.B. Pomeroy of Cortland, New York, about Carpenter and his famous painting. Pomeroy "says that he has heard this story many times from the lips of his uncle, Senator S[amuel]. C[larke]. Pomeroy of Kansas and therefore can vouch for its truth":

> The painting, which was largely executed in the state dining-room of the White House, was finished and presented for final showing in the committee rooms of Senator S.C. Pomeroy of Kansas, which were located in the Treasury Building in Washington.
>
> Mr. Carpenter called in the members of the Cabinet to pass judgement on the picture. In those days most men wore black Prince Albert coats but Mr. Stanton, Secretary of War was painted wearing a short gray coat. Mr. Seward had light colored trousers. Mr. Wells wore a white vest and others were not so noticeable.
>
> When Mr. Stanton saw that the artist had painted him "not dressed up" he was furious. In his tastes Stanton was something of a dandy and his temper rose at this offense. He swore, he raved and assailed the artist, until, as Senator Pomeroy said, "I was scart [sic] to hear such language." None of it moved Frank B. Carpenter. He only grew the madder as curses poured out.
>
> Mr. Carpenter told the Cabinet that they were not obliged to take the picture but it was completed and would not be changed in any particular, and it never was.

According to Carpenter, the cabinet first examined the painting in the State Dining Room and never at the Treasury Building. Among the cabinet members' criticisms noted by the artist was nothing concerning their attire.

As for making changes to the completed painting, Carpenter was way too inclined in that direction and willing to accommodate requested alterations.

Yet, to be historically fair, there may have been some consternation expressed over sartorial coloration. An article in the New York *Herald Tribune* in 1930 claims there was an exchange of words between Seward and Carpenter over "Seward's pants." It seems that Seward protested being painted wearing wide, light-colored trousers with his black coat. Though Carpenter may have explained that "the color composition required a splash of light in the foreground," Seward was not placated by "artistic necessity": "He didn't propose to go down to posterity as an effeminate dandy" because of liberties taken with his "statesmanlike black broadcloth trousers."[12]

It is interesting that the two tales are part of the same manuscript, for the Senator Pomeroy alluded to was the gentleman responsible for the Pomeroy circular of February 1864. This was a confidential document critical of President Lincoln and intended to mobilize Republican support for the presidential candidacy of Kate Chase Sprague's politically ambitious father, the secretary of the treasury, Salmon P. Chase. Upon being leaked to the press, the plan backfired, causing serious embarrassment to Secretary Chase and protestations of innocence by him to Lincoln.[13] This was one of the reasons Mary Todd Lincoln felt justified in sarcastically calling Carpenter's *Emancipation Proclamation* painting "The Happy Family."

Carpenter's anecdotes, on the other hand, tend to be more reliable and accurate in their revelations of Lincoln the man. Case in point is his description of the moment when Lincoln signed the document granting emancipation to slaves then held in the rebel states. In modern times, when presidents sign an important document, it is a "photo op" or "photo opportunity." When Lincoln officially signed the Emancipation Proclamation at noon on New Year's Day, 1863, no photographer, like Matthew Brady, or reporter, like Noah Brooks, was summoned. Very quietly and without fanfare, Lincoln placed his signature on the document in the presence of only Secretary Seward and Seward's son, Frederick. Through Carpenter's book, it is revealed that when Lincoln went to write his name, he held the steel pen with a well-chewed wooden handle for a moment, and then dropped the pen. He explained that for the past three hours he had been shaking hands in a presidential New Year's Day open house receiving line and could barely feel the pen in his hand. Suffering from the occupational hazard of an accessible president, he expressed his concern: "If my name ever goes into history it will be for this act, and my whole soul is in it. If my hand trembles when I sign the Proclamation, all who examine the document hereafter will say, 'He has hesitated.'" In awhile, he picked up the pen, and with firm deliberation wrote Abraham Lincoln, not his customary A. Lincoln. Then, looking up with a smile, he said,

"That will do." Thus, Carpenter revealed Lincoln the man to be concerned about the judgment of history, at the moment he became the Great Emancipator.[14]

That evening, again related by Carpenter, Lincoln shared with Congressman Schuyler Colfax his concern that "three hours' handshaking is not calculated to improve a man's chirography [penmanship]." Then, changing to a tone of steady resolve, Lincoln was said to have continued, "The South had fair warning, that if they did not return to their duty, I should strike at this pillar of their strength. The promise must now be kept, and I shall never recall one word."[15]

Carpenter's book reveals the mercy and compassion of Lincoln. When court-martial cases came across his desk requiring the death sentence, Lincoln, as noted by Carpenter, was inclined "to pardon or commute the majority." He cited Judge Advocate General Holt's impression: "The President is without exception the most tender-hearted man I ever knew."[16]

One particularly interesting example of presidential clemency was provided by a letter to Carpenter, and he chose to include its content in his book. It seems that a 23-year-old soldier, Lorenzo Stewart (alias Shear) from Utica, New York—"scarcely more than a boy"—in September of 1863 mustered in as a private in the 76th New York Regiment, the same Central New York regiment that Daniel Webster Carpenter had joined. By April 1864, Stewart, now absorbed into the 14th New York Volunteer Artillery, was detained in the military prison camp at Elmira, New York. Charged with multiple attempts at desertion and with the murder of one of his guards by poison, he was sentenced to death and his gibbet was erected. An appeal was made to Secretary of War Stanton, but he refused to listen. This was, in Stanton's opinion, a case of a hard-core criminal. The boy's mother then appeared before President Lincoln. Upon examining the record, Lincoln told her he concurred with the secretary of war and that there was nothing he could do. Finally, the assistance of Judge Ira Harris, senator of New York State, was sought. He prevailed upon the president at the Executive Mansion around midnight, only hours from the scheduled time of execution. Lincoln got up from bed to meet Harris, who explained that the boy was "of unsound mind." Because of insanity, he was not responsible for his actions. Harris did not ask for a pardon but only a reprieve "until a proper medical examination could be made." Finding this reasonable, Lincoln ordered a stay of execution immediately by telegram to Elmira and ordered Dr. John P. Gray of Utica to be commissioned to assess the boy's mental health. Clashing with the direct orders of the secretary of war, Lincoln, according to Carpenter, "sent no less than *four* [emphasis is Carpenter's] different reprieves, by different lines, to different individuals in Elmira, so fearful was he that the message would fail, or be too late." The boy was saved "from being executed the next day at dawn." On January 25, 1865, Lincoln commuted Stewart's sentence to "imprisonment in the Penitentiary at hard labor for ten years."[17]

Carpenter cited the daily crush of humanity upon the Executive Chamber[18] and made this observation: "I shall never cease to regret that an additional private secretary could not have been appointed, whose exclusive duty it should have been to look after and keep a record of all cases appealing to executive clemency. It would have afforded full employment for one man, at least; and such a volume would now be beyond all price."[19]

Through Carpenter, the reader gets a rare glimpse behind the scenes of domestic life at the Lincoln White House. For example, he tells of the fire of February 10, 1864, possibly set by an arsonist, which consumed the White House stables and the two ponies that belonged to Tad and the deceased Willie. Carpenter said, "The only allusion I ever heard the President make to Willie was on this occasion, in connection with the loss of his pony."[20] As for Tad, who was most likely developmentally disabled and "suffering much from an infirmity of speech which developed in his infancy," his father doted upon him and gave him complete run of the Executive Mansion. Carpenter observed, "No matter who was with the President, or how intently he might be absorbed, little [eleven-year-old] Tad was always welcome."[21] This prompted Carpenter to do a painting of Lincoln and Tad, similar to the famous photograph of the two done by the Brady studio showing Lincoln reading to Tad.[22]

According to Carpenter's observations, it would appear that Lincoln possessed what is now called a "photographic memory." He marveled at the man's ability to recite lengthy poems from memory as well as whole passages from *Hamlet* and other works of Shakespeare.[23] In spite of "the multitude of visitors" seen daily by this most accessible of presidents, Carpenter was "often amazed at the readiness with which he recalled faces and events and even names."[24] A man he had not seen for twelve years presumed the president could not recall his name. Lincoln, in good humor, responded, "Your name is Flood.... I am glad to see that the *Flood* flows on."[25]

Scattered all through Carpenter's recollections are examples of Lincoln's remarkable sense of humor. Throughout his lifetime, Lincoln demonstrated an ability to commit to memory funny anecdotes. He once told Noah Brooks, "I remember a good story when I hear it, but I never invented anything original; I am only a retail-dealer."[26] These stories and his own wit were useful upon many an occasion: to put off an irate politician, to socially put someone at ease, or to clinch a point in a lawyerly fashion, such as in Carpenter's account of the group that came to the White House just before the fall of Vicksburg. The group urged the president to remove General Grant from his command because of his fondness for whiskey. Lincoln is said to have replied, "By the way, gentlemen, can either of you tell me where General Grant procures his whiskey? Because, if I can find out, I will send every general in the field a barrel of it!"[27]

"In a corner of his desk," wrote Carpenter of Lincoln, "he kept a copy of the latest humorous work; and it was his habit when greatly fatigued, annoyed, or depressed, to take this up and read a chapter, frequently with great relief."[28] Carpenter found that the president had a distinctive laugh: "The 'neigh' of a wild horse on his native prairie is not more undisguised and hearty." During the dark days of the war, a group was waiting to be admitted to see the president when the unmistakable "neigh" could be heard through the partition. One in the group remarked, "That laugh has been the President's life-preserver!"[29] It has been noted that for Lincoln humor was a "tool" for maintaining his mental health while "checking the lengthening mortality lists of a four-year ordeal."[30]

As for Lincoln's physical health, Carpenter expressed surprise at how the president sustained his life, for he noted that it seemed there were weeks in which "he neither ate nor slept," and the president admitted that no amount of rest or recreation "seemed ... to reach the *tired* spot."[31] Furthermore, Carpenter noted the total disregard Lincoln showed toward his own bodily safety. The president voiced objection to escorts accompanying him on his near daily travels at day or night between Washington and the presidential family's summer cottage near the Soldiers' Home. He wanted no guards posted outside the Executive Chamber. A Colonel Halpine observed "the utterly unprotected condition of the President's person, and the fact that any assassin or maniac, seeking his life, could enter his presence without the interference of a single armed man to hold him back." When questioned about the wisdom of taking no precautions, Lincoln simply shrugged it off by saying rather prophetically, "If there were such a plot, and they wanted to get at me, no vigilance could keep them out."[32] Given the opportunity, Eli DeVoe would most surely have disagreed.

Carpenter confirmed what his friend Stoddard knew all too well. The president was the recipient of much hate mail, including death threats. Unnerving as it would seem to be, Lincoln confided to Carpenter how he came to deal with such letters:

> Soon after I was nominated at Chicago, I began to receive letters threatening my life. The first one or two made me a little uncomfortable, but I came at length to look for a regular installment of this kind of correspondence in every week's mail.... It is no uncommon thing to receive them now; but they have ceased to give me any apprehension. Oh, there is nothing like getting *used* to things![33]

In the same way, Lincoln dealt with the barrage of words his many critics fired at him in the newspapers and through the mail. Through Carpenter, Lincoln's classic philosophy made it into print:

> If I were to try to read, much less answer, all the attacks made on me, this shop might as well be closed for any other business. I do the very best I know how — the very best I can; and I mean to keep doing so until the end. If the end brings me out all right, what is said against me won't amount to anything. If the end brings me out wrong, ten angels swearing I was right would make no difference.[34]

Carpenter had critics, too, and not just art critics. When Carpenter's publishers decided in 1867 to issue a new printing of his memoir under the title *The Inner Life of Abraham Lincoln,* Mrs. Lincoln had harsh words: "To think of this stranger, silly adventurer, daring to write a work entitled, 'The Inner Life of Abraham Lincoln.' Each scribbling writer, almost strangers to Mr. L., subscribe themselves his most intimate friend!"[35] And this was from the same woman who just a year earlier had given Carpenter a memento of the late president as a Christmas present — what she said was a "very plain cane ... handled by *him.*"[36]

Praise for *The Inner Life of Abraham Lincoln* did come, however, from one reputable literary figure in 1868. Charles Dickens and Carpenter met for the first time on April 18, 1866. Horace Greeley of the New York *Tribune* feted Dickens at a dinner at Delmonico's. Among the 24 invited guests were the cartoonist Thomas Nast and the artist-biographer Francis B. Carpenter.[37] On his second tour of America in 1868, Dickens wrote to Carpenter on February 15 from Westminster Notch, New York. The great English author thanked him for the book and commented:

> It has interested me exceedingly. I sat down quietly to read some pages of it, an hour after I arrived here: and the book did not leave my hand until I had read it through to the last word. Believe me, Dear Sir, Faithfully yours — Charles Dickens[38]

24

"I Have Certainly Not Stolen a March on Anybody"

Stoddard did not immediately publish books about his White House days. From the 1870s into the early 1900s, he was busily engaged in churning out a slew of adventure books for young boys. Titles like *Chris the Model Maker* and *Lost Gold of the Montezumas* were quite popular, and by 1905, they were described as "the best boys' books published." Homer was the scene for many of them, and "the characters were easily recognized, though under fictitious names, making Homer classic."[1] He also dabbled in "railway, telegraphic and manufacturing enterprises" of the times, which resulted sometimes in the making of small fortunes and then the loss of what had been amassed.[2] Because of unsuccessful speculations or generosity to kin or both, Stoddard seemed to have difficulty hanging onto money—a trait he had in common with Carpenter.

In 1878, Stoddard found himself embroiled in the McGarrahan-New Indria case, an inquiry into corruption involving claims of title in 1861 to a California quicksilver mine. *The New York Evening Post* of March 11, 1878, charged that there was evidence that the secretary to President Lincoln had "used his position to sell Cabinet and other government secrets for effect in Wall Street and for other purposes." In a letter to the editor of the *Post*, Stoddard admitted to openly speculating in gold and stocks during the war which "was the mania of the day," but he flatly denied the corruption allegations. A Senate investigation revealed no wrong-doing by the former assistant secretary.[3]

Six years after this, in 1884, Stoddard published *Abraham Lincoln: The True Story of a Great Life*. This would be the first of six books he would write about Lincoln. Stoddard drew criticism immediately from Nicolay and Hay because Stoddard's major biography had gone to press before theirs.[4] Hay was miffed that Stoddard's work would "take away market value" from his work. Stoddard retorted, "I have certainly not stolen a march on anybody."[5] He assured Nicolay and Hay, twenty years after Lincoln's death, that the market for books on Lincoln was wide open and they would "succeed *enormously*": "Mine seems to find its place. So will yours."[6]

In truth, more ink has been spilled related to Lincoln than any other person in United States history,[7] and Nicolay and Hay's ten-volume biography (1890) found its niche.[8] So, too, did additional works by Stoddard: *Inside the White House in War Times* (1890), *The Table-Talk of Abraham Lincoln* (1894), and *Lincoln at Work: Sketches from Life* (1900).[9] His memories of Lincoln were always filled with affection and humor.

In 1885, Stoddard moved to Hempstead, Long Island. Nine years later, he relocated to Madison, New Jersey. In 1907, while in his seventies, Stoddard completed a massive typewritten, 767-page autobiography, just two years before the centenary of Lincoln's birth. Never published, his *Recollections of a Checkered Lifetime told for his children by William O. Stoddard in his old age* was written mostly from memory and from pieces of personal writing that had survived a fire when he lived in New York.[10] This manuscript was edited by Harold Holzer under the title *Lincoln's White House Secretary: The Adventurous Life of William O. Stoddard* and published in 2007.

Here, Stoddard tends to overplay his role in certain events. He would have the reader believe Lincoln offered him a job, rather than he requested one of Lincoln.[11] Also, he is at odds with historians over the replacement of Vice President Hannibal Hamlin with Andrew Johnson at the Republican (Union Party) national convention in 1864. Stoddard's highly unlikely version has the assistant secretary engineering a "Dump Hamlin" movement at the personal request of President Lincoln.[12] Additionally, although Stoddard maintains his poor health was the motive for his requesting the post of marshal for the Eastern District of Arkansas, there may have actually been other motives at play in 1864. A general election was approaching. Was this a favorable time for a White House staff member to be departing? His sister Kate prevailed upon Senator Ira Harris of New York and Jacob Schermerhorn of Homer to urge the president not to send her brother to a distant former rebel state fraught with "difficulties."[13] The appeal was ignored, but why was the appeal made at all if this is what Stoddard wanted and had asked for?

Historian Daniel Mark Epstein has suggested that "the timing of the appointment, as well as its remote location, strongly suggest a quiet exile or moral quarantine rather than a voluntary career move." For what conceivable reason? Again, Epstein has theorized that given the president's call for the draft and his plummeting popularity in 1864, even among his own party members, "the last thing the president needed in an election year was a stock-jobber and currency gambler running a gold line from the White House to the New York banks."[14] This is plausible, but Lincoln was also thinking of future Southern senators for the Reconstruction period and how to get the ballot into the hands of the freedmen. So is Stoddard's version of the events of 1864 credible? Which explanation carries more contextual weight? According to Stoddard's granddaughter Eleanor, "He is telling the story, and he has a good opinion of himself that never waivers."[15]

On a good many points involving Lincoln, scholars have frequently cited both Stoddard and Carpenter's recollections as reliable primary sources. For example, Stoddard supports Carpenter's view of Lincoln as a man of compassion. He cites the occasion when a letter arrived at his desk addressed to the president from a widow who had sacrificed four sons in battles. She wrote eloquently of her prayerful support of her president and of her country. Noting that the stationery appeared to be blistered by fallen teardrops, Stoddard was moved to take the letter immediately to Lincoln. As Lincoln began reading, Stoddard observed that the president's eyes, like his own, were welling up with tears. Furthermore, both he and Carpenter corroborate the story of Lincoln spending sleepless nights pacing the White House floor, consumed in a personal Gethsemane of anguish over the national bloodletting. This is another iconic image of Lincoln that has survived into the twenty-first century, though Carpenter's account is based on what he saw and Stoddard's is based on what he heard and imagined.[16] (To compare the two accounts, see Appendix F.)

And for those who say Lincoln was a non-believer, Father Keep might have disagreed. While Lincoln refrained from any personal affiliation with organized religion and never publicly accepted the divinity of Christ, his powerful speeches were frequently laced with references to God and to scripture, which Keep most likely would have found to be a reflection of a sincere communion with the divine. In 1861, after reading Lincoln's farewell speech to the folks of Springfield, John Keep wrote Lincoln a letter from Oberlin commending him for his public avowal of trust in God.[17] That trust, along with his compassion, never disappeared from his speeches, as perhaps is best exemplified by the closing of his Second Inaugural Address:

> With malice toward none, with charity for all, with firmness in the right as God gives us to see the right, let us strive on to finish the work we are in, to bind up the nation's wounds, to care for him who shall have borne the battle and for his widow and his orphan (March 4, 1865).

Like Carpenter, Stoddard also noted Lincoln's absolute need for a good joke now and then: "Mr. Lincoln says that he must laugh sometimes, or he

24. "I Have Certainly Not Stolen a March on Anybody" 147

Letter from John Keep and Henry Cowles of Oberlin to the Honorable Abraham Lincoln (courtesy Library of Congress, Lincoln Papers).

would surely die." Stoddard recalled a Sunday during the war when Hay shared a rib-tickling joke with him and Nicolay. The president, hearing peals of laughter, entered the room, sank into a chair, and said, "Now, John, just tell that thing again." So Hay gladly told the story again, and the quartet exploded in guffaws. "Down came the President's foot from across his knee, with a heavy stamp on the floor, and out through the hall went an uproarious peal of fun." All were reveling in the much needed emotional release when a voice interrupted: "Mr. President, if you please, sir, Mr. Stanton is in your room." It was Edward McManus, the old doorkeeper, looking penitent at disrupting the merriment. Stoddard felt compelled to note Lincoln's response:

> The shadow came back to Lincoln's face, and he arose, slowly, painfully, like a man lifting some enormous burden. He even seemed to stagger as he walked out, for not only are each day's burdens heavy, but the worst news of the war has thus far been its Sunday news, and such as brings over Stanton in person.[18]

A weary man bearing an oppressive burden — this was the part of Lincoln the people did not see or know. It fell to William Stoddard to tell them.

On Saturday, August 29, 1925, a few weeks short of his ninetieth birthday, the last-surviving personal secretary to Abraham Lincoln died at the home of his son, Ralph, at 37 Crescent Road in Madison, New Jersey. Plagued with health issues throughout his life, Stoddard wrote to John Hay on January 17, 1895, explaining the cause of his remarkable longevity: "I have been vastly benefited by the free use of olive oil ... a table-spoonful after each meal, with a drop of red wine." Naturally, the down side of a long life is the experience of great loss. Stoddard began to lose his hearing in his forties. He outlived his wife (by twenty-nine years), his sisters, his brothers, two sons in their infancies, three daughters (from tuberculosis), a little grandson, and most of his contemporaries. Finally, the very old man with a well-trimmed beard of gray, who thrived on social interaction and being interviewed by reporters, lost his life. He is buried in Hillside Cemetery in Madison, New Jersey.[19]

William Stoddard in his eighties (author collection).

The up side of Stoddard's long life is that he was able to witness the veneration through the years of Lincoln by poets, essayists, biographers, artists, and sculptors. The *New York Times* eulogized Stoddard in 1925 by noting he had lived long enough to see the name of his friend and employer "accepted everywhere as a synonym for all that is best in democracy":

> He saw England place a statue of Lincoln in front of Westminster Abbey. He saw his name used as a watchword by the soldiers of many nations who fought for democracy in the [first] world war. He saw the nation whose unity Lincoln saved dedicate to his memory as beautiful a memorial as the world contains.[20]

Stoddard's granddaughter, Eleanor, was four years old when he died. She dimly remembers him, but her recollections are fueled by family stories, and the reading of a copy of the two-volume, leather bound original manuscripts. The original is in the Detroit Free Public Library.[21] In 1955, Stoddard's son, William O. Stoddard, Jr., at the age of eighty-two, published *Lincoln's Third Secretary*, a distillation of the weighty autobiography down to one small volume. It added a chapter on the death of Willie Lincoln that did not appear in the original manuscript and the story of the runaway slave in Grandpa Osborn's cellar.[22] Abridged as it was and in a more easily readable novel-like format, it made Stoddard's life known to young readers who frequented Homer's Phillips Free Library. In 1995 Eleanor paid a visit to her grandfather's birthplace in Homer. At the time, the residence was a well cared for bed-and-breakfast owned by Mr. and Mrs. Duane Stevens. She said then that she had been approached by the eminent Lincoln scholar, Harold Holzer, to produce a fully edited version of the original memoir. She welcomed this opportunity "to bring out the kind of reliable edition the work deserve[d]."[23]

The result was *Lincoln's White House Secretary: The Adventurous Life of William O. Stoddard*, edited by Harold Holzer, with illustrations, annotations, and personal comments by Eleanor. The book was published by the Southern Illinois University Press in 2007. While it omits the account of the runaway slave, it contains a never before published description of Stoddard's behind-the-scenes lobbying efforts to get Congress to accept Carpenter's painting as a gift from Mrs. Thompson.[24] At long last, Stoddard's autobiography has been presented and edited through the filter of a historian versed in the politics and culture of mid–nineteenth-century America.

Besides authoring over thirty books on Lincoln, Harold Holzer is the senior vice president for external affairs at the Metropolitan Museum of Art in New York City and is very familiar with Carpenter's paintings. Holzer is highly knowledgeable about Lincoln, in paint and print, and about the remarkable men from Homer who knew him, Stoddard and Carpenter.

25

Homer and the Lincoln Legacy

As part of the year-long 2009 national observance of the two-hundredth birthday of Abraham Lincoln, the community of Homer, New York, festooned with red, white, and blue bunting, made its week-long contribution in mid-May. "Homer's Celebration of Lincoln in Paint and Print," sponsored by the Homer Education Foundation and the Homer Center for the Arts, included an original, one-act play, *Freedom*, which included the character of Eli DeVoe and ended with the actors recreating on stage the *Emancipation Proclamation* painting. Following the play by Homer playwright William Allen, nationally-known Lincoln impersonator James Getty of Gettysburg, Pennsylvania, made history come alive for an enthralled crowd. During the week, one of the local banks distributed over-sized, gold-foiled Lincoln pennies made of chocolate. A patriotic Civil War era parade through the village culminated with a wreath-laying ceremony at Carpenter's grave. A local group of teenaged Civil War re-enactors marched in the parade, camped out overnight on the Homer Green, and fired artillery salvos the next day. Author Jason Emerson spoke at the public library on Mary Todd Lincoln, and the Elizabeth Brewster House served confections from Mary's recipes. The celebration brought forth all of Carpenter's portraits in the village for public display and hosted lectures on May 15 and 16 by Harold Holzer. He spoke with authority and humor about Stoddard and Carpenter and their unique connection to Lincoln. Holzer was also a co-chairperson of the national Abraham Lincoln Bicentennial Commission that enthusiastically endorsed the Homer celebration.

Accompanying Holzer was Eleanor Stoddard and descendants of Stoddard's sister Kate. Descendents of Carpenter joined the festivities and enjoyed Holzer's PowerPoint presentation on their artistic ancestor. Even one descendant of Eli DeVoe was present, Daryl DeVoe, who was closely studied by those eager to gain some sense of what the nineteenth century detective may have looked like. Warmly welcomed by the community, all the descendents participated in the celebration of the Lincoln legacy left to Americans by Stoddard and Carpenter. No descendants of Lincoln were invited because there are none. With the death of Robert Lincoln's last grandchild, Robert Todd Lincoln Beckwith, in Virginia in 1985, the direct line of Abraham and Mary Lincoln ended.[1] Yet, there was a way to get close to the one whose birthday was being observed. At a book signing, people were eager to meet Eleanor Stoddard, for as Holzer says, touching Eleanor's hand means touching the hand that touched *the hand*.[2] The week concluded with the profound sense that it was right and proper that Homer celebrated its three native sons and their descendants in 2009.

In the case of Carpenter's artistic legacy, three more of his portraits came to light during the planning for the bicentennial celebration. One arrived at the Center for the Arts from a church in Poughkeepsie, New York. It was a portrait, in beautiful condition and a stunning gold frame, of the Reverend Henry G. Ludlow. Ludlow (1797 to 1867) was a minister and an active abolitionist and one of those who served on the New York *Amistad* Committee. His church and home in New York City were partially demolished in July of 1834 during furious anti-abolitionist rioting set off, in part, by word that Ludlow had officiated at a mixed race marriage.[3] According to information on the back of the frame, the portrait was rendered in Ludlow's last year of life, 1867, when Carpenter was arguably at the top of his form.

Before this portrait came to Homer, two others arrived in a most interesting manner. In 2008, while the celebration was in its planning stage, a man residing in Homer came walking into Homer's Phillips Free Library on Main Street with two very old paintings in tow. The man had been the friend and caretaker of the late Liona Fisher Hammond Field of Homer. She owned these paintings and more than once had rejected offers to sell them. After she passed away, he stored the two paintings in a closet in his home for the next eight years. Apologetically, he explained to the librarian that he had just discovered the envelope attached to the back of one of the paintings. Inside were Liona's written instructions to give the paintings to the library. What he presented were, in fact, the two oldest known paintings by Carpenter. In need of serious cleaning and restoration, they were portraits of a husband and wife, Justin and Mary Pierce, born in Homer in 1804 and 1807, respectively. Justin was a justice of the peace and was employed at the mill operated by Carpenter's uncle Eli Carpenter. The Pierces lived up the East Hill in Homer, not far from Stoddard's birthplace on Albany Street. Most likely these were some of the paintings Carpenter did before going to Syracuse to hone his portraiture skills

Justin and Mary Pierce of Homer, New York (courtesy Phillips Free Library; photograph by David Quinlan).

under Sanford Thayer. He could not have been more than thirteen or fourteen at the time. Juxtaposed against these two portraits, the Ludlow portrait reveals to even an untrained eye the maturation of Carpenter's portraiture skills over the course of his career.

Amazingly, the man who saved the pair of portraits from oblivion and delivered them to their intended destination was Ronald DeVoe of Homer. While sharing the same last name of Lincoln's rescuer of 1861, Ronald does not share lineage with Eli.[4] Yet, like Eli, he seems to have been the right man at the right place at the right time.

Without Eli DeVoe's actions, there would be no story to tell, according to Homer's David Quinlan, who conceived the idea of "Homer's Celebration of Lincoln in Paint & Print." But there was a DeVoe, and because of him there was a President Abraham Lincoln, who, by his decisive leadership, left behind an intact nation and "a new birth of freedom." In turn, this greatest of American presidents is known and cherished today as the Great Emancipator because of the paint and print of two talented men from Homer, New York — a place which was finally recognized as "a new Lincoln Mecca" in the Fall 2009 issue of The Lincoln Forum *Bulletin*.

Homer can take justifiable pride in not just being their birthplace. To

25. Homer and the Lincoln Legacy

F. Halpin's print of study of Lincoln by Carpenter, donated to the Village of Homer by Grant Watson (photograph by David Quinlan).

use the modern vernacular, Homer was their launch pad. Homer was the place that set DeVoe, Carpenter, and Stoddard on their career paths. One has to ask: What if there had been no Fessenden Nott Otis in Homer to introduce Frank Carpenter to the world of art and no empathetic Paris Barber to nurture Carpenter's need to document people and events through art? What if there had been no proponents of the value of liberal education in Homer, like John Osborn or Samuel B. Woolworth or Father Keep? What if there had been no progressive school on the Green to instill in William Stoddard the virtues of taking a keen interest in public affairs and of acting audaciously upon one's ambitions? What if there had been no life-long relationships established in Homer with Andrew D. White or Theodore T. Munger or Stephen Smith — men of intellect, principles, and connections?

Fortunately, Homer had the people and the institutions in the 1830s and 1840s to make a difference. They combined to create a synergistic force that gave direction and meaning to the lives of three boys from Homer. The story of Eli DeVoe, Francis Bicknell Carpenter, and William Osborn Stoddard is worth passing on. Not only is the account compelling, but it proffers valuable lessons as applicable now as they were over 150 years ago. One of those important lessons can be summed up quite well in these words that are frequently attributed to President Abraham Lincoln:

> *I like to see a man proud of the place in which he lives.*
> *I like to see a man live so that his place will be proud of him.*

Epilogue

As the nation approaches its observance of the sesquicentennial of the Civil War and of the Lincoln administration, is it not ironic that a black man occupies the White House? The forty-fourth president of the United States, Barack Obama, is the first black president. The image evoked is a powerful one when set within the context of the history of race relations in America. Indeed, the significance of the presidential image was foremost with Mr. Obama as he approached the office to which he had been elected in 2008. Appearing Lincolnesque was carefully orchestrated to capitalize upon the parallels that already existed between him and the sixteenth president.

Each man became a lawyer and served in the Illinois State Legislature before serving a single term in Congress. Each burst into prominence upon the national political stage through powerful oratory addressing the existence of division in America. In 1857, in Illinois, Lincoln delivered the classic line, "A house divided cannot stand. I believe this government cannot endure permanently, half slave and half free." Obama captured national attention at the 2004 Democratic National Convention with his keynote address and a plea for unity: "There is not a liberal America and a conservative America; there is the United States of America." Neither did another parallel go unnoticed. Like Lincoln, Obama had as his party's closest contender for presidential nominee the senator of the state of New York. Just as Lincoln appointed his rival Senator William Seward to be secretary of state, Obama appointed Senator Hillary Rodham Clinton to the same cabinet post.

Thus, it was no mere coincidence that Obama chose to make his inaugural trip to Washington in 2009 by the same means used by Lincoln in 1861—by train. Obama commenced his journey at Philadelphia, where Lincoln had stopped to raise an American flag outside Independence Hall, site of the crafting of the Declaration of Independence in 1776. However, Obama stopped at

Baltimore to make the kind of public appearance that had been denied Lincoln. When Obama took the presidential oath of office, he placed his hand on the same Bible Lincoln had used for his inauguration, and as if the symbolic linkage needed further reinforcing in the public's mind, Obama and his family made a media-covered visit to the Lincoln Memorial. An African American president standing in homage before the statue of the Great Emancipator made for a powerful image of the Lincoln legacy fulfilled.

Lincoln may have been one of the first presidents to give conscious attention to his visual presidential image. While Eli DeVoe was one who secured safe passage of Lincoln into Washington, Lincoln was troubled by the cartoon images placed in the press depicting him as a cowardly leader sneaking through Baltimore and into the capital. It was certainly not the presidential image he wanted at the commencement of his administration. Rarely did he turn down an opportunity to sit for a photograph. Along with Mathew Brady, Lincoln, in an age on the cusp of photojournalism, realized the contribution that a presidential image could make not just for the political moment but as historic documentation for the future. Just as he understood the public relations value of having a Brady photograph of an unknown presidential candidate from the West placed in the New York newspapers of 1860 along with his Cooper Union speech, so, too, Lincoln grasped the lasting benefit to be derived from sitting for a portrait in oil by Francis Carpenter in 1864. *The First Reading of the Emancipation Proclamation before the Cabinet* projected a positive presidential image of decisive and resolute leadership. It gave him the heroic stature he did not get to enjoy during his presidency, beset as he was by critics from all sides. Even William Stoddard, a White House staffer for President Lincoln and the first lady, seemed to grasp the importance of his unofficial responsibility as what is now called a PR man. It was a role he continued to play in his concerted effort with Carpenter to get the painting of the Lincoln administration accepted as the national picture by Congress and placed on public display thirteen years later.

Any piece of public art is designed to raise questions within the viewer. Who? What? When? Where? Why? How? This holds true for the *Emancipation Proclamation* painting hanging in the Capitol or appearing as a print by Ritchie in a book or upon a classroom wall. When, for example, a young person, American or foreign, first beholds the presidential image rendered by Carpenter and asks the questions about the past that it seeks to elicit, that becomes a teachable moment. It becomes an opportunity to direct the questioner to the books—to the story that goes with the painting and which answers the question "What does it mean?" Fortunately, both Carpenter and Stoddard, among countless others, provided the story, too. In so doing, the Lincoln captured by paint and print attained a certain immortality. The image became indelibly imprinted upon the brain along with its meaning. As the people of the birthplace of DeVoe, Carpenter, and Stoddard understand, the story of emancipation and presidential image-making still resonates with meaning and gives cause for celebration.

> *"For nothing is absolutely dead: every meaning will someday have its homecoming festival."*
> — Mikhail Bakhtin, *Speech Genres and Other Late Essays* (1986)

Appendix A: *Central Illinois Gazette* Story (May 4, 1859)

Personal

Our Next President.— We had the pleasure of introducing to the hospitalities of our Sanctum, a few days ago, the Hon. Abraham Lincoln. Few men can make an hour pass away more agreeably. We do not pretend to know whether Mr. Lincoln will ever condescend to occupy the White House or not, but if he should, it is a comfort to know that he has established himself a character and reputation, of sufficient strength and purity to withstand the disreputable and corrupting influences of even that locality. No man in the West at the present time occupies a more enviable position before the people or stands a better chance for obtaining a high position among those to whose guidance our ship of state is to be entrusted.

Appendix B: *Central Illinois Gazette* Editorial (December 7, 1859)

Who Shall Be President?

We have no sympathy with those politicians of any party who are giving themselves up to a corrupt and selfish race for the presidential chair, and are rather inclined to believe that the result will be a disappointment to the whole race of demagogues. The vastness of the interests depending on the political campaign now commencing, gives even a more than usual degree of interest to the question: "Who shall be the candidate?" Believing that a proper discussion of this question through the columns of the local papers is the true way to arrive at a wise conclusion, we propose to give our views, so far as formed, and we may add that we are well assured that the same views are entertained by the mass of the Republican party of Central Illinois.

In the first place, we do not consider it possible for the office of President of the United States to become the personal property of any particular politician, how great a man soever he may be esteemed by himself and his partisans. We, therefore, shall discuss the "candidate question" unbiased [sic] by personal prejudices or an undue appreciation of the claims of any political leader. We may add, with honest pride, an expression of our faith in the leading statesmen of our party, that neither Chase nor Seward nor Banks nor any other whose name has been brought prominently before the people, will press individual aspirations at the expense of the great principles whose vindication is inseparably linked with our success. While no circumstances should be allowed to compel even a partial abandonment of principle, and defeat in the cause of right is infinitely better than a corrupt compromise with wrong, nevertheless, the truest wisdom for the Republican party in this campaign will be found in such a conservative and moderate course as shall secure the respect and consideration even of our enemies, and shall not forget National compacts within which we are acting and by which we are bound: and the proper recognition of this feature of the contest should be allowed its due influence in the selection of our standard bearer.

Although local prejudices ought always to be held subordinate to the issues of the contest, it will not be wise to overlook their importance in counting the probabilities of what will surely be a doubtful and bitterly contested battlefield. It is this consideration which has brought into so great prominence the leading Republican statesmen of Pennsylvania and Illinois. If these two states can be added to the number of those in which the party seems to possess an unassailable superiority, the day is ours. The same reasons to a less extent, in exact proportion to its force in the electoral college, affects New Jersey.

From Pennsylvania and Illinois, therefore, the candidates for President and Vice President might, with great propriety, be chosen. It is true that our present Chief Magistrate is from Pennsylvania, and other States justly might urge that a proper apportionment of the National honors would not give her the presidency twice in succession; but, while there are several good precedents for such a course of action, there is one point which outweighs in importance all others: to wit, *We must carry Pennsylvania in 1860*, and if we can best do it with one of our own citizens as standard-bearer, that fact cannot be disregarded with impunity. The delegation from the keystone State will doubtless present this idea with great urgency in the National convention.

Aside from this, there are other points in favor of the two States mentioned, which cannot fail to carry great weight in the minds of all candid and reasonable men. They have both been distinguished for moderation and patriotism in the character of their statesmen, with a few exceptions as any other States. They are among that great central belt of States which constitute the stronghold of conservatism and Nationality. They are not looked upon as "sectional" in their character, even by the South. They, moreover, are, to a high degree, representative States. Where will our manufacturing, mining, and trading interests find a better representative than Pennsylvania? Or what State is more identified in all its fortunes with the great agricultural interests than is Illinois?

The States themselves, then, being open to no valid objection, we come to the question of individual candidates. Pennsylvania has not yet determined her choice from among her own great men, but as for Illinois it is the firm belief of our citizens that for one or the other of the offices in question, no man will be so sure to consolidate the party vote of this State, or will carry the great Mississippi Valley with a more irresistible rush of popular enthusiasm, than our distinguished fellow citizen,

ABRAHAM LINCOLN

We, in Illinois, know him well, in the best sense of the word, *a true democrat*, a man of the people, whose strongest friends and supporters are the hard-handed and strong-limbed laboring men, who hail him as a brother and who look upon him as one of their real representative men. A true friend of freedom, having already done important service for the cause, and proved his abundant ability for still greater service; yet a staunch conservative, whose enlarged and liberal mind descends to no narrow view, but sees both sides of every great question, and of whom we need not fear that fanaticism on the one side, or servility on the other, will lead him to the betrayal of any trust. We appeal to our brethren of the Republican press for the correctness of our assertions.

Appendix C: Gideon Welles's Version of the September 22, 1863, Cabinet Meeting

SOURCE: *Diary of Gideon Welles*, Vol. I, 142–144

The subject was the Proclamation for emancipating the slaves after a certain date, in States that shall then be in rebellion. For several weeks the subject has been suspended, but the President says never lost sight of. When it was submitted, and now in taking up the Proclamation, the President stated the question was finally decided, the act and the consequences were his, but that he felt it due to us to make us acquainted with the fact and to invite criticism on the paper which he had prepared. There were, he had found, not unexpectedly, some difference in the Cabinet, but he had, after ascertaining in his own way the views of each and all, individually and collectively, formed his own conclusions and made his own decisions. In the course of the discussion on this paper, which was long, earnest, on the discussion on this paper, which was long, earnest, and on the general principle involved, harmonious, he remarked that he had made a vow, a covenant, that if God gave up the victory in the approaching battle, he would consider it an indication of Divine will, and that it was his duty to move forward in the cause of emancipation. It might be thought strange, he said, that he had in this way submitted the disposal of matters when the way was not clear to his mind what he should do. God had decided this question in favor of the slaves. He was satisfied it was right, was confirmed and strengthened in his action by the vow and the results. His mind was fixed, his decision made, but he wished his paper announcing his course as correct in terms as it could be made without any change in his determination. He read the comment. One or two unimportant amendments suggested by Seward were approved. It was then handed to the Secretary of State to publish to-morrow. After this, [Postmaster General Montgomery] Blair remarked that he considered it proper to say he did not concur in the expediency of the measure at this time, though he approved of the principle, and should therefore wish to file his objections. He stated at some length his views, which [were] substantially that we ought not to put in greater jeopardy the patriotic element in the Border States, that the results of the Proclamation would be to carry over those States en masse to the Secessionists as soon as it was read, and that there was also a class of partisans in the Free States endeavoring to revive old parties, who would have a club put into their hands of which they would avail themselves to beat the Administration.

The President said he had considered the danger to be apprehended from the first objection, which was undoubtedly serious, but the objection was certainly as great not to act; as regarded the last, it had not much weight with him.

The question of power, authority, in the Government to set free the slaves was not much discussed at this meeting, but had been canvassed by the President in a private conversation with the members individually. Some thought legislation advisable before the step was taken, but Congress was clothed with no authority on this subject, nor is the Executive, except under the war power, — military necessity, martial law, when there can be no legislation. This was the view which I took when the President first presented the subject to Seward and myself last summer as we were returning from the funeral of Stanton's child, — a ride of two or three miles from beyond Georgetown. Seward was at that time not at all communicative, and, I think, not willing to advise, thought he did not dissent from, the movement. It is momentous both in its immediate and remote resolute, and an exercise of extraordinary power which cannot be justified on mere humanitarian principles, and would never have been attempted but to preserve the national existence. The slaves must be with us or against us in the War. Let us have them. These were my convictions and this the drift of the discussion.

Appendix D:
The Preliminary
Emancipation Proclamation
(September 22, 1862)

By the President of the United States of America.

A PROCLAMATION.

I, ABRAHAM LINCOLN, President of the United States of America, and Commander-in-Chief of the Army and Navy thereof, do hereby proclaim and declare that hereafter, as heretofore, the war will be prosecuted for the object of practically restoring the constitutional relation between the United States, and each of the States, and the people thereof, in which States that relation is, or may be, suspended or disturbed.

That it is my purpose, upon the next meeting of Congress to again recommend the adoption of a practical measure tendering pecuniary aid to the free acceptance or rejection of all slave States, so called, the people whereof may not then be in rebellion against the United States and which States may then have voluntarily adopted, or thereafter may voluntarily adopt, immediate or gradual abolishment of slavery within their respective limits; and that the effort to colonize persons of African descent, with their consent, upon this continent, or elsewhere, with the previously obtained consent of the Governments existing there, will be continued.

That on the first day of January in the year of our Lord, one thousand eight hundred and sixty-three, all persons held as slaves within any State, or designated part of a State, the people whereof shall then be in rebellion against the United States shall be then, thenceforward, and forever free; and the executive government of the United States, including the military and naval authority thereof, will recognize and maintain the freedom of such persons, and will do no act or acts to repress such persons, or any of them, in any efforts they may make for their actual freedom.

That the executive will, on the first day of January aforesaid, by proclamation, designate the States, and part of States, if any, in which the people thereof respectively, shall then be in rebellion against the United States; and the fact that any State, or the people thereof shall, on that day be, in good faith represented in the Congress of the United States, by members chosen thereto, at elections wherein a majority of the qualified voters of such State shall have participated, shall, in the absence of strong countervailing testimony, be deemed conclusive evidence that such State and the people thereof, are not then in rebellion against the United States.

That attention is hereby called to an Act of Congress entitled "An Act to make an additional Article of War" approved March 13, 1862, and which act is in the words and figure following:

> "*Be it enacted by the Senate and House of Representatives of the United States of America in Congress assembled,* That hereafter the following shall be promulgated as an additional article of war for the government of the army of the United States, and shall be obeyed and observed as such:
>
> > Article —. All officers or persons in the military or naval service of the United States are prohibited from employing any of the forces under their respective commands for the purpose of returning fugitives from service or labor, who may have escaped from any persons to whom such service or labor is claimed to be due, and any officer who shall be found guilty by a court-martial of violating this article shall be dismissed from the service.
> >
> > SEC. 2. *And be it further enacted,* That this act shall take effect from and after its passage."

Also to the ninth and tenth sections of an act entitled "An Act to suppress Insurrection, to punish Treason and Rebellion, to seize and confiscate property of rebels, and for other purposes," approved July 17, 1862, and which sections are:

> "SEC. 9. *And be it further enacted*, That all slaves of persons who shall hereafter be engaged in rebellion against the government of the United States, or who shall in any way give aid or comfort thereto, escaping from such

persons and taking refuge within the lines of the army; and all slaves captured from such persons or deserted by them and coming under the control of the government of the United States; and all slaves of such persons found (or) being within any place occupied by rebel forces and afterwards occupied by the forces of the United States, shall be deemed captives of war, and shall be forever free of their servitude, and not again held as slaves.

"S<small>EC</small>. 10. *And be it further enacted*, That no slave escaping into any State, Territory, or the District of Columbia, from any other State, shall be delivered up, or in any way impeded or hindered of his liberty, except for crime, or some offence against the laws, unless the person claiming said fugitive shall first make oath that the person to whom the labor or service of such fugitive is alleged to be due is his lawful owner, and has not borne arms against the United States in the present rebellion, nor in any way given aid and comfort thereto; and no person engaged in the military or naval service of the United States shall, under any pretence whatever, assume to decide on the validity of the claim of any person to the service or labor of any other person, or surrender up any such person to the claimant, on pain of being dismissed from the service."

And I do hereby enjoin upon and order all persons engaged in the military and naval service of the United States to observe, obey, and enforce, within their respective spheres of service, the act, and sections above recited.

And the executive will in due time recommend that all citizens of the United States who shall have remained loyal thereto throughout the rebellion, shall (upon the restoration of the constitutional relation between the United States, and their respective States, and people, if that relation shall have been suspended or disturbed) be compensated for all losses by acts of the United States, including the loss of slaves.

I<small>N</small> W<small>ITNESS</small> W<small>HEREOF</small>, I have hereunto set my hand, and caused the seal of the United States to be affixed.

D<small>ONE</small> at the City of Washington this twenty-second day of September, in the year of our Lord, one thousand, eight hundred and sixty-two, and of the Independence of the United States the eighty seventh.

[Abraham Lincoln]

By the President:
William H. Seward,
Secretary of State.

Appendix E: The Final Emancipation Proclamation
(January 1, 1863)

By the President of the United States of America.

A PROCLAMATION.

Whereas, on the twenty-second day of September, in the year of our Lord one thousand eight hundred and sixty-two, a proclamation was issued by the President of the United States, containing, among other things, the following, to wit:

"That on the first day of January, in the year of our Lord one thousand eight hundred and sixty-three, all persons held as slaves within any State or designated part of a State, the people whereof shall then be in rebellion against the United States, shall be then, thenceforward, and forever free; and the Executive Government of the United States, including the military and naval authority thereof, will recognize and maintain the freedom of such persons, and will do no act or acts to repress such persons, or any of them, in any efforts they may make for their actual freedom.

"That the Executive will, on the first day of January aforesaid, by proclamation, designate the States and parts of States, if any, in which the people thereof, respectively, shall then be in rebellion against the United States; and the fact that any State, or the people thereof, shall on that day be, in good faith, represented in the Congress of the United States by members chosen thereto at elections wherein a majority of the qualified voters of such State shall have participated, shall, in the absence of strong countervailing testimony, be deemed conclusive evidence that such State, and the people thereof, are not then in rebellion against the United States."

NOW, THEREFORE, I, ABRAHAM LINCOLN, President of the United States, by virtue of the power in me vested as Commander-in-Chief, of the Army and Navy of the United States in time of actual armed rebellion against the authority and government of the United States, and as a fit and necessary war measure for suppressing said rebellion, do, on this first day of January, in the year of our Lord one thousand eight hundred and sixty-three, and in accordance with my purpose so to do publicly proclaimed for the full period of one hundred days, from the day first above mentioned, order and designate as the States and parts of States wherein the people thereof respectively, are this day in rebellion against the United States, the following, to wit:

Arkansas, Texas, Louisiana (except the parishes of St. Bernard, Plaquemines, Jefferson, St. John, St. Charles, St. James, Ascension, Assumption, Terrebone, Lafourche, St. Mary, St. Martin, and Orleans, including the city of New Orleans), Mississippi, Alabama, Florida, Georgia, South Carolina, North Carolina, and Virginia (except the forty-eight counties designated as West Virginia, and also the counties of Berkeley, Accomac, Northhampton, Elizabeth City, York, Princess Anne, and Norfolk, including the cities of Norfolk and Portsmouth), and which excepted parts, are for the present, left precisely as if this proclamation were not issued.

And by virtue of the power, and for the purpose aforesaid, I do order and declare that all persons held as slaves within said designated States, and parts of States, are, and henceforward shall be free; and that the Executive government of the United States, including the military and naval authorities thereof, will recognize and maintain the freedom of said persons.

And I hereby enjoin upon the people so declared to be free to abstain from all violence, unless in necessary self-defence; and I recommend to them that, in all cases when allowed, they labor faithfully for reasonable wages.

And I further declare and make known, that such persons of suitable condition, will be received into the armed service of the United States to garrison forts, positions, stations, and other places, and to man vessels of all sorts in said service.

And upon this act, sincerely believed to be an act of justice, warranted by the Constitution, upon military necessity, I invoke the considerate judgment of mankind, and the gracious favor of Almighty God.

IN WITNESS WHEREOF, I have hereunto set my hand and caused the seal of the United States to be affixed.

DONE at the City of Washington, this first day of January, in the year of our Lord one thousand eight hundred and sixty three, and of the Independence of the United States of America the eighty-seventh.

[Abraham Lincoln]

By the President:
William H. Seward,
Secretary of State.

Appendix F: Carpenter and Stoddard Describe Lincoln's Sleepless Nights

From Francis B. Carpenter, *Six Months at the White House* (1866), 30–31

During the first week of the battles of the Wilderness he scarcely slept at all. Passing through the main hall of the domestic apartment on one of these days, I met him, clad in a long morning wrapper, pacing back and forth a narrow passage leading to one of the windows, his hands behind him, great black rings under his eyes, his head bent forward upon his breast, — altogether such a picture of the effects of sorrow, care, and anxiety as would have melted the hearts of the worst of his adversaries, who so mistakenly applied to him the epithets of tyrant and usurper. With a sorrow almost divine, he, too, could have said of the rebellious States, "How often would I have gathered you together, even as a hen gathereth her chickens under her wings, *and ye would not!*" Like another Jeremiah, he wept over the desolations of the nation; "he mourned the slain of the daughter of his people."

Surely, ruler never manifested so much sympathy, and tenderness, and charity. How like the last words of the Divine one himself, "Father, forgive them, for they know not what they do," will the closing sentences of his last inaugural address resound in solemn cadence through the coming centuries.

From William O. Stoddard, *Memoirs* (1907) ed. Holzer (2007), 307–309

My mail was a large one. I had been hindered greatly by other duties and it had accumulated, not but what it often compelled me to toil on into late hours.

I had been out to my dinner, long ago. I do not know what had become of Nicolay and Hay. My door was open, however, and at last I saw men come out of Lincoln's office and walk slowly away. I can recall Seward, Halleck, Stanton, but after they had departed I believed myself to be alone on that floor of the Executive mansion except for the President in his room, over yonder across the hall. It was then about nine o'clock for I looked at my watch. It was so silent that I could hear it tick. It seemed as if the rooms and hall were full of shadows, some of which came in and sat down by me to ask me what I thought would become of the Union cause and the country.

Not long afterwards, a dull, heavy, regularly repeated sound came out of Lincoln's room through its half open door and found its way into mine. I listened, listened, and became aware that this was the measured tread of the President's feet, as he walked steadily to and fro, up and down, on the further side, beyond the Cabinet table, from wall to wall, and thought about Chancellorsville, its wounded and its dead, and about the nation and its thousands of broken hearts and about the days and the battles which were yet to come. He must have been listening to a great many weird utterances, as he walked and as he turned at the wall at either end of his ceaseless promenade. Ten o'clock came and I was still at my papers but whenever I paused to endorse one of them or to consider its destiny, I could hear the tread of the feet in that other room. Eleven o'clock came, and it had not really ceased for a breathing space. It had become such a half heard monotony that when, just at twelve o'clock, midnight, it suddenly ceased it was the silence itself that startled me into listening more intently. I did not dare to go and look in upon him, but oh, what a silence that was.

It may have continued during many minutes. Lincoln may have been at his table, writing, but there was a strong, strange impression upon my mind, I know not why, that if I had then looked in I would have seen a strong man kneeling down by one of those chairs. God was with him, anyhow, for He was then and there dealing with that man, helping, caring for him and for the nation.

Then the silence was broken and the sound of the heavy feet began again. One o'clock came and I still had much work before me and Lincoln did not seem to me to be even pausing at the walls. At times his pace quickened as if under the spur of some burst of feeling or impulse of angry energy. Two o'clock came, for I again looked at my watch, and Lincoln was walking still. It was a vigil with God and with the future and a long wrestle with disaster and it may be with himself—for he also was weary of delays and sore with defeats.

It was almost exactly at three o'clock that my own long task was done and I arose to go but I did not so much as peer through the narrow opening of the President's doorway. It would have been a kind of profanity. At the top of the stairway, however, I paused and listened before going down and the last sound that I heard and that seemed to go out of the house with me was the sentry-like tread with which the President was marching on into the coming day.

I went home weary enough but did not go to bed. I remember taking a bath and then a breakfast at Gautier's restaurant, on the avenue. My table was still heavily loaded and I knew fresh duties were at hand. It was therefore not yet eight o'clock when I was once more at the White House, letting myself in by my latchkey. It was a bright, sunlit morning, without a cloud in the sky. On reaching the second floor I saw the President's door wide open and looked in. There he sat, near the end of the Cabinet table, with a breakfast before him. Just beyond the cup of coffee at his right lay a sheet of foolscap paper, covered with fresh writing, in his own hand. I do not now recall how, before I came out, I received so strong an impression, amounting to knowledge, that upon this paper he had written his instructions to General Hooker to rally the army, to take fresh courage, and to fight again at the earliest opportunity. They were really the orders under which General Meade shortly took Hooker's place and marched on to Gettysburg. That long night vigil and combat and victory ought to be recorded forever in the most sacred annals of his country. I knew it had been a victory, for he turned to me with a bright and smiling face and talked with me as cheerfully as if he had not been up all night in that room, face to face with—Chancellorsville.

Appendix G: Remarks of William O. Stoddard of New York (Formerly Assistant Private Secretary to President Lincoln)

(Source: *Lincoln's Third Secretary*, edited by William O. Stoddard, Jr., 222–227)

Before the Joint Committee of the Library, February 24, 1873, with Reference to the Purchase by Congress of Mr. F. B. Carpenter's Picture of President Lincoln Reading the Proclamation of Emancipation to His Cabinet

GENTLEMEN OF THE COMMITTEE:

    Understanding as I do the great value of your time, I promise to detain you but a few minutes. At Mr. Carpenter's request, however, I desire to present a few reasons why his painting, now under your consideration, should become the property of the nation. I must beg your pardon for premising that my own feeling in the matter is very strong. Not only is the artist my warm personal friend of long standing, but my interest in the work began before a pencil was touched to it, as it was my pleasant duty to introduce the artist to President Lincoln for the express purpose of this undertaking. More than that, it was my own hand which made the first copy of the immortal document he has here commemorated, and the scene, the faces and figures of that group of men, arise before me whenever I look upon his canvas, with a vivid distinctness which may go far to excuse the warm enthusiasm I feel in the cause I am pleading.

I need hardly more than refer to the established idea and practice, ever since even the foundations of the Capitol were laid, that it should from time to time be ornamented and embellished with works of art. The popular conviction, however, has in these latter years steadily advanced towards the development of a settled doctrine that such productions of the sculptor's or the painter's genius as found a shrine in this, our national gallery, should be confined to more or less literal representations of men or of events whose prominence in our national history would fairly warrant such special commemoration. The very few exceptions to this rule, in later days, do but emphasize the propriety of its observance. With regard to this picture, then, I would suggest that the history of Anglo-Saxon culture has given the world three great state papers, never to be forgotten, difficult to overestimate. The Magna Carta, indeed, antedates American nationality, but the Declaration of Independence and the Proclamation of Emancipation are our own. Even political partisanship can hardly now be found so bitter as to deny the equal rank of the latter as marking an era of our history, hardly any to refuse a feeling of pride in its worldwide honor and influence.

It will, I think, be confessed that the promulgation of this proclamation was a thing well worthy to be made the subject of a historical painting, and that, too, for preservation in the art archives of the nation. A moment's consideration, then, will suffice to convince you that no other incident connected with that promulgation offers either opportunity or scope for the painter's genius and labor. This was really its publication, for when the great President finished his reading the Proclamation was an assured, if not accomplished fact, and the slaves were free, even to the sad, prophetic man who had signed the edict of their freedom. That Mr. Carpenter has wisely chosen the one scene by which he could best embody and preserve the memory of the great event is no less true, or more, than that he has succeeded in rendering the scene and its actors with rare fidelity. He has achieved a historical painting in every worthy sense of that often-abused term. I am well aware that comparisons are odious, but I must say that when, in passing through the rotunda, I have stopped to look at the "Baptism of Pocahontas," or even at the "Rescue of Smith" by that romantic female, or at the "Discovery of the Mississippi by DeSoto," I have been afflicted by grave doubts of their historical accuracy.

The Columbus on the eastern portico of the abutment suggests a painful question whether, as a matter of fact, the great discoverer ever got himself up in that style and threatened to bowl the world at the head of a half-naked

George Washington out in the middle of the opposite square. I should not now refer to these doubts of mine about these and other of our Capitol embellishments but to give point and force to the fact that this painting of Mr. Carpenter is not open to any such objection. This is the old, familiar, plainly-furnished room, where our statesmen, and our generals, too, so often met in counsel. There is where the great President toiled and suffered through the long, wearisome years of our national agony. Up and down that room I have heard the pacing of his tireless feet deep into the night of sorrow that followed some grave disaster to the arms of the Republic, and out of that room I have seen him come, with the light of hope and faith upon his furrowed face, after some tidings of success.

The mere grouping of these eight figures, artistic and admirable as it is, in its lifelike naturalness, I am assured by one of themselves and by his written approval, is as nearly actual as may be, but the successful grouping is only the first excellence to which I would call your attention. Familiar as I may safely suppose you to be with most, if not all, of the faces upon this canvas, you will hardly require to be told that these faces are of unsurpassed fidelity and artistic merit. There is Mr. Blair, the Postmaster General; it is a good likeness today, in spite of all the changes time has wrought. There is the rugged honesty of Mr. Bates, the Attorney General, the legal advisor of the darker days of Mr. Lincoln's administration. There is Mr. Caleb B. Smith, to whom the vast interests of the Interior were then confided. There is the venerable front of Mr. Welles, under whose management, whatever his critics may say, our navy wrought the quickly succeeding miracles of a war which rendered all old-time sea-fighting obsolete. There are the intellectual dignity and the noble proportions of our good Chief Justice, in whose brain our existing financial system took form, and to whom the care of the national purse came as a summons for the exertion of almost superhuman power. There, too, in the foreground of the picture, as of the occasion, are the figures of Seward and Stanton, the pen and the sword, the wisdom and the right arm of Lincoln's presidency. The man whose subtle prudence and profound statecraft kept Europe at bay, while his co-worker in the War Department wore his strong heart out and freely wasted all life and strength in presiding over the management of our armies. There they are, drawn to the life, and all but speaking for themselves.

So much for the Cabinet as represented in this picture; but I almost hesitate to speak as I would of the central figure of all. There is no other such portrait of Lincoln as this — no other which began and grew under his own roof, with daily studies by the artist, in free and careless moments such as no other could or did ever have. There is not, to my knowledge, any other portrait than this which gives so truthfully the prevailing melancholy of that rugged and powerful face, with the added intensity of meaning in the sad, far-seeing eyes, which the deep thought and feeling of such an hour would surely bring. So satisfied was Mr. Lincoln himself with this and the other portraits upon this canvas, and so deeply did he feel the national import and future interest of the occasion, that it was his own earnest wish that this work should eventually become the property of the nation, as we are proposing at this time.

I have said that the original paper of the Proclamation passed from Mr. Lincoln's hands to mine; but some months—a good many—later, it passed from my custody to the patriotic fair at Chicago, to be sold for the benefit of our wounded soldiers. Bought at a high price and presented to the Chicago Historical Society, it perished amid the pitiless devastation of the great fire, as this picture itself may very probably perish if left to the uncertain protection of private ownership. The paper itself is gone, and so are five of the eight men who met that day to listen to its first reading. Chase, Welles, and Blair yet remain for a time, but Lincoln, Stanton, Seward, Bates and Smith have passed away from among the generation for which they worked so unselfishly and so well. No reproduction of this picture, no rival work, no similar pictorial trophy of the time and the event is therefore possible. The painting is, and must forever be, unique and unrivaled, for it is the truth itself concerning the men whom it represents and the mighty deed they did.

As to the mere price, when the city of New York has a full-length portrait of each succeeding governor of the state painted for the Governor's Room at the City Hall, she pays $5,000, and no first-class artist would do the work for less, even for a private customer. Here are eight full-length figures, or $40,000 worth, and we must bear in mind that this picture was painted at no ordinary cost and outlay by this artist in the beginning, while he has devoted much valuable time to it through all the years that have elapsed since then, till even his own critical and jealous judgment told him the work was done. If thus he now asks an appropriation of but $25,000, it will appear that he is hardly seeking what economy itself could call excessive compensation. He will be paid for his time, his cash outlay, in moderate measure; but there are other elements of value in the picture which he cannot measure in coin, and of which he adds no estimate. I have tried briefly to set them forth.

Permit me, in conclusion, gentlemen, to ask your consideration of one question. Not undervaluing any other embellishment of the Capitol, before what painting or sculpture within these walls, if this shall thus be here, will the people of the next and of all succeeding generations linger with most of genuine interest and with the deepest throbs of patriotic feeling? For this is, after all, the consideration which should govern your present action. Will not black and white alike, the gray-headed and the young together, turn from fanciful, from legendary, from doubtful representations, to stand before this canvas and say, "Here, at least, is truth; thus it actually was, for this was painted on the spot and is a reality"? Imagine some gray-haired veteran leaning on his cane and telling his stalwart sons, "They tell me all the others are good, and no doubt they are, but that's Stanton. I saw him, one day, when I took a dispatch to the War Department. I've seen Seward and Chase, and perhaps some of the rest, but that man there, with the paper in his hand, that's Lincoln. You ought to have seen the boys in our camp cry the day we heard he was assassinated. Congress did the right thing, they did, when they bought that there picture. There isn't another one like it in all the world."

Chapter Notes

Chapter 1

1. In a letter from Homer, N.Y., dated October 3rd, 1866, Carpenter informed the Reverend Dr. Leonard Bacon, a prominent preacher in the anti-slavery movement, that he had "been staying in the country with my family for several weeks." (See Williston Walker source on Bacon.) Carpenter was about to paint Bacon's portrait at his studio in New York City. Carpenter's diary indicates that the exhibition in Homer opened on Saturday evening, September 29, 1866, copy transcribed by Carpenter's grandson, Emerson Ives, in Cortland County Historical Society, Cortland, NY. Anna Moore Knapp, a Carpenter descendant, wrote a biographical piece in *Yesteryears* (June, 1961) which states the painting was "finished in Barber's Hall in Homer" and "displayed there" (8).

2. The opera house on the third floor is believed to be the likeliest place in Barber's Hall (now known as the Barber Block) for an exhibition of a huge canvas for "a couple of days" attended by "fellow-townsmen of the painter" and people from "miles around." (See Frederic B. Perkins, *The Picture and the Men: Being Biographical Sketches of President Lincoln and His Cabinet (1867)*. New York: A.J. Johnson, 1867, 48). After the proprietor, Jedediah Barber, died in 1876, it was also known as the Keator Opera House. Today, the red brick building is in Homer's Historic District, 1–5 Main Street, and the opera house is in need of restoration.

3. Harold Holzer, Gabor S. Boritt, and Mark E. Neely, Jr. "Francis Bicknell Carpenter (1830–1900): Painter of Abraham Lincoln and His Circle," in *The American Art Journal*. Spring, 1984, 75.

4. Carpenter's diary entry for September 29, 1866 (transcribed by Ives) has the tea at Jonah Stone's. Mary Bartlett Cowdrey's notes have the tea hosted by "Mrs. Vernon Stone." Mary Bartlett Cowdrey's notes are in the Cortland County Historical Society, Cortland, NY, a few miles from Homer. Cowdrey, an art historian, archivist, and curator residing in Passaic, NJ, labored for years, starting in the 1930s, to research Carpenter and to catalogue his paintings. She abandoned the project and donated her extensive collection of research materials to the Society in 1953. Succeeding references to her collection will simply use the citation "Cowdrey notes," to not confuse it with the Mary Bartlett Cowdrey papers, Special Collections, University of Delaware Library, Newark, Delaware. The "Cowdrey Papers" are comprised of nine linear feet (nine boxes) of research material on 1,600 American artists of the eighteenth through early twentieth century. See *Who's Who in American Art*. New York & London: R.R. Bowker Company, 1966, 90.

5. Knapp, 11; Carpenter diary entries for September 15 and October 3, 1866, transcribed by Ives.

6. See memoirs of William Osborn Stoddard as edited and annotated by Harold Holzer in *Lincoln's White House Secretary: The Adventurous Life of William O. Stoddard* with commentary by Eleanor Stoddard, Stoddard's granddaughter. Carbondale: Southern Illinois University Press, 2007, 63. Further citation from this source will use the abbreviation Stoddard, II, to distinguish it from the memoirs compiled by Stoddard's son, William O. Stoddard, Jr., and published in 1955. Reference to this earlier publication will use the abbreviation Stoddard, I. A third edition of memoirs edited by historian Michael Burlingame (2000) will be abbreviated as Stoddard, III.

7. Today, a blue and gold New York State

historical marker on Route 11, north of the village of Homer, indicates the site.
 8. Knapp, 7.
 9. This is the birth date cited by the DAB, 60. The birth site is No. 5 Albany Street today. A blue and gold New York State historical marker was placed at the curb on the anniversary of Stoddard's birth in 2009.
 10. Stoddard, II, 31.
 11. Ibid., 29.
 12. Catherine Stoddard Gibson (Stoddard's sister Kate), *Recollections of Kate Stoddard Gibson*, unpublished manuscript, c.1900, 11, provided by her granddaughter, Margaret Tessler, of Albuquerque, NM, June, 2010.
 13. Ibid., 33.
 14. The Charter of the Cortland (later Homer) Academy, dated February 2, 1819, is owned by the Homer Central School District; Stoddard, II, 18–19; the history of the chartering of the Academy is described in Herbert Barber Howe's biography of *Jedediah Barber*, New York: Columbia University Press, 1939, 98–99. This last source will henceforth be referred to as Howe, I, to distinguish it from Howe, II, Howe's biography of Paris Barber, *Paris Lived in Homer* (Cortland, NY: Cortland County Historical Society, 1968). Howe's two biographies were researched, in part, from a collection of hundreds of Barber and Schermerhorn family letters owned in 1939 by Mrs. Katharine Oliver Stanley-Brown of Washington, D.C. These provide valuable insight into life in mid-nineteenth century Homer.
 15. Stoddard, II, 18–20, 22, 66.
 16. Ibid., 33–34; Gibson, 1.
 17. Stoddard, II., 25; Gibson, 5.
 18. Stoddard, II., 29.
 19. Gibson, 9.
 20. Stoddard, II, 31, 51–56, 375; Bertha Eveleth Blodgett, *Stories of Cortland County for Boys and Girls*. First published in the *Cortland Standard*, then in book form in 1932, 248, 254.

Chapter 2

 1. Stoddard, II, 16, 114.
 2. Ibid., 38–39. For a delightful tale of a "skirmish" in 1845 between Homer and the residents of nearby McGraw, NY, over who would use "Old Brimfield" to celebrate the Fourth of July, see Blodgett, 192–193.
 3. Stoddard, II, 29–30.
 4. Ibid., 52–53; remnants of the mill are visible today near the pedestrian bridge over the river located directly in back of the Homer Town Hall.
 5. Gibson, 8.
 6. Stoddard, II., 31; Blodgett, 178; Howe, I, 72; the building still stands.
 7. Howe, I, 142–147.
 8. Stoddard, II, 32.
 9. Ibid., 36, 59–60; Stoddard, I, 27.
 10. Stoddard, II, 40, 59.
 11. Depending on the season of the year, remnants of the hillside quarry are sometimes visible today to the motorist.
 12. Stoddard, II, 56, 59.
 13. Ibid., 41.
 14. Howe, I, 97–98. Years later Adin Webb would pose for his portrait by Carpenter and the building was moved to [No. 87] South Main Street, where it presently is part of a residential structure.
 15. Howe, I, 98.
 16. Amazingly, the Charter of 1819 and the Indenture document have survived to this day; also, see Howe, I, 99.
 17. Howe, I, 102–103; Seymour B. Dunn, "The Early Academies of Cortland County," in *Cortland County Chronicles*, Vol. One. Cortland, NY: The Cortland County Historical Society, 1957, 1970, 60–61; *Catalogue of the Officers and Students of Cortland Academy* for the academic year 1858–59, J.R. Dixon Printer, Homer, NY, 1859.
 18. Howe, I, 102; "Memorial notices and addresses on the character and public services of Samuel Buell Woolworth, LL. D. Pub. under the direction of a committee of the Regents of the University of the state of New York," July 15, 1880, published under the direction of a committee of the Board of Regents by Weed, Parsons & Co., Printers, of Albany, NY, 1883. The full text is on-line at Internet Archive, http://www.archive.org/stream/memorialnoticesa00univ/memorialnoticesa00univ_djvu.txt. Accessed January 30, 2010.
 19. Howe, I, 100.
 20. Howe, II, 11, 19.
 21. Andrew D. White, *Autobiography of Andrew Dickson White*. Volume I. New York: The Century Co., 1905, 6.
 22. S.B. Woolworth to the Honorable William Jessup of Montrose, PA, April 5, 1848, indicating accommodations for his son, Samuel, and another boy had been found in Homer, in a private collection in Homer, NY. A pioneer in the causes of education and temperance in northern PA, Jessup was presiding Judge of the 11th Judicial District of PA from 1838–51. In April, 1861, at the beginning of the Civil War, he was one of the committee of three that was sent by the Governors of PA, NY & Ohio to confer with President Lincoln relative to raising 75,000 men for the Union cause.
 23. Howe, I, 103–104, 107.
 24. Ibid., 104; Blodgett, 131.
 25. Stoddard, II, 34–35.
 26. "History of Homer Academy," in *The Odyssey of 1936*, Homer Academy yearbook, 45, in the possession of Mr. David Quinlan of

Homer, who found it in a garage sale in Ithaca, NY. Upon examination, the yearbook was found to have belonged to Mrs. Doris Merrill, the author's fifth grade teacher, who first formally introduced him to the Civil War as a significant event in American history. Academy graduate, Dr. Salisbury was, also, the originator of the Salisbury steak, a lean chopped beefsteak, which he believed, along with a diet of coffee, could control the diarrhea that so miserably afflicted Civil War soldiers. The information on Amelia S. Quinton is from biographical material provided by Valerie Sherer Mathes, Ph.D., professor emerita at City College of San Francisco, CA, 2009.

27. Stoddard, II, 64–65.
28. Ibid., 65.
29. Ibid., 86.
30. Ibid., 65–66.
31. "One of the famous stories of old Cortland County" has twelve Onondagas angered by Stimson's refusal to give them more "firewater." Fearing harm, Stimson climbed a rope ladder to a loft and pulled the ladder up after him. The frenzied patrons ransacked the log tavern. Supposedly, one of them, thinking in his stupor he was leaping over a fence outside the tavern, actually jumped into a water well. The visitors departed after retrieving their water-logged friend. Stimson's tavern was on the site of the Schermerhorn "Hedges" at 90 South Main Street. Source: Blodgett, 95–96.
32. Stoddard, II, 78.
33. Gibson, 6, 7.
34. The fascinating account of the discovery of a slave singing in the basement of the Osborn residence is the first chapter of Stoddard, I, 25–27.
35. Howe, I, 142; Stoddard, II, 46–47; letter of C.G. Maybury of Winona, MN, describing Don Brown, published in the *Cortland Standard*, December 5, 1902, in the archives of the Cortland County Historical Society, Cortland, NY.
36. Ibid., 26.
37. Howe, II, 18, 68–69; Blodgett, 252–253; a New York State historical marker is at the site today.
38. Oren Cravath's name is one of seventy-eight listed as members of the Cortland County Anti-Slavery Society that organized on April 25, 1837, in Cortland Village, south of Homer. The occasion generated intense debate and bitter feelings in the County. This is known from a little notebook found among the effects of Dr. Caleb Green of Homer, containing the minutes of the Society and comments recorded by its secretary, Simeon S. Bradford. The contents were published as "The Anti-Slavery Society of Cortland County" by Simeon Bradford in *Cortland County Chronicles*, Vol. 2, of the Cortland County Historical Society, Cortland, NY, 1958, 240–246. Dr. Caleb Green was one of the Academy Trustees who had his portrait painted by the young Francis B. Carpenter in the 1840s. He was also a medical mentor to Dr. Stephen Smith, a graduate of the Academy and physician in NYC to Francis Carpenter.

Chapter 3

1. Francis Carpenter's article "The Old Schoolhouse" is excerpted in Benjamin Wisner Bacon, *Theodore Thornton Munger: New England Minister*. New Haven: Yale University Press, 1913, 22–23.
2. This nascent moment in Carpenter's career is described on page 8 of Frederic B. Perkins' book that must have the longest subtitle in the world, *The Picture and the Men: Being Biographical Sketches of President Lincoln and His Cabinet; Together with an Account of the Life of the Celebrated Artist, F.B. Carpenter, Author of the Great National Painting, The First Reading of the Emancipation Proclamation Before the Cabinet by President Lincoln; Including Also an Account of the Picture; an Account of the Crisis Which Produced It; and an Appendix Containing the Great Proclamation and the Supplementary Proclamation of January 1, 1863; Together with a Portrait of the Artist, and a Key to the Picture*. New York: A.J. Johnson, 1867.
3. Transcription of entry in Carpenter's diary, Sunday, June 22, 1851, in Cowdrey notes.
4. Perkins, 8, probably found by him in *American Phrenological Journal*, September, 1856.
5. Ibid., 9.
6. Ibid.
7. Ibid., 9–10.
8. Ibid., 10–11; size of the portrait given in Cowdrey notes.
9. Ibid., 11.

Chapter 4

1. Howe, I, 67–68.
2. Ibid., 71–76, 137–141. The edifice is a privately owned home today at No. 15 Main Street.
3. Letter from Carpenter to a childhood friend, Coleman Hitchcock, August 2, 1894. Published in the *Homer Republican* newspaper, August 6, 1908, 4.
4. Howe, I, 77–78.
5. Howe, II, 57.
6. Ibid., 1, 16–17, 26–29.
7. Ibid., 25.
8. Ibid., 20–23.
9. Ibid., 26–30.
10. Ibid., 32.
11. Ibid., 30–34.
12. Ibid., 54.

13. Ibid., 57.
14. Ibid., 15, 17.
15. Ibid., 57.
16. Ibid., 30.
17. Perkins, 11.

Chapter 5

1. White, 8.
2. Stoddard, II, 66–67, 70; Gibson, 6–7.
3. Stoddard, II, 76–77.
4. Ibid., 118–119.
5. Ibid., 81, 93, 122.
6. Ibid., 67, 75.
7. Ibid., 79–80.
8. Ibid., 80; Gibson, 13.
9. Stoddard, II, 93.
10. Ibid., 113–114.
11. Ibid., 79.
12. White, 13.
13. Stoddard, II, 85.
14. Ibid., 84–85.
15. Ibid., 90, 375.
16. Ibid., 105–106; White, 61–62.
17. Stoddard, II, 106–108.
18. Ibid., 109–110.
19. Ibid., 110.
20. Ibid., 110–111.
21. Ibid., 108. Today, a monument to "the Jerry Rescue," in sculpture, stands in Clinton Square in the heart of the city of Syracuse.
22. Ibid., 104.
23. Ibid., 117.
24. Ibid.; Gibson, 9.
25. Gibson, 11.
26. Gibson, 21–22; Stoddard, II., 131, 134.
27. Stoddard, II, 132.
28. Ibid., 137.
29. Ibid., 122, 138.
30. Ibid., 138–139.

Chapter 6

1. Elliot's portrait of Thayer now hangs in the Skaneateles Public Library, Skaneateles, NY. A salt print of a portrait of Thayer by Elliot is now owned by the Phillips Free Library of Homer, NY, along with an oil portrait Thayer did in 1843 of Carpenter's fifty year old uncle, Eli Sharpe Carpenter. The artist's obituary appeared in *The New York Times*, November 26, 1880.
2. George Knapp Collins Biography of Sanford Thayer in *History Town of Spafford*, 1902, published by Onondaga Historical Association, Syracuse, NY, Dehler Press, 1917, 108–109.
3. Perkins, 11–12; Sanford Thayer's obituary in *American Art Review*, 1881, 169, mentions that he was Carpenter's teacher.

4. Interview with art educator, David Quinlan, of Homer, who had discussions with Westlake Conservators of Skaneateles, NY, July 29, 2010.
5. Ibid.
6. Perkins, 12.
7. It is the brick portion of the Homer Laundry adjacent to the Homer Town Hall today.
8. Howe, II, 58.
9. Howe, I, 154.
10. The book was first published in 1848. The 1860 edition published in New York by Orange Judd & Co. shows Carpenter's sheep drawings on page 131 and 134.
11. Knapp, 9.
12. Howe, I, 106.
13. Howe, II, 59.
14. Howe, I, n. 8, 103.
15. Article in *New York Evening Express*, January 26, 1877, cited in Cowdrey notes.
16. Howe, II, 59; Asaph Carpenter's letter to the editor upon his 50th wedding anniversary, *Cortland County Republican* of Homer, NY, October 6, 1876, cited in Cowdrey notes.
17. Howe, I, 106; Howe, II, 18–20; Keep's letter to Francis B. Carpenter, May 7, 1865, refers to Carpenter's parents as his "friends" and "supporters" "while in Homer," cited in Cowdrey notes.
18. Howe, I, 101.
19. See Nat Brandt, *The Town That Started the Civil War*. Syracuse, NY: Syracuse University Press, 1990.
20. Benjamin Wisner Bacon. *Theodore Thornton Munger: New England Minister.* New Haven: Yale University Press, 1913, 17, 18.
21. David Quinlan, artist, art educator, and resident of Homer, provided researched material on Carpenter paintings now located in Homer, NY.
22. Ibid.
23. Cowdrey notes.
24. Carpenter diary entries for August 18–September 8, 1863, same summer Carpenter hiked up on Mt. Toppin (1841 ft. above sea level), across the valley from the Carpenter homestead, and attended a party at the Schermerhorns on South Main Street, Homer. Transcribed copy by Carpenter's grandson, Emerson Ives, in Cortland County Historical Society, Cortland, NY.
25. Howe, I 99, 109–110.
26. *Minutes of the Trustees of the Academy*, which are also cited in Howe, I, 102.
27. Materials in the archives of the Town of Homer and of the Cortland County Historical Society. A Homer School time capsule unearthed in 2009 contained an article from the January 18, 1893, issue of *The Cortland Standard and Cortland Daily Journal* that made specific

reference to Carpenter's large oil portraits "from nearly fifty years ago" being "among the things saved [during the school fire] that are valued very highly...."

Chapter 7

1. Howe, I, 106; Carpenter and the other 345 students are listed in the *Catalogue of Cortland Academy* for the year ending July 7, 1847, part of the Herbert Barber Howe collection cited in Cowdrey notes.
2. Howe, II, 58.
3. Interview on art history with David Quinlan of Homer, February 20, 2010.
4. Howe, II, 59.
5. Cowdrey notes.
6. Howe, II., 59–60.
7. Cowdrey notes.
8. Perkins, 12–13.
9. Ibid.; Transcription of Carpenter diary entry for May, 1, 1851, in Cowdrey notes.
10. Knapp, 7; Carpenter's mother-in-law was Frances Rollo, according to Cowdrey notes.
11. Cowdrey notes.
12. Entry in the Carpenter Diary, version transcribed by Emerson Ives, copy in Cortland County Historical Society, Cortland, NY.
13. Howe, II, 74.
14. Howe, I, 118, 121–123; Howe, II, 80–82. No.5 Clinton Street is the Paris Barber residence.
15. Entry in Carpenter's diary for June 18, 1852, in Cowdrey notes.
16. Perkins, 16–17.
17. *Cortland County Whig*, August 21, 1851, cited in Cowdrey notes.
18. Perkins, 13; article in praise of the portrait in the *Cortland County Whig* of Homer, NY, June 3, 1852, cited in Cowdrey notes along with notation of portrait's dimensions.
19. Article in *Cortland County Republican*, February 7, 1876, cited in Cowdrey notes.
20. "American Women: A Selection from the National Portrait Gallery," Smithsonian Institution, on-line at http://www.npg.si.edu/cexh/nwomen/lind2.htm. Accessed 30 January 2010. The portrait was gifted to the gallery by Eleanor Morein Foster, in honor of First Lady Hillary Rodham Clinton.
21. The portrait now resides in the Bowdoin College Museum of Art, in Brunswick, Maine. The college claims the painting was done between 1854 and 1855 and came to them as a gift in 1936. During conservation work done in 1988, it was decided that the painting at some point had been removed from its original stretcher, cut, and re-stretched onto a smaller stretcher. It is currently 27" high by 22 1/16" wide, in a plastered, gilt frame, arched at the top. It is inscribed in verso on the canvas at the lower right: "President, Franklin Pierce painted by F.B. Carpenter, 1854–5. At the upper edge: "C.B. '5 37." Stenciled at the upper edge: "Prepared by Charles Roberson/51, Longacre, London."
22. Millard Fillmore to D.A. Boku [?]. Letter from Washington to New York, Oct. 15th, 1852, in collection of Carpenter letters archived at Hildene, The [Robert] Lincoln Family Home, Manchester, Vermont.
23. Perkins, 13–14; Knapp, 11.
24. Letter to a U.S. Senator (?), dated February 2, 1855, in collection of Carpenter letters archived at Hildene, The [Robert] Lincoln Family Home, Manchester, Vermont.
25. Perkins, 15–16.
26. F.B. Carpenter to "My Dear Sir" [name unknown] from NY, Nov. 8th 1853, owned by David Quinlan of Homer, NY.
27. Entry in Carpenter's diary for February 6, 1855, in Cowdrey notes.
28. William Sumner's severe caning in 1856 by South Carolina's Representative Preston Brooks on the floor of the United States Senate (Sumner-Brooks affair) was an event that helped escalate the sectional tensions that led to civil strife.
29. Article in the *New York Press*, July 15, 1890?, in Cowdrey notes, where Cowdrey failed to type in the fourth digit for the year.
30. Ibid., 14.
31. "Francis Bicknell Carpenter" biography, in *Cortland County Republican*, Homer, NY, Thursday, Sept. 30, 1858, 1–2.
32. References to the Carey sisters, whose salon was a gathering place for New York's literati, are sprinkled all through Carpenter's diary, transcribed by Ives.
33. Entries in Carpenter's diary for September 23, 1851, and October 17, 1851, in Cowdrey notes.
34. "Photo-Mural of Village Placed on Wall of Lobby of Homer National Bank," *Cortland Standard*, July 25, 1946.
35. The Carpenter Homestead was listed for sale by the William G. Crandall Agency of Homer in the *Homer Republican*, December 30, 1915, with an asking price of $12,750, transcribed by Betty Bonawitz as part of research done on W.G. Crandall for James Yaman, 2007. Entry in Carpenter Diary, August 7, 1857, as transcribed by Ives, indicates that Carpenter "helped pitch hay."
36. Carpenter diary entries for August 2 and August 4, 1865; October 4, 1867; July 27, 1868; August 5, 1876, transcribed by Ives.
37. Carpenter diary entry for October 4, 1867, transcribed by Ives.
38. "Francis B. Carpenter arrival for summer vacation," reported in *Cortland Standard*, August 16, 1876, which also claimed "Frank gets a

hearty shake from every man he meets," cited in Cowdrey notes. The notes also refer to the diary entry for August 10, 1855, in which Carpenter marvels at the time the train made from New York to Homer: "...can hardly realize I came through so quickly."

39. "Keator Opera House," a history brochure by PK Publishing of Homer, NY, accessed at Homer History Center, February 6, 2010.

40. His portrait and others by Carpenter are now owned by the Cortland County Historical Society, Cortland, NY.

41. Knapp, 10–13; Cowdrey notes. Martius (or Martin) Lynde, who attended the one-room school in Homer with Carpenter, sat, as did other Lynde family members, for portraiture by Carpenter in 1858.

42. Carpenter diary entry for Wed., October 7, 1868, which he proclaimed "a great day for Ithaca." *Cortland County Democrat*, January 28, 1870, a reprint of an article about the commissioning that was published in the Syracuse *Journal*, January, 1870.

43. Knapp, 12.

44. Letter to Cowdrey dated December 2, 1937, in Cowdrey notes.

45. Reprint of article in Ithaca *Journal* of September, 1876, in *Cortland County Republican*, Homer, September 8, 1876, cited in Cowdrey notes.

46. Howe, II, 92. Carpenter's studio was in different locations in New York City at different times. According to a letter to an unknown friend, dated November 8, 1853, he had just moved into a new studio at 359 Broadway "directly over Thompsons Ice Cream Saloon — one of the *two* great resorts here...." Letter is owned by Mr. David Quinlan, Homer, NY.

47. New York *Evening Express*, October 26, 1858, 1, quoted in Cowdrey notes.

48. Ibid.

49. Sitting was in 1863, Cowdrey notes.

50. Reported by New York *Evening Express*, January 26, 1877, cited in Cowdrey notes.

51. *Cortland County Democrat*, August 18, 1876, cited in Cowdrey notes.

52. General Sherman's letter to Carpenter, July 13, 1885, and Whittier's letter to Carpenter, June 20, 1867 (in Ives Collection), as cited in Cowdrey notes.

53. Interview with David Quinlan, art educator, Homer, NY, January 31, 2010; diary entry from June 24, 1851, in Cowdrey notes.

54. Ibid.

Chapter 8

1. Stoddard, II, 138–178.
2. Ibid., 179.
3. Ibid., 165.
4. Ibid., 171–172.
5. Ibid., 161–162.
6. Ibid., 162.
7. Ibid., 175–178.
8. Ibid., 181–182, 188.
9. Ibid., 183, 197, 205.
10. Ibid., 196; DAB, 60.
11. Ibid., 195.
12. Gibson, 22.
13. Stoddard, II, 184.
14. Ibid., 188.
15. Ibid., 190.

Chapter 9

1. Stoddard, III, ix.
2. Stoddard, II, 198–199, 180–181.
3. Ibid., 199.
4. William E. Doster, *Lincoln and Episodes of the Civil War* (New York and London: G.P. Putnam's Sons, 1915), 15, cited in Doris Kearns Goodwin, *Team of Rivals: The Political Genius of Abraham Lincoln.* New York: Simon & Schuster, 2005, 6.
5. Stoddard, II, 206.
6. Ibid.
7. Goodwin, 8.
8. Arthur Bryant, *The American Ideal.* Freeport, NY: Books for Libraries Press, 1969, 63.
9. Stoddard, II, 207, n. 2 on 376–377.
10. Goodwin, 14–15, 191–192.
11. Francis B. Carpenter, "A Day with Governor Seward at Auburn," handwritten manuscript, no date [prob. July 1870 according to Peter Wisbey, Seward House Executive Director, February 2004]. Seward Papers. Rochester, NY: University of Rochester.
12. Goodwin, 231–232; Harold Holzer, *Lincoln President-Elect: Abraham Lincoln and the Great Secession Winter 1860–1861.* New York: Simon & Schuster, 2008, 16–17.
13. This may have been in response to advice from his political ally and friend, Thurlow Weed, who once lived near Homer, in Virgil, New York. Goodwin, 212.
14. Goodwin, 212, 224.
15. Stoddard, II, 208, n.5 on 383.
16. Ibid., n. 2 to chap. 27 on 382.
17. Ibid., 208–210.
18. Stoddard, III, ix–x, n. 16 on 204.
19. "William O. Stoddard Dies; Was Aid of Lincoln," in New York *Times*, August 30, 1925, transcribed copy in archives of Phillips Free Library, Homer, NY.
20. Ibid., n.1 to chap. 27 on 382.
21. DAB, 60.

Chapter 10

1. Stoddard, II, 207.
2. Ibid., 210.

3. Howe, II, 89–90.
4. Ibid., 93.
5. Goodwin, 239–249.
6. Ibid., 250–251.
7. Howe, II, 93.
8. Carpenter Diary, transcribed by Ives.
9. Goodwin, 276–278.
10. Goodwin 277; Holzer, 42.
11. Holzer, 11–12.
12. Stoddard, II, 210.
13. Ibid., 211–212.
14. Abraham Lincoln Papers, on-line through the Library of Congress.
15. Stoddard, II, 212–213.
16. Ibid., 213.
17. For a detailed description of the nation's capital in the Civil War era, see Margaret Leach, *Reveille in Washington*. New York and London: Harper & Brothers, 1941, 5–13.

Chapter 11

1. Stoddard, II, 214.
2. Cited by Holzer, 194.
3. See Holzer (2008) and, in particular, 295–305.
4. Ina Hurlbut Bird, "Eli DeVoe, Scott Road Native, Was Destined to Serve Lincoln at Crucial Time in History," *Homer Post*, February 12, 1932. Today, a New York State historical marker is on the DeVoe birth site, near the Atwater Cemetery on Route 41.
5. For a well-researched book on the subject, see Michael J. Kline, *The Baltimore Plot: The First Conspiracy to Assassinate Abraham Lincoln*. Yardley, PA: Westholme Publishing, 2008.
6. Ibid.; Charles Phillips and Alan Axelrod with Kurt Kemper, "Matsell, George," in *Cops, Crooks, and Criminologists: An International Biographical Dictionary of Law Enforcement*, illustrated edition. New York: Facts on File, Inc., 1996, 101, 102.
7. Michael E.J. Bosak, "The Establishment of the 'Honor Legion,'" c. 2006, on NYPD Police Memorial website, 2010, accessed July 28, 2010.
8. See Michigan Historical Reprint Series, *K.G.C.: An authentic exposition of the origin, objects, and secret work of the organization known as the Knights of the Golden Circle*. First published in February 1862. Paperback reprint published Ann Arbor, Michigan: Scholarly Publishing Office, University of Michigan Library, December 20, 2005.
9. See Kline; David Quinlan provided a transcription of DeVoe's obituary in *The Newark Daily Journal* of Newark, NJ, January 30, 1874.
10. Quinlan notes in Town of Homer archives; Holzer, 377–392; Kline, 189–200.

11. See Kline account.
12. Holzer, 393.
13. See Bird.
14. Holzer, 392–396.
15. Quinlan materials.
16. Kline, 314–317.
17. Bird.
18. Ibid.; as of this date no photographic image or painting of DeVoe has been located.
19. Ibid.; Thomas F. DeVoe (1811–18920, *Genealogy of the DeVeaux Family*, New York: New York Historical Society, 1885, digitized copy provided by the Boston Public Library.
20. "A Noted Detective's Funeral: One of the Men who Frustrated the Plot to Kill Lincoln in Baltimore," in *The Newark Daily Journal*, Friday, January 30, 1874, transcribed copy by David Quinlan of Homer, NY. Today the site of the DeVoe estate is only yards from the Summit Historical Society's headquarters and historical house museum in Summit, NJ.

Chapter 12

1. Holzer, 397–403.
2. Kline, 328, 333.
3. Stoddard, II, 215.
4. See Holzer for entire speech, 463–475. *The Cortland Gazette*, Charles P. Cole, editor, Thursday, March 7, 1861, 2, col. 3 and 4, part of collection of David Quinlan, Homer, NY.
5. Stoddard, II, 6, 216, 234, 385; John Hay would become an outstanding future Secretary of State (1898–1905), being best remembered for the "Open Door" policy regarding China (1899–1900) and more than fifty diplomatic treaties.
6. Goodwin, 345.
7. Blodgett reports incorrectly that the store was owned by Dr. T.C. Pomeroy, 213.
8. Howe, II, 94, 98.
9. The date was April 12, 1861, according to Stoddard, II, 216, 218–222.
10. Stoddard, II, 222–224; Goodwin, 348.
12. "Memorandum of events, 19 April 1861," in *With Lincoln in the White House: Letters, Memoranda, and Other Writings of John G. Nicolay: 1861–1865*, ed. Michael Burlingame. Carbondale: Southern Illinois University Press, 2000, 34.
13. Letter from Washington to Pittsfield, IL, dated 19 April 1861, in Ibid.
14. Stoddard, II, 225.
15. Ibid., 226–227.
16. Stoddard, I, 85.
17. Stoddard, II, 230–231; n. 12 and 13 on 386.
18. The letter to Kitty, along with the account of the medallion, is in Daniel Mark Epstein, *Lincoln's Men: The President and his Pri-*

vate Secretaries. New York: HarperCollins, 2009, 62 & 64.

19. For information on NY 44th Regiment, see "History of Herkimer County, New York." New York: F.W. Beers & Co., 1879. Available on-line at http://herkimer.nygenweb.net/regiments/ellsworth.html.

20. Gibson, 17.

Chapter 13

1. Gibson, 16.
2. Stoddard, II, 232–233. Surely, Stoddard would have a good chuckle at the thoughts of all the future autograph collectors running around claiming to possess Lincoln's autograph when it is really in Stoddard's hand.
3. Ibid., 234–235.
4. John G. Nicolay and John Hay, *Abraham Lincoln: A History*, IV. New York: Century Company, 1886–90, 68–69.
5. Ibid., 69.
6. Comments to Wilson, in *Abraham Lincoln: The Observations of John G. Nicolay and John Hay*, ed. Michael Burlingame. Carbondale: Southern Illinois University Press, 2007, 34.
6. William O. Stoddard, "Face to Face with Lincoln," ed William O. Stoddard, Jr., *Atlantic Monthly*, March 1925, 333. For a thoroughly engaging compilation of the correspondence received by Lincoln at the White House, see Harold Holzer, *Dear Mr. Lincoln: Letters to the President*. New York: Addison-Wesley Publishing Company, 1993, 1995.
7. Mandy Brooke's letter to Mr. Lincoln in 1863 and Kate Stoddard's letter of 1865 are both in the back pages of Gibson, *Recollections*.
8. Stoddard, II., 243–246; Carpenter, *Six Months at the White House*, 281–282.
9. Stoddard, II, 248–250.
10. Ibid., 287.
11. Joshua Wolf Schenk, *Lincoln's Melancholy: How Depression Challenged a President and Fueled His Greatness*. New York: Houghton Mifflin, 2005, 102.
12. Stoddard, II, 317.
13. John Hay to John Nicolay, April 5, 1862, in Tyler Dennett, ed., *Lincoln and the Civil War in the Diaries and Letters of John Hay* (New York: Dodd, Mead, 1939), 40, cited in Stoddard, II, n. 9 on 388.
14. See Michael Burlingame's comments in Stoddard, III, xi–xii.
15. Stoddard, II, 260–262.
16. Ibid., 252.
17. Stoddard, III, 99.
18. Ibid., 98–99.
19. Stoddard, II, 257.
20. Stoddard, III, 154.
21. Recollection of Mrs. John Schermerhorn Fisher of Homer in "Death of Wm. O. Stoddard," *Cortland Standard*, August 31, 1925, transcribed copy in archives of Phillips Free Library, Homer, NY; Blodgett, 182.
22. Stoddard, II, 239–240, 297.
23. Ibid., 252.
24. Gibson, 18.
25. Stoddard, II, 239, n. 2 on 387.
26. Ibid., 273.
27. Ibid., 286, 317.
28. Ibid., 299.
29. Ibid., 241.
30. Ibid., 259–260.
31. Ibid., 307–309.
32. Ibid., 306.
33. Gibson, letter written c. 1865, included in her *Recollections*.

Chapter 14

1. Stoddard, II, 291. A copy of the document written "by a secretary" in the rare books collection at Cornell University may be in Stoddard's hand. From examining the handwriting and noting Stoddard's distinctive "T," the author is of the opinion that it is.
2. Goodwin, 389–396.
3. Cited in F.B. Carpenter, *Six Months at the White House with Abraham Lincoln: The Story of a Picture*. New York: Hurd and Houghton, 1866, 47. Any succeeding references to this source will simply be noted as Carpenter to distinguish it from other sources attributed to him.
4. Cited by Edward Magdol, *Owen Lovejoy: Abolitionist in Congress*, New Brunswick, N.J.: Rutgers University Press, 1967, 342. In a letter dated May 18, 1865, Carpenter informed Lovejoy's widow that Lincoln told him: "'Lovejoy was the *best* friend I had in Congress." The letter, transcribed by Pam Lange, is in the Lovejoy Papers collection of the Lovejoy Homestead, Bureau County Historical Society, Princeton, Illinois.
5. *Diary of Gideon Welles*, Volume I, Boston, New York: Houghton Mifflin Company, 1911, 70–71.
6. August 22, 1862, in Perkins, 24–25.
7. Ibid.
8. Ibid.
9. Ibid., 38.
10. Perkins, 22.
11. Ibid., 38; see Matthew Pinsker, *Lincoln's Sanctuary: Abraham Lincoln and the Soldiers' Home*. New York: Oxford University Press, 2003.
12. Perkins, 26.
13. Blodgett, 250–251.
14. Leach, 289.
15. Goodwin, 481.
16. Perkins, 39.
17. Welles, 143.

18. Carpenter, 89–90.
19. *Lincoln's Sword: The Presidency and the Power of Words.* New York: Random House, Inc., 2006, 142.
20. Stoddard, I, 170.
21. Howe, I, 142, n.17 on 166.

Chapter 15

1. Carpenter, 10–11.
2. Ibid., 12; Carpenter diary entry for Sunday, November 29, 1863, transcribed by Ives.
3. Ibid.
4. Carpenter, 12–13.
5. Perkins, 32.
6. Ibid., 33; Carpenter, 12–14; Carpenter diary entry for December 14, 1863, transcribed by Ives.
7. Cowdrey notes.
8. Francis B. Carpenter to Owen Lovejoy, January 5, 1864, location of original unknown, transcript in the Lincoln Museum collection, Fort Wayne, Indiana, cited by Harold Holzer in his introduction to the edition of Carpenter's memoirs published in 2008 by the White House Historical Association, 7 (henceforth referred to in citations as Carpenter, II); Perkins, 34.
9. Carpenter, 15.
10. Francis B. Carpenter to Theodore Thornton Munger. Letter dated February 22, 1864. Munger Papers, Yale University Library, New Haven, CT.
11. Carpenter, 15–16; Perkins, 34–35; entry in Carpenter diary for the date, transcribed by Ives.
12. Letter from Washington to 653 Broadway, New York, in collection of Carpenter letters archived in Hildene, The [Robert] Lincoln Family Home, Manchester, Vermont; Carpenter, II, 7. This letter was apparently received after Carpenter, in his impatience, had sent a letter of the same date to Lovejoy reminding him that all he needed of the President was "simply a room at the White House ... and a very few sittings" for a painting he had been assured by others would "be immensely popular." The letter, transcribed by Pam Lange, is in the Lovejoy Papers collection of the Lovejoy Homestead, Bureau County Historical Society, Princeton, Illinois.
13. Perkins, 35.
14. Davis represented Cortland and Onondaga Counties [March 4, 1863–March 3, 1867] according to Carpenter diary entry for Monday, Feb. 8, 1864, transcribed by Ives.
15. Keep's commemorative address of the martyrdom of the Rev. E.P. Lovejoy is included in Herbert B. Howe's bound, typewritten volume of source materials on the minister he compiled in 1938 and archived in Phillip's Free Library, Homer, NY.
16. In a letter to the Lovejoy Monument Association, Lincoln wrote of Owen Lovejoy as "my most generous friend," cited in Carpenter, 160.
17. Letter from F.B. Carpenter to Mrs. Owen Lovejoy, dated August 11, 1867, transcribed by Pam Lange, from the Lovejoy Papers collection of the Lovejoy Homestead, Bureau County Historical Society, Princeton, Illinois, where the portrait now resides. Letter to Carpenter from Princeton, Illinois, dated March 28, 1868, in collection of Carpenter letters archived at Hildene, The [Robert] Lincoln Family Home, Manchester, Vermont.
18. Stoddard, II, 63.
19. 18.
20. Ibid., 18–19.
21. Ibid., 19.
22. See Stoddard's opening remarks to the Joint Committee of the Library, February 24, 1873, in which he stated "it was my pleasant duty to introduce the artist to President Lincoln for the express purpose of this undertaking [of portraiture]." This is cited in Stoddard, I, 9.
23. Carpenter, 19–20.
24. Ibid., 148–149.
25. Ibid., 20.
26. Ibid., 20–24.
27. Ibid., 24.

Chapter 16

1. Contrary to the implication of his title for his book, *Six Months at the White House*, Carpenter did not reside at the White House while working on his artistic project. See footnote 353.
2. Carpenter, 30.
3. Perkins, 40–41.
4. Carpenter diary entries for March 25 and 26, 1864, transcribed by Ives. The first poem, said to be Lincoln's favorite because he recited it so often, is by William Knox. The second is by Oliver Wendell Holmes.
5. Carpenter, 46–47.
6. Carpenter, 35–36.
7. Harold Holzer, *Lincoln Seen & Heard*. Lawrence, Kansas: University Press of Kansas, 2000, 28. Henceforth, this book by Holzer will be referred to in abbreviated form as Holzer, HS&D, to distinguish it from other sources authored by Holzer.
8. Stefan Lorant, *Lincoln: A Picture Story of His Life*. Revised and enlarged edition. New York: Bonanza Books, 1975, 163.
9. Harold Holzer, Gabor S. Boritt, and Mark E. Neely, Jr., *The Lincoln Image: Abraham Lincoln and the Popular Print*. Urbana and Chicago: University of Illinois Press, 1984, 2001, 174–175.

10. This account of Carpenter's intercession for the Mounts is documented in the following letters: Wm. Shepard Mount from the U.S. Military Prison, Alton, Illinois, to "My Dear Father," dated January 1864 (copy also sent to Wm. Hoffman, Commissary General of Prisons); S[hepard] A[lonzo] Mount to "Dear Carpenter," dated March 4, 1864; S.A. Mount to "My Dear Friend Carpenter," dated March 28, 1864. These are part of the collection of Carpenter letters at Hildene, The [Robert] Lincoln Family Home, Manchester, Vermont.
11. Issue of March 26, 1864, vol. xviii, no. 443, col. 2b, cited in Cowdrey notes.
12. Perkins, 40.
13. April 30, 1864, at the White House, in Daniel Mark Epstein, *Lincoln's Men: The President and His Private Secretaries*. New York: HarperCollins, 2009, 202.
14. Carpenter, 25.
15. Holzer, LS&H, 13–15.
16. Carpenter, 25.
17. F.B. Carpenter to "my dear friend Mrs. J.H. Munger Homer, N.Y. Nov. 5th, 1872" on paper he claimed Lincoln said "was some of the very paper." In archives of Cortland County Historical Society, Cortland, NY.
18. Carpenter, 25.
19. Ibid., 24–26.
20. Excerpt from a sermon delivered in Homer in 1832, cited in Howe, II, 18–19.
21. To understand the religious underpinnings of the Abolition movement, see David S. Reynolds, *John Brown, Abolitionist: The Man Who Killed Slavery, Sparked the Civil War, and Seeded Civil Rights*. New York: Random House, 2005.
22. Carpenter Diary, transcribed by Ives.
23. (Miss) Bartlett Cowdrey to Miss Ella May Thornton, October 4, 1937. The letter indicates that Carpenter's need for subjects of high moral fiber explains why his subjects tended to be, in many cases, those he knew personally.

Chapter 17

1. Carpenter diary entries for May 4, May 6, and May 28, 1864, transcribed by Ives.
2. Carpenter, 152.
3. Ibid., 153; Will Irwin, "Restoring Lincoln's Study," in New York *Herald Tribune* magazine section, Sunday, February 9, 1930, 2, in collection of Carpenter letters archived at Hildene, The [Robert] Lincoln Family Home, Manchester, Vermont.
4. Perkins, 41; Holzer, LS&H, 7.
5. Carpenter, 54.
6. See Goodwin for Lincoln's dealings with Chase; Carpenter claims to have suggested to Lincoln a replacement for Chase, 84.
7. Perkins, 56–57.
8. Stoddard, II, 63, n. 2 on 397. Stoddard, as art critic, maintained that Smith "never recovered and his portrait is dead, or at least sick, to this very day" (II, 349).
9. Goodwin, 519.
10. Goodwin, 465–466.
11. Holzer et al, 75; Jealousy seeps out in S.P. Chase to F.B. Carpenter, letter from Washington, May 2, 1866, transcribed by Ives.
12. Carpenter, 72–73.
13. Ibid., 73–74.
14. Ibid., 76.
15. Ibid., 90.
16. Carpenter diary entries for Monday, July 25 and Tuesday, July 26, 1864, transcribed by Ives.
17. Interview of David Quinlan, art educator, Homer, NY, January 31, 2010.
18. See Sarah Ellen Blackwell, *A Military Genius: Life of Anna Ella Carroll of Maryland*, ("the great unrecognized member of Lincoln's cabinet"), Vol. 1. Washington, D.C.: Judd & Detweiler printers, 1891. Carroll preferred to be called "Anne." A movie, *Lost River*, came out in 2009, with Fritz Klein as Lincoln and Tami Sutton as Anne Carroll, crediting Carroll with the success of the Tennessee Plan in the western front of the war.
19. Holzer, LS&H, 7–8.
20. Ibid., 22–23.
21. Ibid., 23.
22. Perkins, 41–42.
23. Carpenter, 232–233.
24. Goodwin, 28, 49, 51, 53–54, 132, 179, 256.
25. Perkins, 42.
26. Holzer et al, 23.
27. Perkins, 42–43.
28. Ibid., 47.
29. Ibid., 48.
30. Ibid., 47.
31. Carpenter diary entry for December 31, 1864, transcribed by Ives.

Chapter 18

1. Stoddard, III, 97; Stoddard, II, 307–309, 313.
2. Stoddard, II, 311–312.
3. Ibid., 313.
4. Stoddard, I, 182–187; Stoddard, II., 314–315. Note 1 on 394–395 points out that the New York City "Draft Riots" were, aside from the Civil War itself, "the bloodiest civil disturbance in American history." See Barnet Schecter, *The Devil's Own Work: The Civil War Draft Riots and the Fight to Reconstruct America*. New York: Walker & Company, 2005.
5. Carpenter diary and letters from William, transcribed by Ives, covering July 9–11, 1863. Daniel Webster Carpenter survived the

war, having been promoted to corporal in November of 1863, according to letter from Rappahannock Station, VA, to Frank, dated Nov. 14, 1863, transcribed by Ives.
  6. Entry in Carpenter diary for that date, transcribed by Ives.
  7. Will Carpenter to Frank Carpenter from Gettysburg, PA, July 5, 1863, in diary/letters transcribed by Ives.
  8. Carpenter diary, entry for Sunday, July 12, 1863, transcribed by Ives; Stoddard, I, 184.
  9. Stoddard, William O. *The Volcano under the City: By a Volunteer Special.* New York: Fords, Howard, & Hulbert, 1887, 168.
  10. Carpenter diary, entries for July 14–17, 1863, transcribed by Ives.
  11. Ibid., entry for July 18, 1863.
  12. Howe, I, n.20, 169.
  13. Howe, II, 96–97. Howe calls Glenwood Cemetery Paris' "most lasting contribution to Homer," 96.
  14. Diary transcribed by Ives. The Carpenters returned to Homer in August to inter the remains of infant "Ellie" at Glenwood Cemetery (entry for August 15, 1863).
  15. Carpenter diary entry for August 21, 1863, transcribed by Ives.
  16. Elizabeth Baldwin, "William and Francis Carpenter—Homer Brothers Made History During Civil War Period," *Cortland Standard*, May 22, 1990, 8.
  17. Cited by Baldwin, 8.
  18. Stoddard, I, 186–187.
  19. Ibid., 316–317.
  20. Howe, II, 25, 89–92.
  21. Article appeared in issue of June 26, 1862, cited in Howe, I, 108.
  22. Stoddard, II, 317.
  23. Not all the remains were removed. In 1994, while constructing an elevator shaft at the Homer Elementary School on the Green, skeletal remains of two children from before the 1830s were discovered. Construction halted while archaeologists examined the site. The remains were ultimately removed and reburied with an internment service conducted at Glenwood Cemetery.
  24. Stoddard, II, 317.
  25. Ibid.
  26. Ibid., 321–324.
  27. Carpenter, 130.
  28. Stoddard, II, 317–319.
  29. Ibid., 325.
  30. Ibid., 8, note 22 on 371.
  31. Ibid., 8.
  32. Ibid., 339, 343.
  33. Ibid., 339.
  34. Ibid., 339–341.

Chapter 19

  1. Stoddard, II, 343–345.
  2. This letter of April 22 is among the documents in the Hay Library, Brown University, Providence, RI, cited by Epstein, 230.
  3. Entries for Saturday, April 15 and Monday, April 17, 1865, transcribed by Ives.
  4. Diary entries for April 24 and 25, 1865, transcribed by Ives. Placement of Carpenter's original study of Lincoln next to Lincoln's coffin in NYC cited by Holzer during tour given by Holzer of "Lincoln and New York," an exhibit at New-York Historical Society, New York, March 19, 2010. The exhibit contained this study on loan from the Union League Club of NYC, another original piece by Carpenter, and a copy of the print of *The First Reading of the Emancipation Proclamation.*
  5. Letter dated May 18, 1865, in Lovejoy Papers collection, in Lovejoy Homestead, Bureau County Historical Society, Princeton, IL.
  6. Perkins, 47.
  7. Carpenter, 291–292.
  8. Howe, II, 99.
  9. Holzeer, LS&H, 24.
  10. Ibid., 23.
  11. Holzer et al, 75–76.
  12. Carpenter diary entry for August 19, 1865; C.B. Thomas, "President Abraham Lincoln and His Cabinet Sits in Session in Homer." Excerpts from an account in the Los Angeles *Herald* that appeared in the *Homer Republican* of July 18, 1901, and reprinted in the *Homer Independent*, May 31, 1960, 33, which mistakenly attributed the original *Emancipation Proclamation* painting as the reason for the "material assistance" provided by the men of Homer and an out-of-town visitor.
  13. Perkins, 48; Carpenter diary entry for April 6, 1866, transcribed by Ives; "Two Great Fires, Over Half a Million Dollars Worth of Property Destroyed," *New York Times*, April 7, 1866.
  14. Cited in Holzer, LS&H, 8.
  15. Knapp, 14. Today, the Phillips Free Library of Homer has one, and the Homer Central School District owns two.
  16. Holzer, LS&H, 23–24.
  17. Abraham Lincoln Papers, Library of Congress, available on-line.
  18. Edw. Bates to F.B. Carpenter, letter of October 20, 1864, in collection of Carpenter letters archived at Hildene, The [Robert] Lincoln Family Home, Manchester, Vermont.
  19. Holzer, LS&H, 23–24.
  20. Letter to F.B. Carpenter, from Washington to New York, dated September 17, 1864, in collection of Carpenter letters archived at Hildene, The [Robert] Lincoln Family Home, Manchester, Vermont.

21. Letter to F.B. Carpenter on War Department stationery, dated May 22, 1864, in collection of Carpenter letters archived at Hildene, The [Robert] Lincoln Family Home, Manchester, Vermont.
22. This letter, owned in 1938 by Carpenter's grandson, Mr. Emerson C. Ives of White Plains, NY, is cited on page 225 in the bound typewritten documents on Keep compiled by Herbert Barber Howe and part of the collection of the Phillips Free Library, Homer, NY.
23. Holzer et al, 76–77.

Chapter 20

1. Perkins, 47–48. Carpenter's letter to the Rev. Dr. Bacon of Oct. 3rd., 1866 (cited in chap.1) gives the location of his studio in New York at that time. His studio was at different locations at different times. In 1860, according to Trow's *New York City Directory* for that year, Carpenter's studio was at 442 Broadway, as cited in Cowdrey notes.
2. Knapp, 8; Carpenter netted $55 from the Homer exhibition and $40 from fair-goers at Cortland, according to diary entries for September 29 and October 3, 1866, transcribed by Ives.
3. Ibid., 11. There is a Ritchie print bearing the name C.O. Newton in a private collection in Dryden, NY.
4. Holzer, LS&H, 23.
5. Letter from Paris, France to "My dear Carpenter," transcribed by Ives.
6. Holzer et al, 78.
7. Stoddard, II, 347–348.
8. An observation made by his granddaughter, Eleanor Stoddard, in Stoddard, II, 363.
9. Stoddard, II, 11.
10. Ibid., 348–349.
11. Opening paragraph of Stoddard's testimony, in Stoddard, I, foreword, 9.
12. Holzer et al, 78.
13. Stoddard, II, 349–350.
14. Ibid., 351; Carpenter diary entry for July 9, 1877, transcribed by Ives.
15. Carpenter diary entry for January 10, 1878, transcribed by Ives.
16. Stoddard, II., 350, 352–353.
17. Ibid., 353–356.
18. Ibid., 356.
19. Ibid., 356–358.

Chapter 21

1. Holzer et al, 78; Philip B. Kunhardt III, Peter W. Kunhardt, and Peter W. Kunhardt, Jr., *Looking for Lincoln: The Making of an American Icon*. New York: Alfred A. Knopf, 2008, 220. According to Kunhardt et al., "only once before had a joint session of Congress met to receive a national gift — the 1848 presentation of George Washington's sword and Benjamin Franklin's staff" (220).
2. Stoddard, II, 359.
3. Ibid., 359, n. 16 on 398; Kunhardt et al., 220.
4. Entry in Carpenter's diary for February 11, 1878, transcribed by Ives.
5. Holzer et al, 78; Kunhardt et al, 220.
6. Stoddard, II, 359.
7. Ibid., 359–360.
8. Ibid., 359.
9. Ibid., 360; n. 14 on 398.
10. Carpenter's diary entry for February 15, 1878, in Cowdrey notes.
11. Stoddard, II., 360; Stoddard, I, 228.
12. Cited by Holzer et al, 78.
13. As seen by the author and his family; Stoddard, II, n. 16 on 398.
14. Holzer et al, 80; Stoddard, I, 227.
15. Stoddard, II, 360.
16. Howe, I, 201; Howe, II, 103–104.
17. Howe, II, 99.
18. Ibid., 104–105, for the post-funeral conversation.
19. Ibid., 58.
20. Article in *Cortland County Democrat*, June 24, 1870, cited in Cowdrey notes.
21. Recollection of Theodore Munger's boyhood in Homer, cited in Bacon, 19–20.
22. Carpenter to John W. Hutchinson, January 1, 1891, crediting Hutchinson's song of the 1840s "so popular in my boyhood" with starting "in me the first anti-slavery sentiment and conviction that I can now recall." Letter is referenced in John W. Hutchinson, "The Story of the Hutchinson Family," vol. 2, 360, cited in Cowdrey notes.
23. Carpenter, 9–13.

Chapter 22

1. Carpenter, 30; cited in Knapp, 15.
2. Henry Ward Beecher and Harriet Beecher Stowe were, also, uncle and aunt to Frederic Beecher Perkins, author of the book *The Picture and the Men: Being Biographical Sketches of President Lincoln and His Cabinet* (1867), which has been cited throughout this book.
3. See "Mr. Beecher's Trial," *Harper's Weekly* Supplement, June 5, 1875, 469–472. An original copy was discovered by Gail Servies, a library trustee, in a box in the attic of the Phillips Free Library of Homer, NY, when the building was being cleaned out in preparation for its restoration/renovation in 2006. Ironically, it was brought to the author's attention just before this chapter was to be written.

4. Photocopies of this original newspaper and the previously cited newspaper were provided by David Quinlan from the collection of the Phillips Free Library.
5. Barbara Anne White, *The Beecher Sisters*. New Haven, CT: Yale University Press, 2003, 230.
6. Newspaper report of April 24, 1876, and Carpenter's association with Douglass are in Cowdrey notes, along with a reference to Blodgett (1932), 253.
7. August 27, 79, 2.
8. *New York Tribune*, November 21, 22, 23, 1888 and *New York Graphic*, November 24, 1888, in Cowdrey notes.
9. Article in *New York Tribune*, November 22, 1888, 2, in Cowdrey notes.
10. The meeting with Mrs. Manchester was recorded in Carpenter's diary. It and the letter to MacKaye are cited in the Cowdrey notes. For awhile, James Morrison Steele MacKaye and his family had taken up residence in New York, along with Carpenter and his family, with the wealthy widow Elizabeth Thompson, who patronized the arts and bought the *Emancipation Proclamation* painting. Carpenter, also, provided funding for MacKaye's theatrical projects.
11. Carpenter diary entries for August 6, 1871; October 18–19, 1882; March 23, 24, 26, 1885, transcribed by Ives. Date of deaths of Thayer, Asaph Carpenter, and Almira Carpenter cited in Cowdrey notes.
12. See Arthur Conan Doyle, *The History of Spiritualism*, vol. 2. New York: G.H. Doran, 1926, and Bret E. Carroll, *Spiritualism in Antebellum America*. Bloomington: Indiana University Press, 1997, 248.
13. See Nettie Colburn Maynard, *Abraham Lincoln and Spiritualism during the Civil War*. Ancient Wisdom Publishing, 2009. Originally published in 1891 and reprinted in 1917 under the title *Was Abraham Lincoln a Spiritualist? Curious Revelations from the Life of a Trance Medium*, this revised edition includes much of the original work along with background information and explanations of many of the events described in the book.
14. Stoddard, II, 134.
15. Holzer et al, 82–83. Buttre was another native Central New Yorker; he was born in Auburn, NY, in 1821.
16. Mary Todd Lincoln to Francis B. Carpenter, December 8, 1865, cited in Cowdrey notes.
17. Carpenter diary entries for August 7 and 17, 1865, transcribed by Ives.
18. Francis B. Carpenter to William H. Herndon (Lincoln's law partner), December 4, 1866, reference to Lincoln's comment after sitting for the oil sketch. In the Herndon-Weik Collection. Manuscript Division. Library of Congress. Washington, D.C.
19. Holzer et al, 85.
20. Letter from "Your friend, John Hay" to "My dear Mr. Carpenter," January 22, 1866, in collection of Carpenter letters archived at Hildene, The [Robert] Lincoln Family Home, Manchester, Vermont.
21. Letter to F.B. Carpenter, on Navy Department stationery, dated December 4, 1866, in collection of Carpenter letters archived at Hildene, The [Robert] Lincoln Family Home, Manchester, Vermont.
22. The original letter, dated December 3, 1866, was in the Emerson Ives collection, White Plains, NY, and seen by Cowdrey on June 23, 1837, cited in the Cowdery notes.
23. Knapp, 13–14; Phillips Free Library has one of the prints today. The Homer Village Board owns another, donated by Grant Watson, former Homer pharmacist; it was restored in 2009 by West Lake Conservators of Skaneateles, New York; Christine Laubenstein, "Homer restoring 1864 print by local painter," *Cortland Standard*, May 6, 2008, 3.
24. The photograph is owned by Charles Bernheim of Homer, NY, and the Cortland County Historical Society owns a larger one. The *Alabama* claims refers to charges made by the United States government for damages suffered by the U.S. in the Civil War from depredations on American vessels of commerce by ships fitted out or supplied by British ports. The U.S. received $15.5 million in compensation.
25. Article in *New York Tribune*, December 2, 1891, 7, cited in Cowdrey notes.
26. Knapp, 9.
27. Stoddard, II, n. 15 on 398; David Quinlan contacted the curators of the British Royal Art Collection, who were unable to trace the whereabouts of Carpenter's "Arbitration" painting.
28. Holzer et al, 85.
29. Explanations gained from interviews with Anita Wright, Cortland County Historical Society, January 29, 2010, and David Quinlan, Homer artist and art educator, January 30, 2010. Cowdrey's letter to Miss Ella May Thornton of the Georgia State Library, Atlanta, GA, October 4, 1937, states that "Carpenter used very cheap paint" after 1875 because of his limited funds, copy in Cowdrey notes.
30. Perkins, 17.
31. Advertisement for Ritchie print, inside back cover of Carpenter's *The Inner Life of Abraham Lincoln*. Boston: Houghton, Osgood, 1878.
32. Holzer et al., 86; a copy signed by Carpenter is in a private collection in Homer, NY.
33. Holzer et al, 87; "Funeral of Francis B. Carpenter," in the *Cortland Evening Standard*,

June 1, 1900, 4; "Carpenter the Artist Dead," in *New York Sun,* May 24, 1900, 7; Cowdrey notes.
  34. In the process of cataloging, Cowdrey did find portraits that had been sold through an art gallery in the early 1930s. She noted a portrait of Lincoln sold for $8,500, a portrait of Mary Todd Lincoln for $2,100, and a miniature of Lincoln and Tad for $750.

Chapter 23

  1. This is a view shared by Holzer et al, 87.
  2. Carpenter, 218.
  3. Harold Holzer, Gabor S. Boritt, and Mark E. Neely, Jr., *The Lincoln Image: Abraham Lincoln and the Popular Print.* Urbana and Chicago: University of Illinois Press, 1984, 2001, 113.
  4. Irwin, 2.
  5. (Miss) Bartlett Cowdrey to Miss Rose M. Munger of New Haven, CT, November 30, 1937, in Cowdrey notes.
  6. Diary transcribed by Ives.
  7. Carpenter diary entry for April 14, 1866, transcribed by Ives.
  8. Carpenter, v.
  9. Letter of January 22, 1866, in collection of Carpenter letters archived at Hildene, The [Robert] Lincoln Family Home, Manchester, Vermont.
  10. See Goodwin, 581–582.
  11. "A Story of Lincoln as told by Frank B. Carpenter."
  12. Irwin, 2.
  13. Goodwin, 605–607.
  14. Carpenter, 269–270.
  15. Ibid., 87.
  16. Ibid., 33, 178.
  17. 76th NYSV: "The Cortland Regiment," Roster page, sponsored on-line by the Lt. Col. Andrew Grover Civil War Roundtable. See http://www.bpmlegal.com/76NY/roster-s.htm. Accessed August 18, 2010. Clinton Rice to Fras. B. Carpenter, letter from 503 West 23rd Street, NY, to 653 Broadway, NY, dated April 10, 1866, in collection of Carpenter letters at Hildene, The [Robert] Lincoln Family Home, Manchester, Vermont. Carpenter, 174–176. Lincoln's message to Dr. Gray on April 25, 1864 and his order of commutation to Judge Advocate General Joseph Holt on January 25, 1865, in *The Collected Works of Abraham Lincoln, Vol. 7,* reprint, Rockville, MD: Wildside Press, 2008, 313 and 227, respectively.
  18. Carpenter, 281.
  19. Ibid., 43.
  20. Ibid., 44–45; Carpenter diary entry for the date: "President's stables burned tonight; six horses lost." Transcribed by Ives.
  21. Ibid., 93.

  22. Holzer et al, in *The American Art Journal,* 83.
  23. Carpenter, 50, 52, 58–61.
  24. Ibid., 52.
  25. Ibid., 52–53.
  26. Cited by Carpenter, 235.
  27. Carpenter, 247.
  28. Ibid., 150.
  29. Ibid.
  30. Martin A. Sweeney, "The Personality of Lincoln the War President," *The Social Studies,* Volume LXV, No. 4, April, 1974, 165–166.
  31. Carpenter, 217.
  32. Ibid., 63–67.
  33. Ibid., 62–63.
  34. Ibid., 258–259.
  35. Mary Todd Lincoln to Henry C. Deming, letter dated December 16, 1867, cited in Holzer et al, *The American Art Journal,* 84.
  36. Mary Todd Lincoln to Frank B. Carpenter, December 25, 1866, transcribed by Ives. The cane was said to have Lincoln's name upon it.
  37. Cited in Cowdrey notes.
  38. Cited in Cowdrey notes.

Chapter 24

  1. Seymour Cook, "Early Days in Homer," reprint from the *Homer Republican,* 1905, in *Cortland County Chronicles,* vol.2, Cortland, NY: Cortland County Historical Society, 1958, 190. Stoddard, II, 11.
  2. Ibid., 11–12.
  3. Ibid., 12.
  4. Ibid., 12–13.
  5. William O. Stoddard to John Hay, letter dated March 25, 1885, cited in Stoddard, II., 13.
  6. Smithsonian. Website description of "Lincoln at the Smithsonian," "exhibitions celebrating Lincoln at the bicentennial of his birth in 1809." Washington, D.C.: Smithsonian Institution, Jan. 2, 2009. http://www.si.edu/visit/whatsnew/LINCOLN.ASP.
  7. Stoddard, II, 13.
  8. Stoddard, III, note 1 on 203.
  9. Stoddard, II, 1, 13, 348, n. 2 on 369.
  10. Ibid., 4–5.
  11. Ibid., 338–339; n. 11 on 396–397.
  12. Gibson, 23.
  13. See Epstein, 217–218.
  14. An impression cited in Stoddard, II., 365; for one interpretation of Stoddard's role at the Baltimore convention, see Epstein, 208–212.
  15. Stoddard, II, 246; Carpenter, 30–31; Stoddard, II, 308–309.
  16. Keep to Hon. A. Lincoln, letter dated Feb. 14, 1861, Lincoln Papers, Library of Congress.
  17. Stoddard, III, 93–94.

18. Stoddard, II, 13–14. On May 16, 2009, as part of "Homer's Celebration of Lincoln in Paint & Print," while a wreath was laid at Carpenter's grave in Homer, a similar wreath was laid on Stoddard's grave in Madison, New Jersey, through the auspices of the Madison Historical Society.

19. "In One Life Time," editorial in *New York Times*, August 30, 1925, transcribed copy in archives of Phillips Free Library, Homer, NY.

20. Stoddard, II, 361, n. 2 on 369.
21. Ibid., 9.
22. Ibid.
23. 348–360.

Chapter 25

1. See Mark E. Neely, Jr., *The Abraham Lincoln Encyclopedia*. New York: McGraw-Hill Book Co., 1982.

2. Stoddard, II, dedication page.

3. See archaeological report cited in Lincoln Anderson, "Tales from the crypt: 'Trump bones' shed light on abolitionist believers," online edition of *The Villager*, Vol. 76, No. 34, January 17 – 23, 2007. Accessed June 13, 2009.

4. David Quinlan, a written explanation of how the portraits of the Pierces came to be in the library's collection, 2007, in the Town Archives, Homer, NY.

Sources

Abraham Lincoln Papers, Library of Congress. Accessed online May 18, 2008.
"American Women: A Selection from the National Portrait Gallery," online at http://www.npg.si.edu/cexh/nwomen/lind2.htm. Accessed 30 January 2010.
Bacon, Benjamin Wisner. *Theodore Thornton Munger: New England Minister*. New Haven, CT: Yale University Press, 1913.
Baldwin, Elizabeth. "William and Francis Carpenter — Homer Brothers Made History During Civil War Period," in *Cortland Standard*, May 22, 1990, 8.
Bates, Edwin. Letter to F.B. Carpenter, October 20, 1864. In collection of Carpenter letters archived at Hildene, The [Robert] Lincoln Family Home, Manchester, VT.
Beers, F.W. "History of Herkimer County, New York." New York: Beers, 1879. Source of information on 44th New York Regiment. Available online at http://herkimer.nygenweb.net/regiments/ellsworth.html.
Bird, Ina Hurlbut. "Eli DeVoe, Scott Road Native, Was Destined to Serve Lincoln at Crucial Time in History," in *Homer Post*, February 12, 1932.
Blackwell, Sarah Ellen. *A Military Genius: Life of Anna Ella Carroll of Maryland*, Vol. 1. Washington, DC: Judd & Detweiler, 1891.
Blodgett, Bertha Eveleth. *Stories of Cortland County for Boys and Girls*. First published in the *Cortland Standard,* then in book form, Cortland, NY: Cortland County Historical Society, 1932.
Bosak, Michael E.J. "The Establishment of the 'Honor Legion.'" New York City Police Memorial, http://nypd.police-memorial.com/honor-legion-police-department-city-of-new-york/, accessed July 28, 2010.
Brandt, Nat. *The Town that Started the Civil War*. Syracuse, NY: Syracuse University Press, 1990.
Bryant, Arthur. *The American Ideal.* Freeport, NY: Books for Libraries Press, 1969.
Carpenter, F.B. Personal diary, version transcribed by Emerson Ives, grandson, along with letters from Daniel Carpenter and William Carpenter. Copy in Cortland County Historical Society, Cortland, NY. Not the same as Carpenter Diary entry transcriptions made as part of the Cowdrey notes in the same society.
_____. *Six Months at the White House with Abraham Lincoln: The Story of a Picture*. New York: Hurd and Houghton, 1866.
_____, to Mrs. J.H. Munger of Homer, NY. "This half sheet of paper is one of several that was thrown down on the table one day for me by Mr. Lincoln when I asked

him the *size* of the sheet on which the *Emancipation Proclamation* was written." Also bears Carpenter's signature and the date November 5, 1872. In archives of Cortland County Historical Society, Cortland, NY.

_____, to Mrs. Lincoln. Letter from 96 West 45th Street, New York, dated January 5, 1867, transcribed by Ives, Cortland County Historical Society, Cortland, NY.

_____, to "My Dear Sir" [name unknown]. Letter from New York dated November 8, 1853. Owned by David Quinlan of Homer, NY.

Carpenter, Francis B. "A Day with Governor Seward at Auburn." Handwritten manuscript, no date [circa July 1870], Seward Papers. Rochester, NY: University of Rochester.

_____. *The Inner Life of Abraham Lincoln*. Boston: Houghton, Osgood, 1878.

_____, to Coleman Hitchcock. Letter dated August 2, 1894, to his childhood friend. Published in the *Homer Republican* newspaper, August 6, 1908, 4.

_____, to Theodore Thornton Munger. Letter dated February 22, 1864. Munger Papers, Yale University Library.

_____, to William H. Herndon. Letter dated December 4, 1866. The Herndon-Weik Collection. Manuscript Division. Library of Congress. Washington, D.C.

"Carpenter the Artist Dead." *New York Sun*, May 24, 1900, 7.

"Carpenter's Secret." *The Daily Graphic*, front page, Vol. 7, no. 704, New York, Friday, June 11, 1875.

Carroll, Bret E. *Spiritualism in Antebellum America*. Bloomington: Indiana University Press, 1997.

Catalogue of the Officers and Students of Cortland Academy for the academic year 1858-59. Homer, NY: Dixon, 1859.

Charter of the Cortland Academy, dated February 2, 1819. Removed from storage in Homer's Key Bank vault in 2008, it is now framed and in the custody of the Homer Central School District, Homer, NY.

Chase, S.P., to F.B. Carpenter. Letter dated May 2, 1866. Transcribed by Ives, in Cortland County Historical Society, Cortland, NY.

Collins, George Knapp. "Biography of Sanford Thayer," in *History, Town of Spafford*, 1902, published by Onondaga Historical Association, Syracuse, NY: Dehler Press, 1917, 108–109.

Conan Doyle, Arthur. *The History of Spiritualism*, vol. 2. New York: Doran, 1926.

Cook, Seymour. "Early Days in Homer." Reprint from the *Homer Republican*, 1905, in *Cortland County Chronicles*, vol. 2, Cortland, NY: Cortland County Historical Society, 1958.

Cowdrey, Mary Bartlett. Extensive research notes on Carpenter and transcriptions of selected entries from his diary at Cortland County Historical Society, Cortland, NY, a few miles from Carpenter's boyhood home, accessed February 2010.

"Death of Wm. O. Stoddard." *Cortland Standard*, August 31, 1825, transcribed copy in archives of Phillips Free Library, Homer, NY.

DeVoe, Eli. Obituary, *New York Times*, January 28, 1874, provided by the Summit Historical Society, Summit, NJ.

DeVoe, Thomas F. *Genealogy of the DeVeaux Family*. New York: New York Historical Society, 1885. Digitized copy provided online by the Boston Public Library, http://www.archive.org/stream/genealogyofdevea00devo/genealogyofdevea00devo_djvu.txt.

Dunn, Seymour B. "The Early Academies of Cortland County," in *Cortland County Chronicles*, Vol. 1. Cortland, NY: Cortland County Historical Society, 1957, 1970.

Epstein, Daniel Mark. *Lincoln's Men: The President and His Private Secretaries*. New York: HarperCollins, 2009.

Fillmore, Millard. Letter to D.A. Boku [?], Oct. 15, 1852. In collection of Carpenter letters archived at Hildene, The [Robert] Lincoln Family Home, Manchester, VT.
"Francis Bicknell Carpenter." *Cortland County Republican*, September 30, 1858, 1–2.
"Funeral of Francis B. Carpenter." *Cortland Evening Standard*, June 1, 1900, 4.
Gibson, Catherine. "Recollections of Kate Stoddard Gibson," unpublished manuscript, c.1900, provided by her granddaughter, Margaret Tessler, Albuquerque, NM, June 2010.
Goodwin, Doris Kearns. *Team of Rivals: The Political Genius of Abraham Lincoln*. New York: Simon & Schuster, 2005.
Harper's Weekly, "Mr. Beecher's Trial," supplement, June 5, 1875, 469–472, photocopy of the original owned by Kenny and Cindy Teter of Homer, NY, provided by David Quinlan.
Hay, John. Letter from Paris to Frank B. Carpenter, January 22, 1866. In collection of Carpenter letters archived at Hildene, The [Robert] Lincoln Family Home, Manchester, VT.
Holzer, Harold. *Lincoln President-Elect: Abraham Lincoln and the Great Secession Winter 1860–1861*. New York: Simon & Schuster, 2008.
_____. *Lincoln Seen & Heard*. Lawrence: University Press of Kansas, 2000.
_____. Tour given of "Lincoln and New York," an exhibit at New-York Historical Society, New York, March 19, 2010.
Holzer, Harold, Gabor S. Boritt, and Mark E. Neely, Jr. "Francis Bicknell Carpenter (1830–1900): Painter of Abraham Lincoln and His Circle," in *The American Art Journal*, Spring 1984, 66–89.
_____, _____, _____. *The Lincoln Image: Abraham Lincoln and the Popular Print*. Urbana: University of Illinois Press, 1984, 2001.
"In One Life Time." editorial on William Stoddard, *New York Times*, August 30, 1925, transcribed copy in archives of Phillips Free Library, Homer, NY.
Irwin, Will. "Restoring Lincoln's Study," in New York *Herald Tribune* magazine section, Sunday, February 9, 1930, 2. In collection of Carpenter letters archived at Hildene, The [Robert] Lincoln Family Home, Manchester, VT.
Keep, John, and Henry Cowles. Letter to Hon. A. Lincoln, from Oberlin to Cleveland, February 14, 1861. Lincoln Papers, Library of Congress.
Kline, Michael J. *The Baltimore Plot: The First Conspiracy to Assassinate Abraham Lincoln*. Yardley, PA: Westholme, 2008.
Knapp, Anna Moore. "Francis B. Carpenter: 1830–1900," in *Yesteryears* 4, no. 16 (June 1961), 7–18. Knapp was Homer Village historian and a descendant of Carpenter. Her research was based on material gathered by Mary Bartlett Cowdrey and donated by Cowdrey in 1953 to the Cortland County Historical Society.
Kunhardt, Philip B. III, Peter W. Kunhardt, and Peter W. Kunhardt, Jr. *Looking for Lincoln: The Making of an American Icon*. New York: Knopf, 2008.
Laubenstein, Christine. "Homer Restoring 1864 Print by Local Painter." *Cortland Standard*, May 6, 2008, 3.
Leach, Margaret. *Reveille in Washington*. New York: Harper & Brothers, 1941.
Lincoln, Abraham. *The Collected Works of Abraham Lincoln*, Vol. 7. Reprint. Rockville, MD: Wildside Press, 2008.
Lincoln, Mary, to Frank B. Carpenter. Letter dated December 25, 1866, transcribed by Ives, in Cortland County Historical Society, Cortland, NY.
Lorant, Stefan. *Lincoln: A Picture Story of His Life*. Revised and enlarged edition. New York: Bonanza Books, 1975.
Lovejoy, Owen G. Letter from Princeton, IL, to Carpenter, dated March 28, 1868. In

collection of Carpenter letters at Hildene, The [Robert] Lincoln Family Home, Manchester, VT.
Lovejoy Papers collection in the Lovejoy Homestead, Bureau County Historical Society, Princeton, IL, includes letter from Carpenter to Lovejoy dated January 15, 1864; letters from Carpenter to Lovejoy's widow, dated May 18, 1865, and August 11, 1867.
Magdol, Edward. *Owen Lovejoy: Abolitionist in Congress*. New Brunswick, NJ: Rutgers University Press, 1967, 342.
Mathes, Valerie Sherer, Ph.D. Three-page biography of Amelia Stone Quinton (July 31, 1833 — June 23, 1926), sent to the author on September 15, 2009.
Maybury, C.G. Letter from Winona, MN, describing Don Brown, in the *Cortland Standard*, December 5, 1902, in the archives of the Cortland County Historical Society, Cortland, NY.
Maynard, Nettie Colburn. *Abraham Lincoln and Spiritualism during the Civil War*. Rev. ed. Toronto: Ancient Wisdom, 2009.
Michigan Historical Reprint Series. *K.G.C.: An Authentic Exposition of the Origin, Objects, and Secret Work of the Organization Known as the Knights of the Golden Circle*. Originally published in 1862. Paperback reprint published Ann Arbor, Michigan: Scholarly Publishing Office, University of Michigan Library, 2005.
Minutes of the Trustees of the Academy, 1817–1867. Now in the custody of the Homer Central School District, Homer, NY.
Mount letters: William Shephard Mount to his father, January 6, 1864; Shephard Alonzo Mount to Carpenter, March 4, 1864; and Shepard Alonzo Mount to Carpenter, March 28, 1864. In the collection of Carpenter letters archived at Hildene, The [Robert] Lincoln Family Home, Manchester, VT.
Neely, Mark E., Jr. *The Abraham Lincoln Encyclopedia*. New York: McGraw-Hill, 1982.
"The New Administration." *Cortland Gazette*, March 7, 1861, 2, col. 3 and 4.
Nicolay, John G. *With Lincoln in the White House: Letters, Memoranda, and Other Writings of John G. Nicolay: 1861–1865*, ed. Michael Burlingame. Carbondale: Southern Illinois University Press, 2000.
Nicolay, John G., and John Hay. *Abraham Lincoln: A History*, vol. 4. New York: Century, 1886–90.
____ and ____. *Abraham Lincoln: The Observations of John G. Nicolay and John Hay*, ed. Michael Burlingame. Carbondale: Southern Illinois University Press, 2007.
"A Noted Detective's Funeral: One of the Men who Frustrated the Plot to Kill Lincoln in Baltimore." *Newark Daily Journal*, January 30, 1874, transcribed copy in archives of the Town of Homer, NY.
The Odyssey of 1936, "History of Homer Academy," p. 45.
Perkins, Frederic B. *The Picture and the Men: Being Biographical Sketches of President Lincoln and His Cabinet (1867)*. New York: A.J. Johnson, 1867.
Phillips, Charles, and Alan Axelrod, with Kurt Kemper. "Matsell, George," in *Cops, Crooks, and Criminologists: An International Biographical Dictionary of Law Enforcement*, illus. ed. New York: Facts on File, 1996, 101, 102.
"Photo-Mural of Village Placed on Wall of Lobby of Homer National Bank." *Cortland Standard*, July 25, 1946.
Pierce, Franklin. Letter to a friend (U.S. Senator?), dated February 2, 1855. In collection of Carpenter letters archived at Hildene, The [Robert] Lincoln Family Home, Manchester, VT.
Pinsker, Matthew. *Lincoln's Sanctuary: Abraham Lincoln and the Soldiers' Home*. New York: Oxford University Press, 2003.

Quinlan, David. Interviews on art history, Carpenter's artistic style, and Carpenter's training, January 31, February 20, and July 29, 2010. Mr. Quinlan is an artist and art educator residing in Homer, NY.

_____. Research material on Carpenter paintings now located in Homer, NY, provided in 2008, along with information about detective DeVoe and a transcription of the *Baltimore Times* of April 20, 1865, which dealt with the arrest of Lincoln assassination conspirators. Mr. Quinlan also contacted the curators of the British Royal Art Collection, who were unable to trace the whereabouts of Carpenter's *Arbitration* painting.

Randall, Henry S. *Sheep Husbandry*. New York: Orange Judd, 1848, 1860, with two illustrations of Merino sheep by a young Carpenter.

Reynolds, David S. *John Brown, Abolitionist: The Man Who Killed Slavery, Sparked the Civil War, and Seeded Civil Rights*. New York: Random House, 2005.

Rice, Clinton. Letter to Fras. B. Carpenter, April 10, 1866, in collection of Carpenter letters at Hildene, The [Robert] Lincoln Family Home, Manchester, VT.

Russell, the Rev. James H. Copy of Homer Congregational Church Centennial Anniversary Sermon, July 14, 1963, in Town of Homer historical archives.

Schenk, Joshua Wolf. *Lincoln's Melancholy: How Depression Challenged a President and Fueled His Greatness*. New York: Houghton Mifflin, 2005.

Schecter, Barnet. *The Devil's Own Work: The Civil War Draft Riots and the Fight to Reconstruct America*. New York : Walker, 2005.

Seitz, Don C. *Horace Greeley: Founder of the New York Tribune*. Indianapolis: Bobbs-Merrill, 1926.

76th New York State Volunteers. "The Cortland Regiment." Roster page, sponsored online by the Lt. Col. Andrew Grover Civil War Roundtable, Cortland, NY. http://www.bpmlegal.com/76NY/roster-s.htm. Accessed August 18, 2010.

Seward, William H. Letter to F.B. Carpenter, from Washington to New York, dated September 17, 1864, in collection of Carpenter letters archived at Hildene, The [Robert] Lincoln Family Home, Manchester, VT.

Smithsonian Institution. "Lincoln at the Smithsonian, exhibitions celebrating Lincoln at the bicentennial of his birth in 1809." Washington, DC: Smithsonian Institution, Jan. 2, 2009. http://www.si.edu/visit/whatsnew/LINCOLN.ASP Accessed January 2, 2009.

Stanton, Edwin M. Letter to F.B. Carpenter on War Department stationery, dated May 22, 1864, in collection of Carpenter letters archived at Hildene, The [Robert] Lincoln Family Home, Manchester, VT.

Stoddard, William O. "Face to Face with Lincoln," edited by William O. Stoddard, Jr., *Atlantic Monthly*, March 1925, 333.

_____. *The Volcano under the City: By a Volunteer Special*. New York: Fords, Howard, & Hulbert, 1887.

"A Story of Lincoln as told by Frank B. Carpenter." Unpublished four-page, typed manuscript (writer unknown) containing two accounts of Carpenter and Lincoln, in archives of Phillips Free Library, Homer, NY.

Sweeney, Martin A. "The Personality of Lincoln the War President," in *The Social Studies* 65, no. 4 (April 1974), 164–167.

[Thayer, Sanford.] Obituary, *American Art Review*. 1881, 169.

[_____.] Obituary, *New York Times*, November, 26, 1880.

Thomas, C.B. "President Abraham Lincoln and His Cabinet Sits in Session in Homer." Excerpts from an account in the Los Angeles *Herald* that appeared in the *Homer Republican* of July 18, 1901, and reprinted in the *Homer Independent*, May 31, 1960, 33.

"Two Great Fires, Over Half a Million Dollars Worth of Property Destroyed." *New York Times*, April 7, 1866.
Walker, Williston. *Ten New England Leaders*. New York: Silver, Burdett, 1901.
Welles, Gideon. *Diary of Gideon Welles*. Vol. 1. Boston, New York: Houghton Mifflin, 1911.
White, Andrew D. *Autobiography of Andrew Dickson White*. Vol. 1. New York: Century, 1905.
White, Barbara Anne. *The Beecher Sisters*. New Haven, CT: Yale University Press, 2003.
Who's Who in American Art. New York & London: R.R. Bowker, 1966, 90.
"William O. Stoddard Dies; Was Aid [sic] of Lincoln." *New York Times*, August 30, 1925, transcribed copy in archives of Phillips Free Library, Homer, NY.
Wilson, Douglas L. *Lincoln's Sword: The Presidency and the Power of Words*. New York: Random House, 2006.
Woolworth, S.B. Letter from Homer, NY, to Hon. William Jessup of Montrose, PA, April 5, 1848, in a private collection in Homer, NY.

Index

Numbers in ***bold italics*** indicate pages with photographs.

Abbott, Emma 53
Abraham Lincoln Bicentennial Commission 150
Abraham Lincoln: The True Story of a Great Life 144
Adams, Capt. George A. 110
Alabama claims 133
Allen, Ethan 4, 9
Allen, William (playwright) 150
American Art Union (NYC) 46
Antietam 87, 90; *see also* Chase, Salmon P.; Welles, Gideon
Arbitration Picture 133
Arnold, Benedict 5, 83
Atwater & Kellogg (Homer) 51
Auburn, NY 63, 64, 132

Babcock, Hank 12
Bacon, Almon 17
Bakhtin, Mikhail 156
Barber, Catherine Reid 46
Barber, George J.J. 27, 46, 63
Barber, Jedediah (or "Uncle Jed") 12, 17, *24*, 25–28, 40, *43*, 44, 46, 47, 91, 127
Barber, Jedediah II 45, 46
Barber, Louisa Anna 12
Barber, Lydia Jane Eno 47
Barber, Mary Elizabeth McClellan 28
Barber, Mary Louise 46
Barber, Matilda 12, 28, 46
Barber, Paris 25, 27–30, *29*, 40–41, 53, 63, 64, 75–76, 127–128; assassination of Lincoln and reaction of 117–118; as benefactor of Francis Bicknell Carpenter 30, 45–47, 128, 153; death and burial 127; designs Glenwood Cemetery (Homer) 110, 113, *114*; designs Homer Green 111; designs "King Corn" 127
Barber, Samuel 53
Barber, Watts 27, 76
Barber Block (or Hall) or Keator Opera House 7, 47, 51, 121; *see also* Barber, Jedediah; Great Western

Barbers' cook, Hannah 20, 91
Barker, Luther 118
Barnum, P.T. 48, 53
Bates, Atty. Gen. Edward 60; comments on *Emancipation Proclamation* painting 119; portrait 103
Bates, Therena 76
Beckwith, Robert Todd Lincoln 151
Beebe, Joseph 4
Beebe, Rhoda 4
Beecher, Rev. Henry Ward 129; *see also* Beecher-Tilton Scandal
Beecher-Tilton Scandal 129–131
Bennett, Rev. Alfred 9, *43*, 44
Berger, Anthony 98, 99
Blair, Postmaster General Montgomery 8, 89, 103, 125
Bleeding Kansas 101
Booth, John Wilkes
Bradford, Simeon S. 128
Brady, Mathew 74, 98, 139, 141, 155
Brewster, William 4
Bright, Rev. Edward 19, 85
Brooks, Noah 105, 118, 139, 141
Brown, Don 20
Brown, John 101, 129
Bryant, William Cullen 98
Burgoyne, Gen. "Gentleman Johnny" 11
Burr, Prof. George L. 52
Butler, Gen. Benjamin 125
Buttre, John Chester 132

Carey, Alice 50
Carey, Phoebe 50
Carpenter, Almira 8, 24, 42, 131
Carpenter, Asaph 8, 22, 23–25, 27, 29, 40, 42, 102, 131
Carpenter, Augusta ("Gus") Prentiss 46, 51, 102, 110
Carpenter, Clement DeWitt ("Witt") 110
Carpenter, Pvt. Daniel Webster 109, 140

199

Index

Carpenter, Eli 151
Carpenter, Elliott ("Ellie") 47
Carpenter, Florence Trumball 47
Carpenter, Francis Bicknell 52, 99, 106, 130; advice to artists from 50; *Arbitration Painting* and 133; as art student in Syracuse 39–40 (see also Thayer, Sanford); assassination of Lincoln and reaction of 116–117; autograph 106; Beecher-Tilton Scandal and 129–131; birthplace of 13; Charles Dickens and 143; childhood 5, 8, 22–25, 128; comments on Lincoln's face 129; completes *The Lincoln Family* in Homer 132; critiques in press 48, 53; death, funeral, and burial 134; decline in workmanship 133; on emancipation as historic event 92–93, 100–101, 104, 105, 126; *Emancipation Proclamation* 94, 97, 100, 102–103, 118, 121, 122, 125, 128, 136, 137–138; financial woes 144; first meetings with Lincoln at White House 94–96; Frederick Douglass and 131; Frémont's edict of emancipation supported by 94; government acceptance of painting 121–127; influence of liberation theology 100–101; influence upon Lincoln 98–99; intellectuals painted by 52 (see also Cornell University); last meeting with Lincoln at White House 107; Lincoln and Tad painted by 141; Lincoln lore and 137–139; Lincoln's image in print marketed by 118–119, 132, 133–134; Lincoln's image on currency and 98; on Lincoln's sleepless nights 146, 169; Mary Bartlett Cowdrey and 134; Mary Todd Lincoln and 143; New York City draft riots and 109; opinion of other artists given by 48–49, 49; paintings done in Homer by 24, 40–46, 51–52, 118, 135, 151–152 (see also trustee paintings); photography and 97–99; physical appearance 95; presidents painted by 48; published memoirs 119, 136–137, 139–143; senators painted by 50; on Seward as abolitionist 61; "Seward's pants" and 139; signs painted for Homer merchants by 27; spiritualism and 131–132; Stone-Ivins trial and 131; style of portraiture 53–54; William W. Carpenter's death and 110 (see also Barber, Paris, as benefactor of)
Carpenter, Helen 52, 131
Carpenter, Herbert ("Bertie") Sanford 44, 47, 51, 102
Carpenter, Noah 4, 5, 8
Carpenter, Pvt. William ("Will") Wallace 109–111, 128, 131; death, funeral, and burial of 110; New York City draft riots and 109; portrait 110, 111
Carroll, Anna Ella 104
Carson, Mrs. William W. 133
Caruth, Mr. 33–34
Centennial Exposition at Philadelphia (1876) 127
Central Illinois Gazette 56–62
The Century (NYC) 63
Chancellorsville 86, 108
Chapman, John Gadsby 133
Chase, Kate (Mrs. William Sprague) 137–138

Chase, Sen. Salmon P. 8, 60, 64, 89, 96, 137–139; and jealousy of Seward 103; on Lincoln and emancipation 90; Pomeroy circular and 139; portrait 103, 122
Chris the Model Maker 144
Clough, George L. 23, 39, 49
Cole, Thomas 46
Colefax, Speaker of the House Schuyler 93, 140
Common Sense 3
Compromise of 1850 34
Congregational Church (Homer) 4, 8, 15, 17, 21, 27, 42, 46, 52, 68, 76, 127, 128; dedication 110; and funerals of casualties of Gettysburg 110; William W. Carpenter's portrait and 110, 111; see also Barber, Paris; Keep, John; Schermerhorn, Jacob Maus
Constitution of the United States of America 61, 91, 103
Cooper Union Speech 63, 155
Copperheads 69
Cornell, Ezra 52–53; see also Cornell University
Cornell University 10, 32, 52–53, 127; see also White, Andrew Dickson
Cortland Academy (later Homer Academy) 16–17, 41, 42, 44, 45, 46, 52, 128, 134, 153; charter of 9, 15–16, 42; exhibition day 16–17, 112–113; see also trustee paintings
Cortland County Agricultural Society 28, 40, 121
Cortland County Historical Society 54, 134
Cortland County Republican 127
Cortland Gazette 73
Cotton, John (Rev.) 4
Cowdrey, Mary Bartlett 134
Cravath, Oren 21
Crowded Out o' Crofield; or, The Boy Who Made His Way 32
Cushing, Atty. Gen. Caleb 48

The Daily Graphic (NYC) 129–130
Daily Tribune (of NYC) 131
Darrow, Nathan B. (Rev.) 15
David Harum: A Story of American Life 22
Davis, Jefferson 75, 83
Davis, Congressman Thomas Treadwell 93
Declaration of Independence (document) 6, 104, 154
Declaration of Independence (painting by Trumbull) 105
Delmonico's (NYC) 143
Democratic Party 123
Derby & Miller 118, 120, 126
Detroit Free Public Library 149
DeVoe, Abigail D. Spear 72
DeVoe, Daryl 151
DeVoe, Dct. Eli (aka Davis) 5, 68, 73, 142, 150, 151, 152; birthsite 68; case of the French Railway Company and 71; death and burial in NJ 71–72; role in presidential image-making 72, 127, 152, 154; see also Lincoln, assassination of; Lincoln, assassination plot of 1861
DeVoe, Helena Godwin 4, 5, 68
DeVoe, John 4, 5, 68

Index

DeVoe, Ronald 152
Dickens, Charles 143
Dixon, Joseph R. 127
Douglas, Sen. Stephen A. 58
Douglass, Frederick 131
Dryden (NY) *Herald* 131

Edmunds, Sen. George Franklin 124
Edwards, Jonathan 101
Edwards, Jonathan, Jr. 101
1890 House Museum (Cortland, NY) 44
Election of 1860 64
Elizabeth Brewster House (Homer) 150
Elliot, Charles Loring 39, 48, 50
Ellsworth, Col. Ephraim Elmer 77–78, *77*
Ellsworth's Avengers 78
Emancipation Proclamation (document) 87, 89, 90–91, 104, 105, 113, 128, 134, 163–168; battle at Antietam Creek and 87; Carpenter describes signing of 139; *see also* Lincoln, Abraham; Stoddard, William Osborn
Emancipation Proclamation (painting) or *The First Reading of the Emancipation Proclamation Before the Cabinet* 96, 103–107, 118, 120, 121, 122–128, **126**, 132, 133, 134, 150; accomplishes Lincoln's ambition 107, 155; critiques 100, 103, 104–107, 119–120, 121, 122, 124; effect of Lincoln's assassination 117, 118, 119; and empty chair 104–105; gifted to Congress in 1878 125–126; Halpin print of 132–133, *153* (*see also* Hay, John Milton); as "The Happy Family" 105, 139; Homer, NY and 7, **8**, 121; and Lincoln's portrait 103; as public art and teachable moment 155–156; on public tour 107; readied for transportation 107; Ritchie print 118–120, 121, 133–134; *see also* Stoddard, William Osborn
Emerson, Jason 150
Epstein, Daniel Mark 145
Erie Canal 26, 31
Executive Mansion (or White House) 7, 9, 48, 63, 74–75, 77, 79, 82–84, 86, 87, 89, 94–102, 108, 115, 122, 123, 132, 137–138, 140, 141, 142, 145, 146, 154, 155; work environment in Lincoln's 79–80

Fessenden, Rev. Thomas E. 52
Field, Liona Fisher Hammond 151
Fillmore, Pres. Millard 35, 48
The First Religious Society of the town of Homer 4
Ford's Theater 86, 117
Fort Sumter 75
Frank Leslie's Illustrated Newspaper 100
"Freedom" (one-act play) 150
Frémont, Gen. John C. 50; emancipation proclamation 88, 94
Fugitive Slave Law of 1850 34–35

Gardner, Alexander 106
Garfield, Pres. James A. 48, 123, 126
Garrison, William Lloyd 101
Getty, James 150

Gettysburg 108, 109, 110, 150
Gettysburg Address 90
Glenwood Cemetery (Homer) 110, 113, **114**, 127, 134
Gobright, Lawrence 126
Godwin, Henry 4
Grant, Pres. Ulysses S. 108, 114, 122–123, 141–142
Gray, Dr. John P. 140
Great Western Store 26–27, 32, 41, 47; *see also* Barber, Jedediah
Greeley, Horace 53, 88, 102, 143
Green, Dr. Caleb **43**, 44, 47
Gunpowder River Bridge 69

Halpin, Frederick W. 132–133, **153**
Hamlin, Vice-Pres. Hannibal 64, 67, 145
Hannum, David 22
Harpers Ferry, VA 101, 129
Harpur, Robert 3
Harris, Sen. Ira 140, 145
Harvard University 93, 106, 131
Hay, John Milton 75, 79, 82, 87, 113, 115, 137, 144–145, 147, 148; inquires of Halpin print 132
Hayes, Pres. Rutherford B. (Pres.) 123
The Hedges (Homer) 14
Hempstead, Long Island 145
Henry, William "Jerry" 35; *see* Jerry Rescue of 1851
Herald Tribune (New York) 139
Herndon, William 64, 65, 77; letter from Stoddard **65**
Hillside Cemetery (in Madison, NJ) 146
Hiscock, Sen. Frank 133
Holzer, Harold 145, 149, 150–151
Homer, NY: as birthplace and launch pad of DeVoe, Carpenter, and Stoddard 152–153; and "Homer's Celebration of Lincoln in Paint and Print" (2009) 150–151, 152; listed in National Register of Historic Places 1; as "a new Lincoln Mecca" 152; as "place of the silversmith" 9
Homer Center for the Arts 41, 150, 151
Homer Central School District 44, 134; *see also* Cortland Academy; trustee paintings
Homer Education Foundation 150
"The Homer Festival" 111–112
Homer Green (or Common) 1, 4, 15–17, **20**, 40–42, 51, 52, 110, 111–**112**, 127, 128, 150, 153
Homer History Center at Key Bank 51
Homer Republican 117
Howard, Robert 17
Howe, Sen. Timothy 123
Howland, William 41
Hoyt, James W. 32–33
Huffman, Pvt. Wesley 10
Hurd and Houghton 137

The Independent (NYC) 134, 136–137
The Inner Life of Abraham Lincoln 143
Inside the White House in War Times 145

Jackson, Andrew 106
Jerry Rescue of 1851 (Syracuse, NY) 6, 34–35, **36**

Index

Johnson, Vice-Pres. Andrew 145
Jones, Anna 54

Kane, Baltimore Police Chief George 69–70
Keep, Rev. John or "Father Keep" 5, 12, 16, 28, 29, 30, 41–42, *43*, 47, 94, 100–101, 102, 110, 128, 153; comments on *Emancipation Proclamation* painting 119–120; letter to Lincoln in 1861 from 146, *147*; *see also* trustee paintings
Kennedy, John (Superintendent of NYPD) 68–69, 111
Knights of the Golden Circle 69

Lamon, Ward Hill 70
Lane, Frederick A. 93
"The Last Leaf on the Tree" 97
Leavitt, David 47–48
Lee, Robert E. (Gen.) 87, 108, 117
The Liberator 101
The Life, Public Services and State Papers of Abraham Lincoln 136–137
Lincoln, Abraham: assassination of 7, 116; assassination plot of 1861 67–72; in Carpenter's memoirs and published writings 136; 139–143, 146; changing emancipation policy of 87–90, 96; Col. Ellsworth and 77; conscious of presidential image-making 155; critiques the *Emancipation Proclamation* painting 105–107; departs from Springfield 67; discusses emancipation with Cabinet 89–90; on emancipation as historical event 104; first inaugural address 73; as first subscriber for Ritchie print 119; Frémont and 88; funeral procession in New York City 116–117; gives opinion of Gen. Grant to Stoddard 114; as Great Emancipator 6, 94, 118, 123, 127, 136, 140, 152, 155; interest in Shakespeare 86, 97, 141; letter from Mandy Brooke 81; lore involving Carpenter and 137–139; nominated as presidential candidate 63–64; poetry and 59, 97; photograph by Alexander Gardner *74*; photograph by Brady *85*; physical appearance 59, 60, 95; presidential burdens 80–81, 140–143, 146–147, 169–171; Reconstruction and 146; second inaugural address 146; sense of humor 60, 90, 95, 141–142, 146–147; Seward's advice and 89, 90, 96; speech at Cooper Union 63, 155; spirituality 146; in Stoddard's memoirs and published writings 146; and the Union 88, 91, 104, 126, 140
Lincoln, Edward Baker 67
Lincoln, Mary Todd 64, 67, 70, 82–83, 143, 150; comments on the *Emancipation Proclamation* painting 105, 120, 139; Kate Chase and 137–138; and mood swings described by Oliver H. Browning 82; photograph by Brady *85*; séances at the Executive Mansion 132
Lincoln, Robert Todd 67, 93, 133, 151
Lincoln, Thomas ("Tad") 67, 98, 141
Lincoln, William ("Willie") 67, 132, 141, 149
Lincoln at Work: Sketches from Life 145
The Lincoln Family 132
The Lincoln Forum Bulletin 152

Lincoln's Third Secretary 149
Lincoln's White House Secretary: The Adventurous Life of William O. Stoddard 145, 149
Lind, Jenny 48
Little York Lake (NY) 51
Long, Dr. Crawford W. 131
Lost Gold of the Montezumas 144
Lovejoy, Rev. Elijah 94
Lovejoy, Congressman Owen 88, 93–94, 95; portrait 94; and son's letter to Carpenter 94
Ludlow, Rev. Henry G. 151, 152
Luther, Martin 101
Lynde, Martius 22, 52

Mac Kaye, Steele 131
Madison, NJ 145, 148
Magna Carta 101
Marchant, Edward Dalton 100
Marcy, Gov. William L. 48
Matsell, George Washington 68
May, Joe 33
May, Rev. Dr. Samuel J. 33
McClarey, John 1
McClellan, Gen. George B. 114
McGarrahan–New Indria case 144
McManus, Edward 147
Mechanics Hall (Homer) 40, 44, 117
Metropolitan Museum of Art (NYC) 149
Military Tract (NYS) 3
Morrill Act 52
Morse, Samuel F.B. 53
Mount, Shepard Alonzo 98
Mount, William Shepard 98
Mount, William Sidney 49, 50, 98
Mouquin's (NYC) 123
Munger, Rev. Dr. Theodore T. 17, 22, 33, 42, 45, 51, 100, 101, 132, 133, 134, 153
Myers, Matthew 34

Nasby, Petroleum V. (pen name of David Ross Locke) 89
Nash, Frances 52
Nash, Sylvester 29, 52
Nast, Thomas 143
National Academy of Design (NYC) 48, 93
Native Americans 18–19
New London, CT 113
The New Prima Donna: The True Story of Emma Abbott 53
New York City draft riots of 1863 108–111
New York Evening Post 98, 144
New York Times 105, 119, 125, 134, 148
New York Tribune 53, 88, 93, 100, 102, 143
Newton, C.O. 121
Nicolay, John G. 75, 76, 79, 82, 113, 115, 118–119, 125–126, 144–145, 147; comments on *Emancipation Proclamation* painting 121

Obama, Pres. Barack 154–155; and linkage to Lincoln 154–155
Oberlin College 5, 42
"Oh! Why Should the Spirit of Mortal Be Proud" 97

Index

The Old Granite State 128
157th New York Regiment 109
Onondaga Lake (NY) 32
Opdyke, Gen. Emerson 125
Osborn, Amelia Cotton 4, 9, 15
Osborn, John (or Squire) 4, 6, 9, 11, 15, 17, 18–21, 27, **43**, 44, 149, 153; death 36; prophetic thoughts 37
Otis, Dr. Fessenden Nott 23, 50, 127, 153; accompanies Carpenter to Gettysburg 109

Panic of 1837 10, 26
Panic of 1873 121, 122
"Passage Through Baltimore" by Volck **71**; *see also* Lincoln, assassination plot of 1861
Philadelphia, Washington & Delaware Railroad 70
Phillips Free Library (of Homer) 46, 54, 138, 149, 151, 152
Phipps Union Seminary 9
Pierce, Benjamin ("Benny") 48
Pierce, Pres. Franklin 36, 48
Pierce, Justin 151, **152**
Pierce, Mary 54, 151, **152**
Pinkerton, Detective Allen 68–71, 73
Plymouth Church (Brooklyn) 129
Pomeroy, Sen. Samuel Clarke 138
Pomfret, CT 8
Porter, Misses at Halsted Hall 37
Potomac River 67, 76, 81, 83, 108
Powell, Lewis Thornton (aka Lewis Paine or Lewis Payne) 71, 117
Preble, NY 109
Presidential election of 1860 64
Protestant Reformation 101

Queen Victoria 133
Quinlan, David 134 152
Quinton, Amelia Stone 17

Randall, Hon. Henry S. 26, 41, 52
Raymond, Henry J. 136
Recollections of a Checkered Lifetime Told for His Children by William O. Stoddard in His Old Age 145, 149
Republican Party 57, 61, 122, 123; National Convention of 1860 63–64; National (Union Party) Convention of 1864 145
Richmond, NY 9
Rights and freedom 3–6, 94, 101
Ritchie, Alexander Hay 118
Rogers, Will 22
Rothschild, Baron 71

Salisbury, James (Dr.) 17
Sampson, Det. Tom (aka Thompson) 68–71; *see also* Lincoln, assassination plot of 1861
Samson, George Washington 12
Schermerhorn, Anna (Mrs. John Fisher) 84
Schermerhorn, Jacob Maus 12, 14, 75, 84, 145
Scott, Gen. Winfield 35–36, 69
Scroggs, John Walker ("Doc") 56, 57, 59–60, 66, 84

Sesquicentennial of the Civil War 154
76th New York Regiment 109, 140
Seward, Frederick 69, 139
Seward, William H. 60–61, 63–64, 69, 71, 75, 88, 99, 116, 117, 139; assassination of Lincoln and reaction 117; comments on *Emancipation Proclamation* painting 103, 119, 139; on emancipation proclamation 89, 126; "Higher Law" speech 61, 63; portrait 103, 104, 122, 138–139
Shattuck, Pvt. Morris I. 110
Sheep Husbandry 41
Sherman, Gen. William Tecumseh 53
Sherman Block (Homer) 40
Sherry's (NYC) 133
Sinclair, Samuel 93
Six Months at the White House with Abraham Lincoln: The Story of a Picture 119, 137, 139–143, 146
Skaneateles Lake (NY) 39, 51
Smith, Sec. of the Interior Caleb B. 103, 124
Smith, Dr. Stephen 17, 47, 109–110, 133, 134, 153
Smithsonian American Art Museum and Art Inventories Catalog 134–135
Soldiers' Home 89, 142
Spafford, Carrie 77
Spiritualism 131–132
Sprague, Sen. William 137
Springfield, IL 64, 65, 67
Stanton, Sec. of War Edwin M. 8, 83, 96, 140, 147; comments on *Emancipation Proclamation* painting 138; portrait 103, 122, 138
Stanton, Elizabeth Cady 100
Stephens, Congressman Alexander 123, 126
Stevens, Mr. and Mrs. Duane 149
Stevens, Judge Henry 52
Stewart (aka Shear), Pvt. Lorenzo 140–141
Stimson, Maj. Enos 19
Stoddard, Amelia 9; death 36–37
Stoddard, Catherine (or Kate) 9, 12, 33, 57, 66, 81, 84, 85, 115, 145, 150; attends play with Lincoln 86
Stoddard, Charles 9
Stoddard, Eleanor 146, 148–149, 150–151
Stoddard, Frances M. Bolles 37
Stoddard, Henry (or Harry) 9, 38, 66, 76, 85, 108, 115; in D.C. Rifles 76, 79; New York City draft riots 108–110
Stoddard, John 9
Stoddard, Julia 9; death 37
Stoddard, Ralph 148
Stoddard, Sadie 127
Stoddard, Samuel Prentice 9, 26, 31; remarriage 37
Stoddard, Sara Ann Osborn 9; death 36
Stoddard, Susan Eagleson Cooper 122, 127
Stoddard, William O., Jr. 149
Stoddard, William Osborn **148**; assassination of Lincoln and reaction of 116; as assistant personal secretary to the Lincolns 79–87, 95, 97, 113, 145–146, 155; autobiography of 145; ballot for freedmen of Arkansas and 115; birthplace of **13**, 151; and Carpenter as reliable sources on Lincoln 146; as chief clerk in the

Index

Dock Department of NYC 122; childhood in Homer 6, 9–21, 31; Col. Ephraim Elmer Ellsworth and 77; coming of age in Syracuse 31–38, *36* (inset); comments on the *Emancipation Proclamation* painting 8, 122, 124; complains about Carpenter 8; D.C. Rifles and 76; death and burial in Madison, NJ of 148; "Dump Hamlin" movement and 145; endorses Lincoln for President 60, 61–62, 157–160; and experiences out West 53–66, *57*; and financial woes 144; and first meetings with Lincoln in Illinois 59–60; as "Game Stoddard" 32; gold and stock speculation and 85, 108, 144, 146; inspects federal troops for Lincoln 115; introduces Carpenter to Lincoln 94–95; and last meeting with Lincoln in White House 115; on Lincoln's compassion 146; on Lincoln's need for a good joke 146–147; on Lincoln's sleepless nights 146, 170–171; lobbies the Government to accept the painting 121–125, 127, 155; makes copies of Emancipation Proclamation 9, 87; as marshal of Eastern District of Arkansas 115–116, 122, 145; Mary Todd Lincoln and 82–83, 84, 85–86; New York City Draft Riots and 108–111; *New York Examiner & Chronicle* and 85; organizes Fourth of July celebration in Washington 108; published writings 85, 122, 144–145; Rambler's Club and 32; returns to Homer in 1863 111–113; seeks job from Lincoln 65–66, 74–75, 145 (*see also* Herndon, William); spiritualism and 132; testifies before the Joint Committee of the Library on February 24, 1873 122, 172–176; tests firearms with Lincoln 81–82; Thanksgiving dinner speech by 114; University of Rochester and 37–38, 57; and vacation of 1863 113; as witness to veneration of Lincoln 148; World's Fair (1853) and 33

Stoddard & Babcock (bookseller) 31, 37
Stone, Mrs. Jonah 8
Stowe, Harriet Beecher 34, 129
Summit, NJ 68
Surratt, Mary 71

The Table-Talk of Abraham Lincoln 145
Taney, Chief Justice Roger B. 105
Thayer, Sanford 39, 49, 51, 131, 152
Thirteenth Amendment 7
Thompson, Elizabeth 123, 125–126, 149
Tilton, Theodore 129; *see also* Beecher-Tilton Scandal

Tioughnioga River 10, 11, 12, 26, 51
Todd, Amos 4
Tower's blacksmith shop 27
Treaty of Washington (May 8, 1871) 133
Trustee Paintings 41–44, *43*, 134
Twain, Mark (pen name of Samuel L. Clemens) 51
Twiggs, CSA Gen. David E. 125
Tyler, Pres. John 48

Uncle Tom's Cabin, or, Life Among the Lowly 34
Underground Railroad 21, 37
U.S. Capitol Building 66, 73, 107, 127

Vicksburg 98, 108, 141
A View of Homer 50–51; *see also* Otis, Fessenden Nott
The Volcano Under the City 110

War Powers of the President (William Whiting) 106
Ward, Artemus (pen name of Charles Farrar Browne) 89–90
Washburne, Congressman Elihu B. 70
Washington, D.C. 66, 67, 82, 107, 108, 113, 122, 123
Webb, Maj. Adin 15
Webster, Sen. Daniel 34, 53
Welles, Sec. of the Navy Gideon 88, 107, 125–126; critiques Halpin print 132–133; on Lincoln and emancipation 90, 161–162; portrait 103, 138
West Urbana (later Champaign), IL 56, 84
Wheadon, Henry 132
Whig Party 14, 35
White, Andrew Dickson 10, 32, 52, 128, 133, 153; *see also* Cornell University
White, Horace 26, 32, 66
Whittier, John Greenleaf 53
Wigwam (Chicago) 63–64
Wilkeson, Samuel 100
Williams family (Homer) 14
Wilson, Douglas L. 90
Wilson, Matthew Henry 106
Wisdom's Gate (or Temperance Tavern) 12
Wolff, Edward 85
Woolworth, Calvin 22, 51, 52, 133, 134
Woolworth, Samuel Buell 16–17, 41, *43*, 45, 153; *see also* trustee paintings

www.ingramcontent.com/pod-product-compliance
Ingram Content Group UK Ltd.
Pitfield, Milton Keynes, MK11 3LW, UK
UKHW042001140426
5217IPUK00015B/914